T0215485

Artificial Intelligence and Music Ecosystem

Artificial Intelligence and Music Ecosystem highlights the opportunities and rewards associated with the application of AI in the creative arts.

Featuring an array of voices, including interviews with Jacques Attali, Holly Herndon, and Scott Cohen, this book offers interdisciplinary approaches to pressing ethical and technical questions associated with AI.

Considering the perspectives of developers, students, and artists, as well as the wider themes of law, ethics, and philosophy, *Artificial Intelligence and Music Ecosystem* is an essential introduction for anyone interested in the impact of AI on music, including those studying and working in the creative arts.

Martin Clancy is a Research Fellow at Trinity College Dublin, the Founder Chair for the IEEE Global AI Ethics Arts Committee, and a Certified Ableton 11 Live Trainer.

Artificial Intelligence and Music Ecosystem

Edited by Martin Clancy

Routledge
Taylor & Francis Group

LONDON AND NEW YORK

Cover image: Boris SV / Getty images

First published 2023
by Routledge
4 Park Square, Milton Park, Abingdon, Oxon OX14 4RN

and by Routledge
605 Third Avenue, New York, NY 10158

Routledge is an imprint of the Taylor & Francis Group, an informa business.

British Library Cataloguing-in-Publication Data
A catalogue record for this book is available from the British Library

Library of Congress Cataloging-in-Publication Data
Names: Clancy, Martin, editor.
Title: Artificial intelligence and music ecosystem / edited by
    Dr. Martin Clancy.
Description: Abingdon, Oxon ; New York : Routledge, 2022. | Includes
    bibliographical references and index.
Summary: "Artificial Intelligence and Music Ecosystem highlights the
    opportunities and rewards associated with the application of AI in
    the creative arts. Featuring an array of voices, including interviews
    with Jacques Attali, Holly Herndon and Scott Cohen, this book offers
    interdisciplinary approaches to pressing ethical and technical questions
    associated with AI. Considering the perspectives of developers, students
    and artists, as well as the wider themes of law, ethics and philosophy,
    Artificial Intelligence and Music Ecosystem is an essential introduction
    for anyone interested in the impact of AI on music, including those
    studying and working in the creative arts"— Provided by publisher.
Identifiers: LCCN 2022015706 (print) | LCCN 2022015707 (ebook) |
    ISBN 9780367405786 (hardback) | ISBN 9780367405779 (paperback) |
    ISBN 9780429356797 (ebook)
Subjects: LCSH: Music—Philosophy and aesthetics. | Artificial
    intelligence. | Music and technology. | Music—Social aspects. |
    Music—Moral and ethical aspects.
Classification: LCC ML3800 .A74 2022 (print) | LCC ML3800 (ebook) |
    DDC 780.285/63—dc23/eng/20220502
LC record available at https://lccn.loc.gov/2022015706
LC ebook record available at https://lccn.loc.gov/2022015707

ISBN: 978-0-367-40578-6 (hbk)
ISBN: 978-0-367-40577-9 (pbk)
ISBN: 978-0-429-35679-7 (ebk)

DOI: 10.4324/9780429356797

Typeset in Times New Roman
by Apex CoVantage, LLC

Contents

Contributors

Jacques Attali was born on November 1, 1943. Special adviser to the president of France François Mitterrand for ten years, he is the founder of four international institutions: Action contre la faim, EUREKA, BERD, and Positive Planet. He has also conducted several orchestras worldwide (Paris, Grenoble, London, Jerusalem, Shanghai, Astana, Montreal, Lausanne, Brussels, and Helsinki). Jacques Attali has written more than one thousand editorials for *L'Express* magazine and is the author of more than eighty books, which have sold nine million copies and have been translated into twenty-two languages. He is currently a columnist for *Les Echos* newspaper.

Martin Clancy is a Dublin-based musician, academic, and events producer. He is currently a research fellow in the School of Creative Arts, Trinity College Dublin, and was awarded his doctorate on the financial and ethical implications of AI music in 2021. Martin is a founder member of the Irish band In Tua Nua and, while an artist in residence at New York's Seaport Music Festival 2009–2011, had a series of top 40 hits in the US Billboard Dance Charts. Martin is a certified Ableton trainer and the founder chair of the IEEE Global AI Ethics Arts Committee. He co-manages the Irish artist Jack Lukeman.

Scott Cohen began his music career in the late '80s in independent and major label artist management. Scott Cohen cofounded the digital distribution company the Orchard in 1997, which Sony Music now owns. In 2019, Scott Cohen became the chief innovation officer at Warner Music Group. He is an outspoken proponent of AR, VR, blockchain, and AI. He is also the cofounder of CyborgNest, a company exploring the interface of biological and digital intelligence. Scott sat on the British Phonographic Industry Council for many years and sits on the boards of several cutting-edge companies like Sound Diplomacy. Scott is a human rights activist and strict vegan.

David Cope is a professor emeritus of Music at the University of California at Santa Cruz. His books on the intersection of music and computer science include *Computers and Musical Style, Experiments in Musical Intelligence, The Algorithmic Composer, Virtual Music, Computer Models of Musical Creativity*, and *Hidden Structure*, which describe the computer program Experiments in Musical Intelligence, which he created in 1981. Recordings of EMI's music comprise *Bach by Design, Classical Music Composed by Computer, Virtual Mozart, Virtual Bach,* and *Virtual Rachmaninoff.* Cope is also a notable visual artist with many paintings on display around the world.

Jennifer Edmond is an associate professor of digital humanities at Trinity College Dublin, a codirector of the Trinity Center for Digital Humanities, the director of the MPhil in Digital Humanities and Culture, and a funded investigator of the SFI ADAPT Centre. Over the past ten years, Jennifer has coordinated a significant number of inter- and transdisciplinary research projects, worth a total of almost €9m in research funding. Jennifer also serves as President of the board of directors of the pan-European research infrastructure for the arts and humanities DARIAH-EU.

Holly Herndon is an American composer, musician, and sound artist based in Berlin, Germany. Her music is primarily computer-based and often uses the visual programming language Max/MSP to create custom instruments and vocal processes. Holly Herndon studied composition at Stanford University and completed her PhD at Stanford University's Center for Computer Research in Music and Acoustics. Holly Herndon received an MFA in electronic music and recording media at Mills College and won the Elizabeth Mills Crothers award for Best Composer in 2010. Other notable projects involve collaborations with Jlin, Hieroglyphic Being, Rene Hell, and the Iranian philosopher Reza Negarestani, as well as performances with the media group.

Andre Holzapfel is an associate professor at KTH Royal Institute of Technology–Sweden and conducts research in music computing and ethnomusicology. His work here was supported by the Swedish Research Council (2019–03694) and the Marianne and Marcus Wallenberg Foundation (MMW 2020.0102).

Rujing S. Huang is currently a presidential postdoctoral fellow at the University of Hong Kong, where her research crosses boundaries between (ethno)musicology, sound studies, and classical Chinese philosophy.

Mick Kiely is an expert on 'automatic music generation' (AMG). He has over thirty years of experience in all media, music composition, and live performance. Mick's particular focus is on music production. He cofounded and became the CEO of the AI music company Xhail Technologies in 2012. Mick is one of Ireland's most productive and versatile musical composers, and his extensive music catalog boasts global placements from TV and film productions to major corporate advertising. He cofounded Games Music Ireland, a nonprofit organisation designed to support Irish composers, and designed the game composers training module for Windmill Lane Studios, Trinity College Dublin, and Griffith College Dublin.

Artur Osipov is a classically trained pianist and won numerous Russian piano competitions. Artur has a BE in computer science from Moscow Aviation University and a BA (Hons) in music production from Griffith College Dublin.

Artur has over ten years of experience developing AI music systems and is Secretary of the IEEE Global AI Ethics Arts Committee. He worked as a composer/producer in Ireland and East Europe in the last seven years. In 2021, Artur won the Provost PhD Scholarship in Trinity College Dublin. His PhD research project, entitled 'Language, Culture and the Empowerment Gap of Artificial Intelligence,' uses methodologies at the border of the digital humanities and science and technology studies.

Miller Puckette obtained a BS in mathematics from MIT (1980) and a PhD in mathematics from Harvard (1986). As a researcher at IRCAM, he wrote Max, a widely used computer music software environment. Miller Puckette joined the music department of the University of California–San Diego in 1994, where he is now a professor. He is currently developing Pure Data ('Pd'), an open-source, real-time multimedia arts programming environment. Puckette has collaborated with many artists and musicians, including Philippe Manoury (whose Sonus ex Machina cycle was the first major work to use Max), Rand Steiger, Vibeke Sorensen, Juliana Snapper, and Kerry Hagan.

Richard Savery is a Macquarie University research fellow in Sydney, Australia. His research focuses on developing artificial intelligence and robotics, using music and creativity as a medium to program better interactions, understandings, and models. He completed a PhD in music technology (minor in human computer interaction) at the Georgia Institute of Technology, in the Robotic Musicianship Lab with Gil Weinberg, and an MFA at the University of California–Irvine in integrated composition, improvisation, and technology. He has also worked as a composer for many video games, films, and ads, such as Fast Four, featuring Roger Federer.

Aljosa Smolic is a professor of creative technologies at Trinity College Dublin. His research group V-SENSE focuses on immersive XR and deep learning for visual computing by combining computer vision, computer graphics, and media technology. He was a senior research scientist for Disney Research Zurich and the head of the Advanced Video Technology group. With Fraunhofer Heinrich-Hertz-Institut (HHI) Berlin, he headed a research group as a scientific project manager. He has published over 250 peer-reviewed papers and filed over forty patents.

Bob L. T. Sturm is an associate professor of computer science at KTH Royal Institute of Technology–Sweden and specialises in signal processing and machine learning applied to music. His work here was supported by MUSAiC (ERC-2019-COG No. 864189).

Gil Weinberg is a professor in Georgia Tech's School of Music and the founding director of the Georgia Tech Center for Music Technology, where he leads the Robotic Musicianship group. His research focuses on developing artificial creativity and musical expression for robots and augmented humans. Among his projects are improvising robotic musicians and prosthetic robotic arms for amputees that restore and enhance human musical skills. Weinberg has presented his work worldwide in venues such as the Kennedy Center, the World Economic Forum, and Ars Electronica. He received his MS and PhD in media arts and sciences from MIT.

Gareth W. Young is a postdoctoral research fellow on the V-SENSE project at Trinity College Dublin. His research focuses on evaluating creative uses for extended reality technology (XR). This research includes studying the design and use of XR technology in innovative practices, focusing on the interface between the user and the platform. Gareth's role is to observe and record how users interact, and design new approaches for using XR in innovative and creative ways.

Acknowledgements

Thanks to Hannah Rowe at Routledge for commissioning the book and making the process calm and straightforward. Thank you for early direction and assistance, to Anna McPartlin, Helena Mulkerns, James L. Smith, Rome Thomas, Kerry Hagen, and Vicky Sheckler. Many thanks also, Vasileios Gourgourinis, Tony Keville, Daniela Modrescu, Leo Hofnug, and Chris Buckley. Special mention to Susan Kane and Myra Clancy for their ongoing encouragement and support.

A successful transdisciplinary project builds on disciplinary expertise. I am therefore indebted to Greg O'Neill, John C. Havens, and Anna Barcz, respectively, for the legal, ethics, and philosophy chapter mentorship. Thanks also to David Hughes for his addendum interview to the legal chapter. To Ruth Barton, Catriona Curtis, Eve Patten, and Jane Ohlmeyer at the Long Room Hub Arts and Humanities Research Institute, Trinity College, for providing a research home for three years and a window to a new world. Also, a special salute to Artur Osipov, whose cynicism and boundless enthusiasm kept this book on track.

This work is about its contributors, most of whom are giants in their fields yet still found time to respond to an email from an Irish PhD researcher. Go raibh maith agaibh go léir ó mo chroí ceoil.

Billie, get your lead; it's time for a long walk.

Martin Clancy, Dublin, January 15, 2022

Introduction

Artificial intelligence (AI) presents a unique opportunity for musicians to shape and transform existing modes of creative expression. It raises questions regarding the role of the human artist and related economic and philosophical issues. In response, multiple voices from leading AI practitioners in the arts, industry, and academy present transdisciplinary perspectives on emerging ethical and technical questions. Contributors who begin within fields of expertise have been encouraged to fence step and address what matters most. Indeed, it is a research responsibility in a work of this kind (one that involves near-future societal tests) not to avoid the most taxing question: What needs to happen next?

This book highlights pathways to the affordances and rewards available while attempting to address these issues with à la carte neighbouring chapters offering supplementary topics. It is designed in sequence, bookended by chapters dedicated to the future. In Chapter 1, economist and philosopher Jacques Attali confirms AI as the *composing* technology he predicted in *Noise* (1977) and points to the following stages of human and music evolution. In Chapter 2, David Cope, whose work since the 1980s has shaped the possibilities of computer creativity, reflects on the meaning of music. In Chapter 3, Miller Puckette, the inventor of Pure Data and Max languages, candidly argues how programmers should explore new musical ideas. In Chapter 4, Armenian pianist and computer scientist Artur Osipov draws on the commonalities between music theory and computer programming. In Chapter 5, American musician and sound artist Holly Herndon discusses how AI continues to inform her work and considers its impact on the music industry and creative practice. In Chapter 6, Georgia Tech's Gil Weinberg and Richard Savery present a 'human-first deep learning design' for embodied AI music robotics. In Chapter 7, Ajosa Smolic and Gareth W. Young examine approaches for AI and music within immersive XR environments such as virtual and augmented realities. In Chapter 8, the president of DARIAH, Jennifer Edmond, reviews the adoption of AI with music from the standpoint of data. In Chapters 9 and 10, Martin Clancy presents the legal challenges of AI to music copyright and considers the application of global AI ethics reports for a fair and sustainable music ecosystem. In Chapter 11, Rujing S. Huang, Andre Holzapfel, and Bob Sturm build the review of AI ethics into a genuinely global perspective through a series of interviews with AI music practitioners in Asia and India. In

DOI: 10.4324/9780429356797-1

Chapter 12, AI music start-up CEO Mick Kiely delivers a passionate call to arms in response to AI music generation. In Chapter 13, Warner Recording Group Chief Innovation Officer Scott Cohen provides insight into our past and future engagement with new technologies. In Chapter 14, Martin Clancy presents a new and robust theoretical model to underpin an ethical AI 'fair trade' mark to support a fair and sustainable music ecosystem.

Nothing could be further from the intent of our book than to offer a bleak and dystopian appraisal; however, much that follows is troubling, especially when contemplating the future work possibilities for those now beginning in music. As the final edits to this work are drafted (January 2022), it is difficult to detach reflections on AI from the financial impact that COVID-19 has had globally on music makers. The pandemic has revealed the economic fragility of the music ecosystem *before* the full implementation of many technological provocations considered in this book.

In the end, why should music matter so much? Suppose Jacques Attali is accurate that music is a herald for social change and what happens in music happens here first. Indeed, the cycles of twenty-first-century technological disruptions provide evidence that Attali is once more correct. Then, in that case, our present musical entanglements with AI may produce wisdom for both the broader macroeconomic and the environmental ecosystems, and that is something surely worth our embrace, curiosity, and vigilant suspicion.

It may be that a renewed global appreciation of the music ecosystem's economic brittleness will stimulate initiatives to invigorate human-centred values within music, though that is said with as much hope as forecast. Nevertheless, we should remain playful and open-hearted when engaging with AI technologies; as Holly Herndon writes, 'Things will get a lot crazier!' and Scott Cohen's mind-boggling chapter indicates how near that 'crazy' future is. Therefore, it is shrewd for music makers to continue reimagining innovation and influencing its destination, as this book intends to do through a fresh transdisciplinary approach to AI and the music ecosystem.

Bibliography

Attali, J. (1985) *Noise: The political economy of music* (Vol. 16). Manchester University Press. UK.

1 The Future

Interview with Jacques Attali

Martin Clancy

- *You wrote in the 'Art, The Last Bastion of Freedom Against Artificial Intelligence' (2019) that the governance of AI industries would largely determine the course of the twenty-first century. Can you expand on why did you say this?*

AI is one of the last avatars of the digital era. Furthermore, the digital era is not the final world of the twenty-first century. After, we will have other factors, such as the questions raised by nanotechnologies, which will be significant. The neurosciences are going to be very important. And last, but not least, a field that will be fundamental is biomimetics, which involves how a human being imitates nature, and it is not far from AI. However, it is necessary to ask what is the actual overall trend in which AI is only a tiny part.

Since the beginning of humankind, the overall development has been the artificialisation of nature and the artificialisation of everything we do as a service. For instance, we have artificial eyes. Since a human being was created, the different tools that we use are a way of artificial activation – a service given from person to person. For instance, much later on, we can say that a car is a way for the artificialisation of what had previously been performed by a horse. Similarly, audio recording is a way to artificialise the act of singing. We can see that human beings transform any of their services into different artefacts. It is beneficial as it increases productivity while also reducing the pain and difficulty of doing many tasks. However, it is also disadvantageous because the artificialisation of nature has created many environmental problems. AI is the rudimentary beginning of the artificialisation of the brain. This tendency aims to target the whole artificial realisation of the brain through developing strong AI[1] compared to contemporary weak AI. The process will transfer individual knowledge from brain to brain, and it links neurosciences to AI using technologies that are already under scrutiny. After this, the sciences will be driven towards the transfer of memories, and the very concept of memories, will be a transformative idea. This will affect two primary services which are currently a high cost for humans – health and education. Health will begin to be transformed into artefacts. When we transform a service into an artefact, we reduce the cost and transform it into a source of profit. It will be done with health, not only through drugs but also with many new policies and medical devices.

DOI: 10.4324/9780429356797-2

This approach does not currently exist in education. We do not have any tool to plug knowledge directly into our brains. However, AI is the first embryo of that approach, and its trajectory extends into the long term. The whole of the twenty-first century leans towards that goal, one which positions the brain to swallow the vast amount of coming knowledge, culture, and music. Indeed, a tremendous amount of information of different kinds is coming. If we want to absorb it, we need to be in a position to artificialise or multiply the leverage of our capacity to plug our brain into something more significant.

Later on, this process will be followed by something more: the ability to transfer knowledge and our conscious consciousness. If you think about it, you will see that if I transfer my consciousness, and the consciousness of myself, either to someone else or to a hologram, I become an immortal. AI is a tiny facet of the historical journey towards achieving immortality through the process of artificialisation. Which is the principal trend of humankind's history that I have tried to explain from one book to another. However, it is also a naive trend because it is precisely as you say, as you think I am mortal. Still, my computer is immortal because it will last beyond me as an artefact, but it is not alive and therefore is not mortal. Therefore, we want to become artefacts in order to be immortal. AI is just a tiny dimension of this long historical process. We have to stop that process at a particular moment. It is fascinating to see that music, as always, is ahead of the process. Music is ahead because music is consistently using and more easily using the different new technologies than any other field. After all, music is pure software, by the very nature of music; as I said in *Noise*, forty years ago, music is like finance or mathematics, pure speculation of mind. Music can explore the possibility of a technology or creativity more easily than someone who is embedded in needing physical changes, such as physics or any kind of artefacts, and therefore, music is ahead of all other artefacts because it is a pure speculative brain artefact.

- *You have written frequently about transhumanism and, earlier in this interview, referenced strong AI.[2] When we speak about the implications of AI, prohibition is often mentioned. In* Noise, *you state that prohibition, especially with music, does not work, so perhaps we have to encourage ethical responsibility in its place. Many intriguing new music tools are emerging from companies aiming to develop strong AI. These music tools resemble your earlier depiction of future technologies; for instance, Google Wavenet can recreate the voice of deceased singers through unsupervised machine learning. What is your position regarding the ethics of transhuman immortality?*

First, as I said earlier, we had the aim of immortality – the aim of humankind. We consider that aim through creating medicines that raise life expectancy, and we also look at it through other paths. Furthermore, as I mentioned, the transfer of self-consciousness is the best way to envisage immortality for the moment. And of course, it is pretty normal to try to reach it. However, would immortality be only for a happy few, while the rest of humanity is being destroyed and used as slaves? That is certainly a possibility because, as has been explained by many past theologians, it is tough to imagine ten billion immortal people. For such immortals, could they give birth? And if they give birth, do they give birth to immortal people or not? If they give birth to immortal people, then where will we put all of this humankind? It is, of course, impossible. Therefore, as soon as you consider the practicality of immortality, you see that it is impossible, except perhaps for some happy few, hidden somewhere. Alternatively, killing, in a colossal nightmare, the whole of humankind is a concept of pure silliness. Fortunately, these prospects are not for today; maybe we can imagine in the third millennium, and I have written science fiction novels on how man can become eternal, move to other stars, colonise a planet, and leave immortals around the galaxy.[3] As a logic, when possible, the pursuit of immortality is the primary human quest and is the real engine of history.

I wrote a biography of Marx,[4] and we have to reflect on Marx's statement that the struggle of the classes is the engine of history. However, I disagree; instead, the pursuit of immortality is the quest of humanity and history. The artificialisation of nature is the path chosen by humankind to achieve the quest for immortality. I wrote a science fiction novel[5] based on this concept. It contains a story about how AI should be mastered using laws that have been developed that could be put in charge avoid the dangers of the technology.

Firstly, Asimov's laws, which I am sure you know.[6] Those three, but there are four more laws. Who develops AI for use in lethal instruments? Drones are using AI. In ten years from now, a drone the size of a tennis ball, with a camera and a weapon, will be able to come into your house, recognise you, and kill you. If it is under the control of a human being, then that is permittable; it is your weapon. However, without any human management, a bad AI could determine, well, this man is beginning to think that he needs to destroy me (the AI), then I am going to kill him. When the AI becomes able to escape from or even kill its creator, that is a significant danger. That concern is part of Asimov's laws – to not allow an AI to harm its creator. Regulation under these laws is complex to put in place because the laws have to be totally universal. Otherwise, there is no control.

Furthermore, while it is true that we have almost succeeded in having global control over nuclear, biochemical, chemical, and biological weapons, it is not perfect. However, AI weapons are not yet under such control. I know many people are working on that, and they are developed without control.

- *The EU has developed the concept of trustworthy AI, separated into high- and low-risk[7] AI. High-risk AI threatens mortality. However, does low-risk AI, for instance, concerning culture and music, require regulation?*

No, except, though, as we know, technologies used in one field can be applied later in another – for instance, music. Research in music can hide the process of military activity.

- *In* Noise, *do you refer to music in service to a surveillance society? What is your reflection?*

Noise was written forty-four years ago, and it is amazingly valid.

- *Arguably, many of the future concepts in* Noise *are no longer speculative. For example, you wrote about the centrality of music copyright to the economy of the music industry. Can music copyright, copyright, or IP, founded on solely human creativity, withstand the legal challenges AI presents?*

Yes, I think so. Copyright is an artefact. By nature, information is free. If I give you information, an idea, I still am it. Therefore, it is free by nature. However, to grant copyright, we need to create an institutional artefact. Copyright is not like bread or water, which is rare. By its nature, if I give you a glass of water, then I do not have that glass of water. Whereas if I give you an idea, I still have the idea. If I give you a piece of music, I still have the piece of music. Therefore, it has to be an artefact, and there is no copyright without institutions.

Furthermore, the question is, will the institution be strong enough? However, as the English know better than others because they have been pioneers of it, there is no law without judges, police officers, and jails, under the control of a parliament, if possible; therefore, with no copyright, there are no jails. And we hope there is no change without parliament. Thus, copyright is linked to an active fact, which is the legal structure of a country.

- *The exclusivity of intellectual property as a solely exclusive human activity has been challenged in recent court cases with contrasting decisions. As this is a judge-made law, its rulings are highly interpretable.* Noise *traces historic French development of music copyright; curiously, SACEM[8] recognised an AI (AIVA) as a composer in 2017.*

The head of SECAM is a close friend of mine. I know them very well. Yes, the artefact will be part of creativity – that is for sure. It is another step of artificialisation; we have to live with artefacts as partners.

- *If we make the artefacts partners, can artefacts become sole copyright owners?*

There is always someone or a team behind the artefact. I think it would be perilous if we give rights to artefacts without a human being or human gene behind it. As a fundamental principle, you should always have a human being or human team owning or controlling an artefact. An artefact should not be owned by itself.

- *Therefore, would you agree that legal personhood should not be extended to technology?*

That would be a step towards transforming us into an artefact, which is very dangerous. If we do that, we accept that these artefacts will have a right to vote, which is not wise. For then, we are no longer the master of our planet. I understand, and I hope that we are not the sole master of our planet and share that power with other living species. However, this should not be the case with artefacts. There is a real danger of creating artefacts as another kind of species with rights, and maybe higher rights or equivalent to ours.

Furthermore, it is interesting to see that it is once again with music that it is beginning to happen. I do have a frontline key question for the future. Will an artefact become a creator? If it is a creator, will it be considered a subject of law and rights? My answer is no. It should not.

• *The COVID pandemic exposed the existing economic fragility of the music ecosystem. What responses can the industry use to engage with new technologies to create future economic opportunities for the music ecosystem?*

I see many things that are possible. First, we can have a theatre with fewer people in the room. However, we have a vast number of cameras. And this will be seen live by many people who can attend the concert at home, either on television or through virtual glasses, which I think would be in the future, because more people will be able to attend a concert. The COVID pandemic will speed up the process of creating VR and 3D technologies. I see a moment where we will be at home with glasses and attend a concert as if we were not at home. And without being there. Furthermore, we can attend a concert in Hong Kong or in Washington from whatever angle you can imagine. I am sure we stick with technologies that will speed up this transition as it was during the black plague or many of the other opportunities we encountered.

We see music as consolation, a consolation for loneliness, a consolation for lack of emotions, and a surrogate for many dimensions. This desire is more needed than ever during the time of loneliness; what we have for music is more needed than ever. It is time for music, not the time for lamenting for music; it is the time for music.

• *You are a musician. Are you a musician of the composing network? What future AI musical tools would excite you in your creative practice.*

I am not a composer. I am an interpreter, a conductor, and a very bad pianist. I am happy and proud to conduct symphonic orchestras around the world. You asked if I had a musical dream? I dream of conducting a symphony orchestra of ten thousand musicians with the help of AI. It would be wonderful to conduct a virtual orchestra of ten thousand musicians playing a different score. Of course, not the same score. That would be fascinating, because we cannot afford to have more than one hundred musicians. Even when we have forty musicians available, you are thrilled as a conductor. However, to conduct a symphonic orchestra! Ten thousand musicians are playing, like, in the middle *Metamorphosen* of Strauss. Twenty-three different scores, but not twenty-three in my dream, but twenty-three thousand scores!

- *In* Noise, *you wrote that 'the technology of the composing network has yet to be invented.' Does AI represent attributes of the composing technology?*

Yes, it does. It is a shame that I am known mainly for a book which is more than forty years old in which I forecast that we are going to go back to the way we compose. It is a pity as it is one of my rare books only translated into English. All the others are translated into Japanese, Korean, and many other exotic languages.

Still, we are going to compose ourselves, and each of us will become composers. For that to happen, we will need to create new instruments, beginning with hardware and whatever can be digitised. AI is another dimension of it, which is a multiplying effect of computing. Low validity and budget provide us with a massive amount of vertigo that you have seen in interviews with people who do many things. Of course, it will be possible for anyone to compose like Tchaikovsky and do what Tchaikovsky could not do because he died. We love that concept. We will have two hundred symphonies by Tchaikovsky and nine hundred symphonies by Beethoven, and nobody will be able to tell if it is not specifically Beethoven. This is one of the phenomena that will be achieved through AI. We do not know if the mechanics of AI can escape from the pure imitation of music. By the way, this is also true for literature. We shall see new books by Charles Dickens or Victor Hugo, and it will be tough to distinguish from the original works. We will see singers, and not only Pavarotti, but whoever the dead star you wish to name. We will see them come back and sing new songs.

Therefore, AI will be part of what I call *artificialisation*. The distinction between reality and virtuality, reality and fiction, and reality and art; these distinctions will disappear. If you look at art, art is a reality only if it is in the past. A work of art by Mozart is a reality. A work of art that is not yet written is not a reality. However, the distinction between reality and fiction will disappear. It follows that we will have much more future creativity, and many different things will happen. What kind of world will it be? It is challenging to say now. However, I will say that there is a trend in which each of us will listen predominately to ourselves. As a result, we will be a world of narcissist individuals looking only at themselves or friends who have been approved. We can witness the embryos of this development in TikTok and Instagram.

The second dimension is that some occurrences that we cannot yet know will appear, and we will go through the whole process as we see happening in social networks. Some things go through and succeed primarily by touching the emotions. This means that emotions are the last resort of consciousness. If we want to estimate what we will not be able to artificialise in the future or what will be the most difficult to artificialise, then it is emotion. Emotions are the last refuge of the nonartefact, and that is why music should stay as proof that we are alive. The last evidence that we are alive and not yet an artefact.

Notes

1 Sloman, A. (1993) Prospects for AI as the general science of intelligence. *Prospects for Artificial Intelligence*. 1–10.

2 Strong AI is defined as 'being able to match human intelligence and having the ability to make decisions independently, like humans.' – James, A.P. (2020) Towards strong AI with analog neural chips. *2020 IEEE International Symposium on Circuits and Systems (ISCAS)*. 1–5. doi:10.1109/ISCAS45731.2020.9180545.

3 Attali, J. (1989) *La Vie éternelle*. Paris: Fayard.

4 Attali, J. (2007) *Karl Marx Ou L'esprit Du Monde*. Paris: Fayard.

5 Attali, J. (1989) *La Vie éternelle*. Paris: Fayard.

6 Clarke, R. (1993) Asimov's laws of robotics: Implications for information technology-part I. *Computer*. 26 (12), 53–61. doi:10.1109/2.247652.

7 European Commission (2021) Regulatory framework on AI. *Shaping Europe's Digital Future*. https://digital-strategy.ec.europa.eu/en/policies/regulatory-framework-ai.

8 Suchi, R. (2019) An AI completes an unfinished composition 115 years after composer's death. *VICE*. www.vice.com/en/article/neakqm/an-ai-completes-an-unfinished-composition-115-years-after-composers-death.

2   AI Music

On the Meaning of Music: Music Is a Language without a Dictionary

David Cope

Meaning

Meaning, in the context of this chapter, will be defined as *the use, purpose, or significance of something*. As vague as this definition may initially seem, it will provide us with a three-pronged rack upon which we can hang our hats and dig deep into the fundamentals of musical 'meanings.' The manifold ways in which we use music for accompanying dance and films, creating personal emotions and beauty in our lives, purposes such as specifically engaging music for commercials, relaxing on long journeys, or keeping callers from falling asleep while waiting for a human voice to wake us, and the significance of important performances that we hear while attending concerts or listening to music via the internet.

As an example, perceiving a sudden, extremely loud blast of not immediately recognisable sound holds meanings for most humans. 'Danger' comes to mind, as do words like 'run,' 'escape,' 'fear,' and many other related terms. While it was traditionally not defined as music, the second half of the twentieth century proved that many composers of the avant-garde considered it so. Is it possible that other less-blatant sounds such as those found in more traditional music could be analysed in like manner, especially by those who are familiar with such music, and thus derive meaning from what they hear? Could artificial intelligence be used to help determine meanings from a more global perspective? Furthermore, could such translations then enhance our understanding and appreciation of such music (Juslin & Sloboda, 2011)?

Since the early days of collegiate musicology courses, and to some degree, the same for music composition, great distinction has been made between programmatic and absolute music, the former indicating music framed around a recognisable story or obvious sonic memes, and the latter formed around a structure such as a fugue or sonata allegro form that likely does not lend themselves easily to emotional interpretations. *Programmatic* music, filled with sometimes obvious and sometimes less-obvious stories and emotional situations, tends to take the road of less intellectual challenges. On the other hand, classical music of, say, the baroque tends to embrace *absolute* concepts, and thus, academic education formed the main subjects and works of that tradition.

The battle between Hanslick and Wagner is justly famous, but it may stand as exemplary of two very different attitudes toward music that have vied for

DOI: 10.4324/9780429356797-3

dominion in the history of Western music from Plato to the present day. Wagner is heir to the tradition of romantic composers and idealist philosophers that holds that music can be expressive of the profoundest human concerns. According to Hagel, Schopenhauer, and Nietzsche, music provides access to the nature of reality itself; romantic composers such as Berlioz and Schumann thought of themselves as expressing deep insight into human subjectivity. By contrast, Hanslick exemplifies an attitude toward music that stresses the musical work as an autonomous entity divorced from the extramusical world, a structure of forms that can be studied in an objective, quasi-scientific way.

(Robinson, 1997: p. 2)

In this chapter, we will investigate many ways in which music can affect and influence listeners of both types and combinations of the two, thus allowing for communicating more meaningfully the composer's and performer's intents to an audience. Computational analytics can greatly enhance our abilities to research how precisely music can affect the emotional and/or logical aspects of communication. There are, of course, many other techniques which attempt to define, recommend, or deter readers from concepts such as musical hermeneutics (studies of interpretation or translation), which tend to create a bridge between the two. In both cases, the author will describe digital methods to discover and compare while analysing, and then reveal how their timing and placement make sense or don't based on the meanings of music (Mayer, 1961).

Note that music with lyrics provides distinct meanings for listeners, with the accompanying music assumed to substantiate these meanings rather than having meanings of their own. Thus, all but *'Dies Irae'* in this chapter do not have lyrics, and even *'Dies Irae'* does not use those lyrics when appropriated in most classical music.

Music

Music is often defined as 'vocal or instrumental sounds or both that are combined in such ways as to produce beauty of form, harmony, and expression of emotion.' The problem raised by such definitions is that to one person the results may be beautiful, and to another ugly. No two people are alike in their tastes. One cannot define music as only beautiful or only ugly. Many people would call contemporary music ugly, for instance, yet others quite beautiful.

A better definition of the word *music* would be 'sound created to be music,' yet even that broader and simpler characterisation falls short, given that birds, for example, create beautiful and musical calls but in no way would they consider what they've produced as music. Clearly, sounds borrowed from other birds gathered in assumed random orders by mockingbirds are a 'music to the ears' and again more likely to be some kind of communication between those of similar origins.

The best definition of *music*, therefore, would be 'sounds that anyone wishes to call music.' While this definition seems somewhat arbitrary, it ultimately makes sense since it allows freedom for each individual to broaden their musical horizons and please their minds and ears.

Artificial Intelligence

Artificial intelligence and *computers* have nearly synonymous meanings these days, though certainly they have their differences. For example, Google Definitions defines *AI* as 'the theory and development of computer systems able to perform tasks that normally require human intelligence, such as visual perception, speech recognition, decision-making, and translation between languages.' Each of these specialties most certainly fall under the AI bandwidth, yet many others do as well. Machine learning, for example, as in deep learning and earlier artificial neural networks, had helped in achieving extraordinary advances in recent years. In fact, the aforementioned tasks often require DL and ANNs in their learning processes. On balance, computer learning software accounts for most of the programs needed for strong scientific research.

> Hod Lipson of Columbia University says that 'the more intelligent AI becomes, the more sophisticated its art will be.' Kevin Warwick of Coventry University studies cyborgs. He says, 'Creativity in machines is there, whether we humans understand it or not. If we can figure out how memory works, then chips will go beyond memory, and will improve our creativity enormously.' Douglas Eck of Google tells me, 'Technology is special because it gives us AI, and AI may create things so beautiful that we may care differently about them.' Murray Shanahan of Imperial College in London was the technical adviser on the film *Ex Machina*. He states emphatically, 'In principle, because the brain obeys the laws of physics, computers can do anything the brain can do.' Blaise Agüera y Arcas of Google says provocatively, 'When we do art with machines I don't think there is a very strict boundary between what is human and what is machine.'
>
> (Miller, 2019: p. xxiii)

Computer analysis of music, in particular, requires significant combinational processes. For example, counting intervals in melodies between two works by different composers can cause complexities that the analysis of only one composer would not. As an example, Elgar and Chopin typically, but not always, tend to use wide intervals (Elgar) and mostly small intervals (Chopin) in their melodies. Using string instruments with mutes as Elgar does often makes his larger intervals less jagged, while, for example, Chopin's, with his emphasis on major and minor seconds, are far more jagged when performed with staccato dots on each note. Humans will quickly discover these differences, while computers will need some kind of actual sonic form of information in order to make the distinctions clear to those providing the analytical data.

The AI program that attempts to predict human emotional reactions to the music discussed in this chapter has at its centre an interchangeable database and a minimal number of words to use in response to its analysis (one hundred available words, from which typically one or two are chosen based on its analysis). The program is further equipped with several analytical techniques, each of which is tied to all the possible words. Since these word choices represent analysis, they are based on simple counts of findings and the final evidence derived from those which match the most unusual features of the work being analysed given the music of its time (in other words, reactions of audience members during the historical period of its first performance).

Following this sentence is a basic outline of the software program that attempts to define an appropriate generalised verbal description of how audiences would emotionally accept or reject what they feel is noteworthy music.

MIDI ≫
translate to numbers ≫
counts per classification ≫
cultural impact ≫
translate to words ≫
(1 to 2 words per work output)

While this may appear somewhat simplistic to many, the author tends to code straightforward programs that achieve the required goals rather than join those who prefer to work with off-the-shelf, more-popular software.

MIDI (Musical Instrument Digital Interface) files for works in public domain are available from many sites on the internet at no or very little cost. These files can then be organised according to whatever needs users have and be double-checked so that the original MIDI presents no errors. It's also important to ensure that the MIDI file results from a non performed version. Simple counting code will produce all possible numbers of particular appearances, which are then ranked according to the cultural norms of the time of composition. Finally, the amounts are tallied, and the translation to words takes place based on those counted. In short, the process of music-to-words identifying particular reactions gives users opportunities to compare various works for their emotional and/or logical content at the time of first performances.

The biggest frustration with this process is that of the mental states of listeners. Is she/he so experienced in the musical style of the work being heard, having listened to it so many times, as to become bored or even having never liked the piece from the first time it was heard? Worse yet, is the individual listener one that judges music according to her/his own values or assumes, as so many do, that the culture in which they have been raised in is right no matter what? These audience members represent the core of any meaning that music has, and tests depend almost entirely on the accuracy of their responses to prelistening questions. A few misevaluations can easily prevent research from any manner of accuracy.

Many people, even those familiar with one or more styles of music and those who conduct, perform, and/or compose at high levels of precision, consider music an abstract art form without explicit meanings, without semantics as languages possess. Certainly, music has no dictionaries, as languages do, to provide meanings for individual notes, groups of notes, motives, phrases, and so on, to guide audiences to a story or at least occasional sonic glimpses of meaning. There are, however, many different ways to understand music in meaningful ways, ways in which music can be appreciated beyond just being dramatic, beautiful, ugly, or boring.

Emotion versus Logic

Emotional states of consciousness, or what are typically called emotional feelings, are traditionally viewed as being innately programmed in subcortical areas of the brain, and are often treated as different from cognitive states of consciousness, such as those related to the perception of external stimuli. We argue that conscious experiences, regardless of their content, arise from one system in the brain. In this view, what differs in emotional and non-emotional states are the kinds of inputs that are processed by a general cortical network of cognition, a network essential for conscious experiences. Although subcortical circuits are not directly responsible for conscious feelings, they provide nonconscious inputs that coalesce with other kinds of neural signals in the cognitive assembly of conscious emotional experiences. In building the case for this proposal, we defend a modified version of what is known as the higher-order theory of consciousness.

(LeDoux & Brown, 2017)

Current research in neuroscience suggests that emotion and logic derive from the same origins in the human brain. This suggests that dopamine, serotonin reuptake inhibitors, and other contributing factors are not just fundamental to emotional reactions but logical ones as well. Now the questions become centred on the balance between the factors. Logic overrun by emotional reactions to music could still involve all features, though out-of-balance relationships can distort our abilities to understand the primary and true impact on the listener (Margulis, 2018). Add this to the cultural and personal knowledge and experience attained with the music, which makes analysis of reactions almost indecipherable (Sacks, 2008).

Thankfully, there are many other indicators that can reveal listener reactions. For example, physical, and thus visible, hints such as disgusted facial indications or tensed body reactions can provide valuable and sometimes obvious negative responses, with smiles or relaxation visible as positive accompaniments. One need not undertake MRI (magnetic resonance imagery) scans or similar procedures to identify the nature of responses. Many researches in related fields, for example, simply ask patients for their reactions and compare those simple responses with the aforementioned visual responses for verification.

Neuroscientists have discovered that listening to music, particularly at a young age, can physically alter the human brain, influencing future perceived meanings. The younger the listener is when encountering these meanings, the more influencing they can be to future interpretations of meanings.

Watching audiences at concerts can often be valuable tests if it's nothing for one listener sleeping and for another visibly reacting positively to the music being played. Few members of such audiences take time to visibly lie about their hatred or love of the music. One-on-one Q and A can also, on the other hand, prove much more difficult to judge (Levitin, 2007).

Musical Examples

In this section, you will find references to 'AI' tests and results that involve groups of people – members of undergraduate and graduate classes over decades – unwittingly taking 'tests' of a few minutes' time that made their way into this chapter. There were no reasons for these students to be other than truthful and candid in their responses, and while these were not scientifically rigorous, they provided enough evidence of accuracy to be quite useful.

There are three primary participants in the musical experience: the composer, the performers, and the listeners. Each has many roles to play, and each makes extraordinary contributions to the meaning of music. The composer inaugurates the process and provides what meanings she or he wishes to impart through the performers to the audience in the music when it's been completed. The performers' job is to as best as possible impart what the composer has composed to the listeners, who must give it their best to understand or waste the money they've paid to attend the concert. For most of the rest of this chapter, the emphasis (not the sole rationale) will be placed on the second two of these three participants. In other words, this chapter, at least from now on, will concern what many call 'performance practice,' the understanding of how the composers' wishes are implemented by performers and audiences, realizing as we do that only with the three participants working together can any true understanding of meaning take place.

In an ideal world, these four common musical patterns would lead to the following subjective expectations in experienced listeners:

1. Pitch proximity Listeners would expect an ensuing pitch to be near the current pitch.
2. Regression to the mean as the melody moves farther away from the mean or median pitch, listeners would increasingly expect the next pitch to be closer to the mean.
3. Downward steps Listeners would expect most intervals to be descending steps.
4. Arch phrases Listeners would expect phrases to begin with ascending pitch sequences and to end with descending sequences. (Huron, 2007: p. 93)

Some of the meanings of music are buried in hundreds of years of tradition, revealing musical form shared by hundreds of composers and performers of the first rank. Luckily, music theory can analyse certain meanings in music. The following expose some of that theory, since meaning in music cannot be discussed without it. However, this is not a chapter on music theory, or of any other, more academic aspect of music. The meaning indicated by music theory, while important, certainly, is not at the core of this chapter. What is at the core is the revelation of why certain music can so deeply affect our emotions and logic in the ways that it does. How, in fact, this music can sound so abstract in one sense and yet so revealing in another. How, unlike any other art form, music can so capture us in seemingly impossible ways even when we have no desire for it to do this.

There is one symphony among all others in the classic repertoire that has, since its premiere, been heard in whole or in part by most of the world's ears, and this symphony is Beethoven's Fifth. A great many people have heard it in its entirety numerous times, and others, likely in the minority, at least recognise it by its first four notes.

The first performance of Beethoven's symphony took place on December 22, 1808, in Vienna at a famous concert which also featured the premieres of his *Symphony No. 6, Piano Concerto No. 4,* and *Choral Fantasy.* We obviously have no recordings of this concert or any others of that time, but the score was certainly available, as it is today. Beethoven was the pianist for the concerto and several other pieces on the program and given credit as conductor even though many in the audience knew that the orchestra had refused to participate in rehearsals under his baton. The length of the concert was reported to be four hours.

Today, Fifth Symphony is on the programs of most orchestras of the Western world within their schedules every four or five years, with standing-room-only crowds attending. The four-movement work is a noteworthy opening to concerts, and the program notes take advantage of Beethoven's growing hearing problems to make the work seem superhuman, a composer composing a work that he himself cannot hear.

Contemporary audiences are often so aware of the bravura of the first four notes of this work that many listen closely to how these passages are performed by conductors and, in this case, the musicians themselves that they often critique the entire work on how these first notes have been prepared.

Interestingly, Beethoven's motive is today quite pinned to a similar motive in Haydn's *Military Symphony (no. 100),* one of his London Symphonies Since Beethoven studied with Haydn for a short time, such a relationship might not seem so far-fetched even given their often-disgruntled meetings and letters. Mahler's Symphony is a more obvious appropriation in that his opening solo is longer, rises instead of falls, opens his symphony with the motive being performed by trumpet solo, and uses triplets instead of eighth notes, unlike like Beethoven's version.

Haydn's *Miracle Symphony (no. 96)* and Mozart's *Piano Concerto (no. 25, K. 503)* show that 'short-short-short-long' rhythms were a regular part of the musical language of composers of Beethoven's time and previously. Many other works by Beethoven are also unified with this motive, such as the *Appassionato* piano sonata, the Fourth Piano Concerto, and the Fourth String Quartet, Opus 74.

These three examples play particularly important roles in performance practice and the manner in which performers, particularly conductors, can dictate many of the features of meaning in music to their audiences. For example, many performances and/or recordings of performances can bend to the conductor's personal preferences by playing the Beethoven opening three eighth notes as triplets and accenting as such, while others performing the Haydn and Mahler triplets as straight eighth notes, thereby ignoring the intent of the composer of the piece.

Listeners' discoveries of appropriations (borrowing passages from other works without revealing the source) can often be very important in communication of meaning in works of music, as composers such as Berlioz, Ives, and too many others to count have proven.

'*Dies Irae*' is a Latin melody attributed to Thomas of Celano of the Franciscans (1200 – c. 1265) based on a medieval Latin poem characterised by its accentual stress and rhymed lines. The title '*Dies Irae*' translates to 'Day of Wrath' in English. No other composer used this theme more than Rachmaninov, who sneaked it nearly into every musical work he composed, in one variation or another, sometimes just once, and on other occasions quite a bit more than once (Berlioz saved his for the last movement of his *Symphonie fantastique: Épisode de la vie d'un artiste. . .en cinq parties* [*Fantastical Symphony: An Episode in the Life of an Artist, in Five Parts*] *Op. 14,* composed in 1830). Because this theme is so well-known, its meaning can be considered literate in the sense that it's understood verbally as well as musically. To understand the function of histories such as this and how they can play serious roles in the meaning of the related music requires the revelations that accompany these histories.

Appropriation represents a simple way of communicating ideas wherein an experienced listener can interpret the listened-to music she/he is experiencing. Of course, recognising appropriations requires familiarity with the music one likes, a good ear to recall having heard a certain passage likely in disguise, and knowing something about the passage to interpret it. Many composers want listeners to identify the appropriations they use as a part of their compositional style and make them obvious as opposed to hiding them.

The entire output of Sergei Rachmaninoff contains direct references as well as variations and inclusions of sections of Gregorian chants (more on this soon to come). Igor Stravinsky is also well-known for his appropriations, mostly from Russian folk melodies and for stating blatantly that 'good composers borrow and great composers steal.' Even J. S. Bach, although not of his doing, orchestrated a keyboard concerto by Antonio Vivaldi which is now often declared composed by Bach rather than the composer he so admired.

Pitches, at least those of the classical-tradition modal and tonal music, reveal an inner capacity to predict next notes, harmonies, counterpoint, and manifold other important meanings with which those listeners who have no idea what's going on as well as those that do can more precisely understand the architecture of the music they are hearing. These meanings originated in the modes founded in the medieval and earlier periods of music history.

The number of modes varied from four to eight, and eventually twelve, and these were generally sung in unison by male choirs in the Catholic Church, the rhythm having been derived from a cantor that followed scores where the rhythm was derived from the distance horizontally between each melodic note.

Rhythm provides the backbone of music, as important to its meaning as are pitches in the form of melody, harmony, and counterpoint.

> Rhythm organizes time. In music, as a time-based acoustical language, rhythm assumes a central syntactical role in organizing musical events into coherent and comprehensible patterns and forms. Thus, the structure of rhythm communicates a great deal of the actual, comprehensive 'musical meaning' of a musical composition. At the other end of the musical communication process, rhythm also modulates the attention of the listener in the relationship to the perception of musical events. Rhythm guides the human brain to make sense of acoustical patterns and shapes by directing focus to important moments in the unfolding of the music.
>
> (Thaut, 2005: p. 6)

Articulation refers to specific attitudes performers will take towards the attack, length, connectivity, and dynamic of a pitch in a score. *Tempo* indicates the speed within which the attendant musical rhythm should proceed. It is indicated at the beginning of a work, usually by a type of note, followed by an equals sign and a number indicating the number of beats per minute. Tempo may instead be marked by Italian names, allowing more performer freedom.

To reveal some of the meanings of these parameters at least, we must decide whether music contains semantic or emotional contexts, some combination of the two, or something else entirely. We shall assume, for this chapter at least, that music consists of sounds that emit emotive feelings rather than semiotic constructs (the gestures, images, and objects notated in scripts sharing a semiotic importance equal to a spoken text).

Two broad concepts stand between success and failure. First, a work of music more than likely will have several different emotional passages or sections. The order of the emotions somehow paints a picture of what the composer feels or felt as the work was being composed, and the order of these requires as much authenticity as does each of the musical passages. Second, a proper balance between the music created by the length in terms of timing has to function effectively.

If the aforementioned do not exist, then the analysis is wrong, and a different approach must be taken. Determining this will depend on the programming of the computer. To accomplish this feat, we will use twenty fragments of music from the medieval to the contemporary periods, each demonstrating the researcher's personal judgements, which require the listener's personal, social, cultural, and experiential experiences with such music, and thus there exists a delicate balance between universal and individual understandings. There further exists the mental states provided by each listener that make any agreement between any two participants almost impossible to predict.

Let us begin with Edward Elgar's *Enigma Variations* (less known by its complete title: *Variations on an Original Theme, Op. 36, 'Enigma'*), completed in 1899.

Most striking in the melody (violin 1) is the number of leaps versus stepwise motion. The melody also consists of six groupings of four notes each separated by quarter rests, making it all the more disjointed. The computer program that analysed this passage used forty different analytical processes and ranked them according to unusual features based on 1,200 themes, averaging these so that unique aspects rise to the top. Interestingly, the rhythm is, by bar, first two eighths, followed by two quarters, and the next measure the reverse of that, providing three balanced two-measure groupings. The resulting computational analysis centres on these intervallic contrasts and thus outputs its resultant emotional value as 'confusing' (not far from an 'enigma,' from the title of the work). There are many other features of the theme upon which the variations are built, but computer analytics brought the above to the fore.

The simplistic AI associated with this research project provided a rather-straightforward response when queried: 'sad' and 'lonely,' no doubt influenced by the minor key and the slow tempo. When compared to human responses, the results did not match with the computer's guesses, but about 30% matched synonyms with the other 70%.

Tchaikovsky's *Romeo and Juliet* (*Overture-Fantasy*) was completed in 1880 (the third and final version). After a lengthy, held, apparent dominant seventh chord (about the 1/3 point in the piece), instead of resolving to the logical tonic, the music takes an unusual resolution as a German augmented sixth chord to a tonic 6/4 in another key, signalling a dramatic and unpredictable modulation from D major to Db major, where a dominating melody takes over and most listeners grab their mental stability for dear life. Known by many as the 'love theme' or the 'most beautiful musical passage in history,' the singular use of this progression in this work provides a lynchpin for the music's relationship between the two main characters.

The AI here proved much more accurate, with nearly 100% using the word *beautiful* or an acceptable substitute. Those that listened to the whole piece returned to the 30% mark, no doubt due to the highly varied tempos, dynamics, rhythms, and so on.

Not to be outdone, Anton Bruckner's Seventh Symphony's (1883) second movement's main theme repeats many times before the same kind of chromatic resolution takes place. In both this and Tchaikovsky's use, the relationship between the original key and the new key is about as distant as they can get, and the attentive first-time listener will be completely surprised.

Computer analytics, by comparison with dozens of other works from the same period, declares that these particular pieces of music use the augmented sixth chords sparingly and with diligent care. The word used by the program, *surprise*, does indeed describe the first-time listener's reaction well but doesn't clearly or accurately define the moment of arrival with the emotional content it holds – that of significant change and beauty of voice-leading and stepwise motion.

Orchestration can also signal many verbal and real meanings, such as birds (birdcall used in Respighi's *The Pines of Rome*), imitation of various animals with particular standard instruments (Prokofiev's *Peter and the Wolf* and Saint-Saëns *Carnival of the Animals*), and many others for which music owes many of its initial programmatic sources.

Stravinsky, initially famous for his work *Le Sacre du Printemps* (*The Rite of Spring*), was well-known for his use of the upper range of the opening bassoon solo (note the high D, an octave and second above middle C, for a basically bass-sounding instrument), which extended the instrument's previous capabilities by at least a major third, giving attendees a sound that no one had heard before.

Only one of the 'subjects' was familiar enough with Stravinsky's ballet to say she liked it, with the others finding it, as one said, similar to the orchestra 'tuning up.'

Dynamics can also play a major role in listener emotional reactions to performances. As can be seen in Beethoven's Fourth Piano Concerto, second movement, the strings begin loud and the piano soft (though how softly requires waiting until its second entry). The movement then proceeds with performances of the two distinguished parts' (soloist and string accompaniment) entrances coming closer to one another until they overlap slightly, with the dynamics more or less changing places. The message here (from both the author and computer) begins with anger and ends with placation. What's astonishing here is the more or less obvious theatrical domination over classical-tradition musical form: from a more standard A-B-A or similar structure to a dramatic and even before-its-time cinematic accompaniment (Powell, 2010). Furthermore, Beethoven's work (1806) precedes Berlioz's *Symphonie Fantastique* (1830) by twenty-six years.

The AI results with all humans listening to the entire movement proved a success to the extent that the group pronounced almost unanimously that the music meant an argument slowly calming to agreement, or hate turning to love, and the AI similarly producing but one word, that of *commencement*.

In contrast, Bach tends to use forms in a strict manner in which the beauty of his contrapuntal abilities lends a kind of singular quality to his works, particularly those of many multiples of movements, such as *The Well-Tempered Clavier*. Most of those hearing the music deemed it a puzzle being solved rather than a piece of music. The AI agreed with them. The leader, however, someone with a high degree of familiarity with the fugal form and the difficulty of succeeding like Bach did, intensely disagreed with everyone else in the room.

Strict forms in music history were popular long before Bach, especially the isorhythmic motets of Machaut discussed previously. The title, appropriately enough, translates to 'My End is My Beginning.' Bach composed many similar examples of highly structured compositions but quickly returned to his first love: the fugue. The Machaut approach, apparently, did not give him the joy that composing more freely derived contrapuntal music. Interestingly enough, the computer program designed for translating music's many various parameters into emotions found no particular words to describe the listeners' reaction to such pieces.

György Ligeti's *Atmosphères* (1961) produces much the same reaction from computer analysis. A work made world-famous by its appearance in Stanley Kubrick's *2001* (1968) film, it consists of extraordinary cluster chords typically formed by groups of similar instruments (i.e., woodwinds, brass, strings) precisely notated as opposed to Penderecki's similarly constructed early works but notated graphically rather than traditionally (see score to *Threnody to the Victims of Hiroshima* [1961]).

Carlo Gesualdo da Venosa (1566–1613), aside from being a double murderer (his wife and her lover having been found in bed together by her husband, Gesualdo), wrote the most chromatic and forward-looking vocal music, not matched until the late nineteenth century. His works remain unique in music history. Modal centres briefly remain coherent, but phrase cadences often make sudden leaps from one mode to a chromatically distant mode. For example, the middle phrase beginning in measure 2 initiates from a straightforward A-minor triad to a phrase ending in a C#-major triad at the cadence in measure 5 (the soprano top note respelled from a more properly E# to a more readable F natural). A diminished first-inversion triad on D# abruptly interrupts the difficult-to-analyse centre-phrase mode. Within 3 and 1/2 measures, Gesualdo manages to chromatically use nine of the twelve pitches, interestingly predating the work of Arnold Schoenberg in his twelve-tone school of thought (some three hundred years apart). The AI analysis of this remarkable differential, and aware of how unusual Gesualdo's work was, surprisingly output a strange combination of emotional descriptions, those being 'shock' and 'beauty.' Most student listeners classified the music as twentieth century in origin.

The masterpiece by Claude Debussy titled *Prélude à l'après-midi d'un faune*, known in English as *Prelude to the Afternoon of a Faun* (1894), demonstrates striking and often-lengthy silences, use of unusual instruments for its time (two harps, bells), immediate repetitions of motives as if in pairs, highly chromatic and complex harmonies, parallel voice-leading in harmonic changes, and extremes of dynamics. Once again, the AI involved in this study of emotions in human reactions to music produced interesting output from Debussy's masterpiece roughly ten minutes in length by outputting the words *sound painting* and *delicate*, both of which seem appropriate to the work and the probable reactions of audiences during its first performance in the year of its completion (Jourdain, 2008).

For this work, the AI produced the words *lazy* and *dissonant*, which did not agree with the responses of any of the subjects, who often agreed with one another with *sleepy* and *relaxing* or synonyms of such words.

The conclusion of the first movement of Mahler's Fifth Symphony provides a perfect example of how music notation can be difficult, if not impossible, to interpret. After quite a soft ending (ppp) with a solo flute, the violas, cellos, and basses are notated with octave-separated pizzicato lowest C naturals. To this point, their dynamic had been *pp*. On these three simultaneously plucked notes, however, the pitches are labelled with *sf* or *sforzando* (a sudden or marked entrance). To the untrained eye, *sf* might be taken to imply *f* (forte: loud), but as *The New*

Grove Dictionary of Music and Musicians and other reference works confirm, during Mahler's time, at least, *sf* had no dynamic implication at all, indicating only that the composer wanted the note reinforced or accented within the prevailing dynamic. Most orchestras and attendant conductors, however, assume that *sf* means loud, in fact, very loud, so they perform it that way. One conductor, who shall remain nameless here, understood the marking to be relative. In other words, he conducted it as an *sf* in *ppp* rather than *fff*. Thus, the movement ended with a very quiet pizzicato rather than a sudden burst of sound as in the other, more fashionable approaches. The question, then, is, who's right and who's wrong? Unless one can find a recording of Mahler conducting his Fifth, or a clever musicologist who finds a similar situation in another of Mahler's works with an *sf* in *pp* that might clear the situation, we will forever be confused by this situation (the ending of a movement being critically important regarding its meaning).

Conclusion

Most people tend to think of music as having meaning, and most of these people think of meaning in its literal sense. The fundamental aspects of 'meaning and music' are lost, however, due to the singularity of the word *meaning*. Music has *meanings*. Some listeners can derive similar meanings, but rarely do two have identical ones. Most audiences coming from different cultures definitely still get meaning from music, but those meanings often bear little resemblance to one another. Couples who've been together for decades still find not just different meanings from the same work but different emotions and logical messages as well. More astonishing, many individuals discover that their reactions to the *same* piece heard at different times in their lives produce contrary results depending on how they feel, their mood before they hear the piece, and what time of day they hear it. Whether music is primarily emotional or logical depends almost exclusively on local situational circumstances (Thaut & Hoemberg, 2014).

How can music have meaning, then, when each individual hears in that music different meanings and different to the point of no one having the same experience? We are used to meaning having a close-knit messaging, as in language. Music is the joy of feeling and thinking in unique ways that differ between the rest of the world's population and ourselves (Samama, 2015). To make things more interesting, these meanings arrive by both emotional and logical processes. We learned this *before* we were born; that in the baby's listening as we do to our mother's heartbeat, stable sometimes and radically changing at other times, these heartbeats contain messages of fear, love, anger, sleep, tenderness, and so on. It's our first contact with the real world, and neuroscientists tell us that these moments must be amazing for the newborn child. Don't imagine for a second that the mother's heartbeat does not get through to the yet-unborn child; it does, and it helps prepare that child for her/his life to come.

What we do know about music sans lyrics is that it's credibly and authentically self-conflicting for most people. No matter the rationale or the take on it by individuals with different backgrounds and different knowledge, it moves us in often very deep ways. It can recollect, can determine immediate connections, and is as mental as it is physical. It's a process to communicate even if that communication is different for each individual. There are some pieces of music that will regenerate memories and others that can change a listener's life forever. Its effects on our minds and bodies can be astounding and sometimes equally devastating, but no matter the results, music changes everyone and does so by being itself, a devastating and timeless art, that living without it, at least for many, is like living without life itself.

Bibliography

Beethoven, v.L. (1806) *Piano Concerto No. 4*.

Berlioz, H. (1993) *Symphonie fantastique*.

Bruckner, A. (1833) *Symphony No. 7 in E Major*.

Debussy, C. (1894) *Prélude à l'après-midi d'un faune*.

Huron, D. (2007) *Sweet anticipation: Music and the psychology of expectation*. Cambridge, MA: MIT Press.

Jourdain, R. (2008) *Music, the brain and ecstasy: How music captures our imagination*. New York: William Morrow.

Juslin, P.N. & Sloboda, J. (2011) *Handbook of music and emotion: Theory, research, applications*. New York: Oxford University Press.

Kubrick, S. (1968) 2001: A Space Odyssey. Metro-Goldwyn-Mayer. USA.

LeDoux, J.E. & Brown, R. (2017) A higher-order theory of emotional consciousness. *Proceedings of the National Academy of Sciences*. 114 (10), E2016. doi:10.1073/pnas.1619316114.

Levitin, D.J. (2007) *This is your brain on music: The science of a human obsession*. London: Penguin Books Ltd.

Ligeti, G. (1961) *Atmosphères*.

Margulis, E.H. (2018) *The psychology of music: A very short introduction*. Oxford: Oxford University Press.

Mayer, L.B. (1961) *Emotion and meaning in music*. Chicago, IL: University of Chicago Press.

Miller, A. (2019) *The artist in the machine*. Cambridge, MA: MIT Press.

Penderecki, K. (1961) *Threnody to the Victims of Hiroshima*.

Powell, J. (2010) *How music works: The science and psychology of beautiful sounds, from Beethoven to the Beatles and beyond*. New York: Little, Brown and Company.

Robinson, J. (1997) *Music and meaning*. Ithaca: NCROL.

Sacks, O. (2008) *Musicophilia: Tales of music and the brain*. New York: Vintage Books.

Samama, L. (2015) *The meaning of music*. Amsterdam, Netherlands: University of Amsterdam Press.

Thaut, M.H. (2005) *Rhythm, music, and the brain: Scientific foundations and clinical applications*. New York: Routledge.

Thaut, M.H. & Hoemberg, V. (2014) *Handbook of neurologic music therapy*. Oxford: Oxford University Press.

3 The Developer

What Do Music Software Developers Do?

Miller Puckette

Introduction

As will be seen by glancing at my references section,[1] what follows is not scholarly writing. Instead, it is a first-person reflection on what it means to use a computer to make music. In my forty-one years working in electronic music, I have taken many moments to reflect on what it is I am trying to do. If I had a clear answer to that question, I feel I would have little trouble sharing it. Nevertheless, I am still hard at work and do not yet have that answer. The practical side of the question could be stated thus: What are the minimal number of features a software system could have to enable a majority of musicians who use electronic means to achieve whatever they want or need to do? The more abstract side of the question is this: What is a musical object, and what does it mean to make or manipulate one? In what follows, I will lay out the terminology and thoughts with which I approach the question at both levels.

I have acted primarily as a designer in my work, despite having no formal design training. My design methodology is straightforward: I live from concert to concert and frequently work with musicians with more profound musical knowledge and skills than mine. My early work at the Massachusetts Institute of Technology (MIT) and Institute for Research and Coordination in Acoustics/Music (IRCAM) (1979–1994) was almost exclusively in collaboration with composers and often closely involved a music performer. Our roles were the well-established ones that would have been recognisable, say, to anyone at the Westdeutscher Rundfunk (WDR) studio in the early 1950s.[2] The role that I filled (that of the designer) was twofold, developing new techniques and applying them to a specific piece of music.

In the years since, as the world of electronic music became less Eurocentric and the boundaries between vernacular and 'art' music fell away, the three roles of designer, composer, and performer have broken down. The stages of preparation of a concert are no longer as demarcated as they once were. Improvisation now coexists with preplanned composition. Nonetheless, the routine holds. Collaborative, time-pressured work with others possessing complementary skill sets, followed by the post-performance weeks of cool-headed reassessment, correcting mistakes, and replacing any stopgap solutions with more thoughtful ones. Lastly,

DOI: 10.4324/9780429356797-4

attempting to generalise the new tools in the service of other projects and an effort to distil the experience into lessons that might inform the next production. A well-trained designer will recognise all this as precisely what they are supposed – *not to do*.

The results take shape over years and are not so much a fixed entity, such as a piece of software, but as a creative practice, involving a combination of the finished and unfinished, central and peripheral pieces of data, along with the knowledge of how to wield it, part of which is codified and part of which becomes folk knowledge. This knowledge is part of a more general culture that encompasses not only the tools and a memory of how they can be wielded but also more normative ideas about what makes a good or an imperfect realisation of a piece of music, and opinions as to how musical projects can best incorporate electronics. As an example of the latter, consider the use of electronics to imitate traditional musical instruments. On the face of it, this sounds like using margarine instead of butter. Why not just use butter, unless it is to save money and put a farmer out of work in favour of a distillation column? However, if you can make a synthesiser sound like a traditional musical instrument, you can, for instance, put it in dialogue with an acoustic one, always somewhat inferior but capable, on the other hand, of doing things the analogue cannot. Some uses of imitative synthesis might be interesting, but others are undoubtedly dull. A nuanced opinion would take these complexities into account.

The distinction between the roles of 'researcher' and 'realiser' is also breaking down. At IRCAM, for instance, I was always considered a researcher, and my job was to write software and develop algorithms for composers to use, such as a score follower or a real-time phase vocoder. In contrast, other employees (at that time called 'tutors' or 'musical assistants' but now called 'computer music realisers') were supposed to work directly with composers on musical projects. Although it was called 'research,' everything I did combined some well-known ideas with some original ones, often, as in the score follower, in a way that would be subsequently hard to separate. When some tool I made seemed particularly interesting, such as my 'explode' object,[3] I would write a short paper about it. However, my purpose was not research as such, although almost everything I built eventually landed in music production, usually one that I had in mind when developing it. I frequently would drop in unannounced at IRCAM's studios, where composers and their assigned realisers were at work, to ask what they were doing and offer advice and programming help. Many of the realisers (such as Cort Lippe, Zack Settel, Arnaud Petit, and Thierry Lancino) were composers in their own right and were sometimes offered IRCAM commissions. We would talk about their projects, which were often more technologically ambitious than those of the invited composers. When I saw that someone wanted to do something I did not know how to do with the existing software, I went back to my own machine and made something, usually the same day. If I saw that my solution could be made general enough to serve more than one musical project, I then baked it into the software system so everyone at IRCAM could access it. The realisers all knew what each other was doing, so word spread quickly whenever a new feature came online.

I am writing all this to show that what I was up to was not a proper software project. My work crystallised into two published systems, Max and Max/FTS. (Max and its offshoots have been commercially available since 1990, and Max/FTS is still functional, although IRCAM does not use or distribute it.) Nevertheless, the whole of my product was (and still is) a complicated mixture of code and culture. The practical and ethical matters I raise in the passages that follow do not specifically relate to software but rather to that mixture of code and culture.

The Pure Data Environment

Shortly after leaving IRCAM to join the University of California–San Diego (UCSD), I began working on and distributing a new software environment called Pure Data. I could easily have continued to contribute to Max and/or Max/FTS, but I had ideas that did not fit easily into that paradigm, and seeing that personal computers were now fully audio and video capable, I felt that a fresh start was needed. Among the many people I worked with on Pure Data were the composers Rand Steiger, Andrew May, Michael Theodore, and Kerry Hagan, performers Elizabeth McNutt and Juliana Snapper, visual artist Vibeke Sorensen, and fellow researcher/designer Mark Danks. My primary purposes in writing Pure Data were to first expand the available media from audio and MIDI to video, computer graphics, and network communications and, secondarily, to rethink the role of musical score and real-time process in music software. In the first aim, my work finds parallels in the later development of Max/MSP and Jitter. It now seems clear (if perhaps for reasons that are not yet understood) that software written to address real-time problems in music performance can also be well suited to all sorts of other real-time computing problems as well, notably live video.

My second purpose is more abstract and still largely unachieved. Although at the outset I aimed to make an environment for composers to use, I ended up making what amounts to a musical instrument: something that you tinker with during production but which is played in a concert. While there are ways to sequence predetermined actions in Max and Pure Data, the true power of both environments lies in their reactivity and the flexibility with which that reactivity can be specified. What I did not do was write an editor for entering musical scores. To do so in a way the composers around me would use, I would have needed to build Western musical culture into the software, in the form of staves, clefs, quarter notes, pitch names, etc. This process struck me as privileging old-fashioned ideas about musical composition, which would not only be a snub to non-Western musical practices but would also hamstring even strictly Eurocentric composers. After all, the whole purpose of electronic music was to emancipate ourselves from the limitations of traditional instruments, and in that respect, making a musical score editor would be a giant step backwards. Besides, I could not read music, so I would have had a colossal task in front of me.

Moreover, many other people were already writing powerful, common-practice music editors. Instead, with nontraditionally notated pieces by Xenakis, Stockhausen, and others in mind, I wanted (and still want) to make a musically interpretable 'draw' or 'paint' program. My first stab at this – Pure Data's 'data structure' facility – has so far proven too cumbersome for broad adoption. However, I would like to propose it as an incitement for some future researcher who can at least learn from my mistakes, and perhaps I can still figure out a way to make the paradigm more usable from within Pure Data.

Some Design Choices

Many of the decisions I made developing Pure Data (and Max before it) came out of the sense that electronic music, as I saw it practised in the 1970s, suffered from the lack of a precise and reliable musical instrument. A world of recording studio practice had all the precision and sonic capacity one could wish for, but none of it was realisable in real-time. Moreover, the existing real-time tools, which mostly took the form of synthesisers and stomp boxes, were limited in sonic range. Like many others, I had some experience playing music with family and friends, and I wanted to make some kind of an all-powerful electronic musical instrument, as versatile as the recording studio but able to turn a musician's real-time intuition into sound. I was only twenty when I got started, and such a grandiose project did not seem as crazily overambitious, even megalomaniacal, as it does in retrospect.

The first requirement for such a musical instrument would be to act as an analogue computer or as a patchable analogue synthesiser, in which a fixed network of processing modules communicates through interconnecting wires. This idea was already well established in both studio-based and live electronic music practice. In addition, it was a common procedure to add some sort of triggering mechanism for describing instantaneous state changes at discrete moments in time. In the design of both *Puckette* (1988) and *Pure Data* (1997), I focused on those state-changing moments, defining them as simply as possible as variable-length messages, each carrying an implicit 'trigger' occurring at a logical time. The system's state is held in 'objects' whose interconnections route the messages sent among them. It often happens that a message does not need any data at all but only needs to exist for its triggering effect. Rather than using an empty string to represent such a message, I chose the token 'bang,' which seemed a good name for something with no parameters and zero duration.

Over the more than thirty years of the development of Max and Pure Data, three critical elements were introduced on top of this basic structure. First, it gradually became practical to incorporate audio signals directly into the same patching language used for message-based computations. This brought to the fore the problematic nature of the interface between the two, which, although well defined, is often hard for practitioners to understand and manage. Second, it transpired that the real-time, reactive nature of Max and Pure Data made them useful in live situations other than pure musical performance. They have both acquired a wide range of input/output possibilities and media besides audio, notably graphics (via the Gem package, originally by Mark Danks) and video, and have found use in other forms than concert music, both performed and installed. Finally, as the state of the objects themselves has become more multifarious, various data visualisation and editing tools have been added: arrays, collections, cue lists, and in Pure Data, heterogeneous linked lists. A computer scientist would describe both Max and Pure Data as application-specific graphical programming environments for real-time multimedia. I think the paradigm's true gist lies in how scheduling and message-passing are done in the two programs.

The Blank Page as a Software Design Ideal

Every software developer has to make trade-offs between ease of use and neutrality. One way to make a program easy to use is to make one gesture do the work of many. The designer predicts which sequences of gestures are more likely than others and provides shortcuts for those sequences. Assuming you have all possible keystrokes bound to some action or another, each new shortcut introduced displaces whatever action was previously bound to the action. In choosing which shortcuts to provide, the software developer nudges the artist towards a particular set of choices.

An example would be Western pitch notation, in which 'C3' has become shorthand for 261.62 Hz. To introduce such a shorthand would be to nudge the artist towards the Western-tempered scale. This design decision privileges Western culture above non-Western ones and is somewhat problematic (although the issue is complicated because the computer itself is a product of the West). Nevertheless, even in the 1980s, when most composers at IRCAM would not have raised cultural hegemony as an issue, the very fact that they were using computers to make music implies a desire to specify things with greater freedom and precision than Western musical practice, for example, by limiting us to that twelve-tone tempered scale had accustomed them to. Although many software designers thought otherwise, my conclusion was that it would be wrong to provide Western pitch names as shorthand for the raw numbers.

In retrospect, my principle of not nudging has in some ways not so much de-Europeanised my software, as it has simply rendered it unavailable to some populations. I have heard from musicians from locales without access to high-quality public schooling that Pure Data is hard to use because it assumes a reasonably strong mathematics background. For such a user, the shorthand would have been an enormous help. Even if we manage to avoid such limiting (and possibly Westernising) shortcuts in our software design, there remains the problem regarding all the shortcuts that we simply are not aware we are making. We cannot talk explicitly about all the tacit assumptions that go into a design, but we can be pretty sure they exist and that at least some of them are pretty fundamental. It remains that they cannot be seen, not because they are too small, but because they are ubiquitous.

The Space of All Possible Music

A figurative way to consider software design is to imagine that the software has a range of possible outputs that can be reached, say, with the musician's given amount of effort. We could (reductively) model the musician as a bitstream of a fixed possible maximum length whose possible values represent each possible input she could generate in a specific fixed interval of studio time. The software, whatever it is, would produce some output or another for each possible input. So we then can try to imagine the set of all possible pieces the software could realise. If we remove the issue of redundancy (two inputs possibly leading to the same output, which we really should not ignore but will nonetheless), then any such software system whose input is the user's stream of data and whose output is sound has the same number of possible outcomes. Our problem is then to make this set, whose cardinality is limited, include, as a point, each one of every possible musician's possibly desired piece of finished music. Put in these terms, it all sounds easy enough.

To accomplish this, we need simultaneously to eliminate bias (which can be thought of as making our output set cover specific musicians' desired musical outputs at the expense of others) and to make the set as sparse as we can so that our fixed number of points 'covers' as significant a field of possibilities as possible – this is achieved by allowing small changes in input to make significant changes in output. Nevertheless, of course, we somehow have to avoid falling into the trap of introducing biases via the shortcuts mentioned above. Furthermore, here we arrive at what appears to me to be a paradox. To make the software expansive, in the sense that a slight input change, one sparing in its demand on the user, can result in a relatively significant output change sufficient that the set of all possible outputs can be as extensive as possible, we thus ought to automate whatever we can. That is, we ought to make it possible to specify large gestures using compactly contained instructions. However, how is this different from providing the convenient shortcuts – a tendency I have denounced a few paragraphs earlier? It is hard to imagine in this context a way in which the expressive power of an input language could not be a manifestation, at bottom, of the designer's preconceived and presumably heavily biased notions of what good music is.

I think that, in practice, most software designers, myself included, almost circumvent this problem by working directly with the musicians our software is intended to serve and, if we wish to avoid bias, seek the broadest possible representation among our collaborators. This could cause worry because my career has unfolded in only the most exclusive citadels of Western electronic musical practice.

My fretting over issues of bias is not only, and perhaps not even primarily, for ethical reasons – vital though they may be – but also to avoid excluding one population even more remote than any currently existing on earth, which is our future selves. My motivation can be cast in purely selfish terms: to ensure the longevity of my creations, to make waves, as far-reaching as I can, across time.

Preservation

Another matter I worry about is how a musician can make a permanently performable piece of live electronic music. It is commonplace to assume this is impossible because of ever-changing technological tools. This is a fallacy. Though some technologies do indeed fall out of use and availability (the 8-track tape cassette player, for example), others get frozen in place. An excellent example of this is the QWERTY keyboard. It is pretty clear now that we are stuck with this one, even though we would like to use a more ergonomic key layout. However, this stuckness brings a real advantage: anything that relies on the QWERTY keyboard design will never have that connection pulled out from under it.

We might describe the evolution of technology as a growing, shifting mass, parts of which congeal and harden into permanence, while others are still appearing, changing, and disappearing. This permanently fixed mass may be only a tiny part of the whole of current technology at any one time, but over time it grows to encompass a working set of technologies that is, if not everything we want, enough to do plenty with. Technologies such as the QWERTY keyboard, the C programming language, and the IPv4 network protocol will likely remain with us forever.

To become *QWERTified*, technology needs to become inescapably ubiquitous and frozen in time. Max and Pure Data, considered together as a programming paradigm, threaten to become the QWERTY keyboard of electronic music. They have already become so in the first respect mentioned above: there is no escaping them. Their ubiquity now raises the question of their permanence urgently: Have they frozen yet? Can a piece be realised using some version of Max or Pure Data and remain playable into the distant future?

The best answer I can give is partial: any composer or other artist who truly wants to can do a pretty good job of future-proofing a realisation of a piece of electronic music. This is especially true of Pure Data, whose development can make archival music documents, often at the expense of ease of use or feature-richness. It is even practical to make a test bed that verifies that a specific patch performs precisely as it did at some point in the past. To achieve this, the composer arranges a performance of the piece and captures the inputs of all personnel needed to play it: microphone signals, key and mouse events on computers, MIDI bytes, network packets, and anything else. These are all stored, with time tags, in files. The composer also records all the audio outputs of the computer during the performance. Then, at any time in the future, the same inputs can be fed into any desired version of Pure Data on any desired hardware, and if the outputs match, the new software and hardware have been verified to play the piece correctly.

This would not be possible if Pure Data were not written deterministically. Its single-threaded realisation has no race conditions, and its treatment of time is virtualised, so differences in CPU execution time do not alter the execution of a patch. This result comes at some expense in I/O latency and available CPU resources, especially because audio is computed in a single thread per PD instance. Other commercial and open-source programs can run more CPU instructions per second than PD can, but as far as I know, they do so at the expense of determinism. The open-source licensing of Pure Data is an additional reason that composers should be able to put some trust in their patches' longevity. There is no built-in reason that an open-source program should be more stable than a closed-source one, but at least the composer knows that, if necessary, the code can be retrieved and recompiled.

This is not so true of, for instance, the 1988 version of Max. I have a private copy of the source code, and I think I could recompile it for a virtualised Macintosh Plus computer if there were a good reason for me to do so, but I would not have permission to distribute either source or a running program. This particular question is moot since I do not think anyone has a 1988-era Max patch they want to run. Nevertheless, the fact remains that one cannot count on the availability of old code, not only because it might be hard to get running again, but mainly because of copyright restrictions that will complicate any attempt to distribute 1988-vintage Max before at least 2060. Having a carefully written, open-source, deterministically executable program is only part of what is needed. In addition, the composer must carefully keep track of whatever external dependencies the work depends on. For Max or Pure Data, these take the form of dynamically linked extensions that often come from third parties. There are thousands of these extensions floating in the ether, and it is often necessary to use some of them to realise one's musical ideas. Such extensions are often not strictly needed but can make the composer's job easier, thereby increasing productivity (and who does not want to be more productive?). However, to make a realisation long-lasting, everyone working on it must weigh the cost of that convenience in terms of the piece's exposure to potentially nonpermanent external code. Whatever choices are made, the source code to all such external extensions, as well as the source code to Pure Data itself, should be archived as part of any piece's realisation, and just to be on the safe side, the piece should be tested against regenerated binaries as part of the process of verification and archiving the piece.

Furthermore, even all these conditions are not alone sufficient to keep a piece of music alive. The unwritten artistic goals gave rise to the piece, whose knowledge might greatly help a future performer play it well. In the best case, a performance practice would emerge. Like everyone else in the new music scene, we software designers should think harder about this than we have so far. I think we do a much better job of recording our doings than, say, a musician a hundred years ago would have, but there remains an unknown amount of knowledge that is not captured and that future musicians and musicologists will wonder about.

Authorship and Ownership

Why would anyone willingly write a piece of software for someone else to use? I can think of two answers, of which my answer tends towards the first one: to be acknowledged as having done something cool. This is the same impulse that drives the artist: the desire to make a thing that others will somehow be touched by and, usually, will bring a measure of recognition to the work's maker. There might also be internal motivations that lead us to create software, or art, 'for its own sake,' but I think an unflinching look at such a motive would show that it is just an internalisation of a desire for status, even if it is only in the form of some kind of self-satisfaction.

The second possible motivation is, of course, money. Although the two coin sides are hopelessly entangled (status can bring money, and vice versa), it is helpful to think of them as essentially antagonistic needs. To extract money from someone by writing software or creating art, one needs for it to be rare. If the art is in physical form, this can be assured by simply making a product of high quality, difficult to reproduce or surpass. However, in the non-physical class, to which software and most aspects of music belong, the cost of duplication is negligible, and so, if money is to be collected, the copies must be made artificially scarce. However, this is the opposite of what must be done to satisfy the first of the two motivations: the lower the work's price (assuming rational consumers and conveniently forgetting Thorstein Veblen's observations to the contrary[4]), the larger a public can and will access it.

Artificial scarcity is accomplished by setting up both practical and legal obstructions to copying. Of the practical barriers, the most widely used today are what is called 'digital rights management' (DRM), through which a publisher contrives to make it possible to view an object on a screen or hear it from a loudspeaker without allowing the viewer to replicate the experience later or on other screens or speakers possibly owned by other people. This requires all sorts of contortions and ultimately can add significantly to the cost of producing and distributing an artefact.

I do not have hard numbers, but I think that, at least in the case of software, the cost of distributing it in a pay-walled, digital-rights-managed way will always exceed the cost of writing and maintaining the software in the first place. A rational software designer should ask if this was worth it. The commercial distribution model has many other commerce related costs that simply vanish if we distribute software for free. I do not know how to quantify this, but speaking for myself only, I would hate spending such quantities of time on activities that ultimately restrict peoples' access to my work.

Adding to this consideration is the worry that DRM would undoubtedly make it harder for future musicians to run my software since it is essentially a form of obfuscation. As mentioned above, one can also put up legal barriers to those who might wish to access creative work, of which the most prominent is copyright. There is an entire industry devoted to legal wrangling over copyright, and the sorts of questions that have to be considered (such as in a famous legal battle over a three-chord progression in *'Stairway to Heaven'*) can achieve full-on absurdity. The entire edifice is built on an act of artificial reification: the idea that a bitstream that represents a work – for instance, an executable file – is, ontologically, a substance that can be owned, bought, and sold. This is, of course, law. You can apparently say anything you want in law.

Copyright is, however, a useful idea for a different reason, one that does not require that we 'own' a thing but only that we 'hold copyright' on it, and that is control over attribution. While I do not think that an artefact's creator has any right to tell someone else that they cannot make a similar, even derivative, arte-fact, I do wish to clarify which artefacts came from me and which did not. I do not want anyone else to be able to sign my name on their product. I do not worry about the possibility that someone could claim that they had done a thing that I actually did; I can always point to my earlier copy of the same (or a similar) artefact. Nevertheless, the opposite sin, attributing to me something I did not do, needs some kind of control. Happily, this can be accomplished without the need for legal intervention: I can simply digitally sign all my work. I have not gone to the trouble yet, since I do not think this will ever be an issue. However, if some rogue actor starts impersonating me, that's when I'll start signing my output.

What's So Special About Music?

Many of the issues I have raised here are abstract and would have similar implica-tions for other digital art forms or even some other act of culture-making. How-ever, music seems to play a unique role in our fumbling attempts to figure out what is what in the world of software design. It is not just that music, being a fine art, evades understanding or even definition. Even among the arts, music seems the most mysterious. For all the library shelves of writing about it, all we know about it are observational descriptions of certain regularities in the data. We seem to be nowhere near a good explanation of what is going on when we make or listen to music or where its power comes from.

This puts the software developer in a strange position. When we try to figure out what a musician requires from a piece of software, there is often no way the need can be articulated; perhaps it is not known to the musician. When something is making a musically flat, uninteresting sound, there is no way to know how it could be changed into something more alive. If only the software were already made, we would have heard that it was doing some desirable new thing. However, when we inevitably lack that example, because we are trying to make something that does not exist yet, there is no language available to describe what it will be. Physical instruments, both orchestral and non-Western, evolve exceedingly slowly, and over history, many decades have gone by without introducing much of anything new.

Nevertheless, since about the mid-1960s, with the introduction of the commer-cial modular synthesiser, there has been an explosion of invention, today primar-ily reliant on processors for real-time control and/or audio computation. And yet I do not think we really know, at the bottom, what we are doing. I doubt we ever will. My job remains a pretty interesting one.

Notes

1 No reference section was provided by the author for this chapter.
2 120years.net (2014) WDR Electronic Music Studio, Werner Meyer-Eppler, Robert Beyer & Herbert Eimert, Germany, 1951. *120years.net*. https://120years.net/wordpress/wdr-electronic-music-studio-germany-1951/.

3 Puckette, M. (1990) *Explode: A user interface for sequencing and score following.* Geneva: ICMC.
4 Veblen, T. (2005) *Conspicuous consumption.* New York: Penguin.

Bibliography

Puckette, M. (1988) *MAX.* https://cycling74.com/products/max/.
Puckette, M. (1997) *Pure Data.* http://puredata.info/.

4 The Student

Shortcuts Guide to Music Theory

Artur Osipov

Introduction

This chapter explores how technological advancement altered the concept of the necessary 'basic' knowledge of the discipline's software development. As an example of its influence within the creative arts, the music industry will be considered.

It has been noted 'that as the student becomes skilled, he depends less on abstract principles and more on concrete experience' (Dreyfus & Dreyfus, 1980: p. 17) to learn. This observation is explored within music education and composition, emphasising the issues encountered by AI software programmers. Dreyfus contends that when acquiring a new skill, a student will progress through five distinctive stages: 'novice, competence, proficiency, expertise, and mastery.' The software developer needs increasing degrees of 'basic' music theory knowledge to develop the desired AI program in each stage. So that the student is capable of 'experiencing moments of intense absorption in his work, during which his performance transcends even its usual high level' (Dreyfus & Dreyfus, 1980). To achieve mastery, the student must transcend the standards of the prior four stages by drawing on profoundly personal experiences that shape the desire for originality. Moreover, a willingness to bend and shape the rules of music theory to achieve this target is essential. Leonard B. Meyer, in 'Exploiting Limits: Creation, Archetypes, and Style Change,' states that:

> The most significant and valuable achievements in the sciences have resulted from the falsification of existing theories and the promulgation of new ones based on previously unformulated concepts or unimagined relationships.
>
> (Meyer, 1980)

These mastery achievements are well-known, and figures such as Galileo, Kepler, Newton, Darwin, Mendel, and Einstein have become regarded as 'exemplary cultural heroes' (p. 177).

Sometimes, it is possible to transcend the limitations of the field and achieve mastery without prior knowledge of the expected standards. The music industry is an robust example of such a practice. There are many significant songwriters and

DOI: 10.4324/9780429356797-5

musicians in the history of popular music who, without any conception of formal music theory, could rely only on their emotional perception and experience of the music. Paul McCartney (McGovern, 2021; Wallis, 2018) has acknowledged that he does not understand music theory; Sting (Beato, 2021) focuses primarily on the emotional feeling while composing. Similarly, J. Dilla famously used the MPC sampler not as suggested by the machine's manual (using quantise function et al.) but instead instinctively created a new playbook where audio samples were imperfectly *cut*, retaining the rough edges to frame his *broken* rhythmics (Charnas, 2022; Questlove, 2013; Vlk, 2021). The J. Dilla catalogue of unique hip-hop instrumentals would inspire a generation of acoustic drummers (Stadnicki, 2017) set on reaching a new level of technical mastery. Each of these musicians created from a different Dreyfus stage; however, this supposed limitation did not prevent any of them from producing an inspiring musical legacy. This paradox is critical to our understanding of the dynamic between the AI programmer and the implementation of musical theory.

Music Theory

> The majority of music students graduate with little to no experience, let alone significant grounding, in the essential creative processes of improvisation and composition represents one of the most startling shortcomings in all of arts education.
>
> (Snodgrass, 2016)

Jennifer Snodgrass's quote emphasises a recurring problem with studying music theory. A typical undergraduate music course can only cover fundamentals such as 'terminology, labels, etc.' (Rogers, 2004). Therefore, by the time students are ready to go deeper into music theory, they have already reached the end of the curriculum. Snodgrass further points out that this teaching approach is outdated compared to the progress made in recent years in pedagogy (Snodgrass, 2020). The length of the course is contingent on the fact that students usually quickly tire of the amount and type of knowledge provided in the first years of study. Memorising various scales and key signatures and the accompanying sets of sharps or flats can become repetitive and dull. It also has to do with the fact that it is not enough to memorise all the essential elements, but it is vital to practice ear training to recognise them. It takes time and precision.

Let us examine two styles of music: tonal and post-tonal. Tonal music is the most commonly used. Examples are predominant in Bach, Mozart, and Western pop music. For this chapter, the definition 'tonality as a system in which pitches are organised hierarchically around a tonal center, or tonic' (Roig-Francolí, 2021) is used. This combination of particular notes is unique to this key signature. Tonal music was prevalent for three centuries before 1900. Its influence was such that the elements developed during that period are still used by composers (Trainor & Trehub, 1994) and in AI training datasets. Its sound and harmony are elemental (tonal) in its core, and the majority of its copyright long expired and is now available in the public domain. Circa the end of the 1800s, the tonal system had 'become so strained by chromaticism' that further system development was impossible (Kostka & Santa, 2018: p. 1) a twentieth-century transition, therefore, was inevitable.

As mentioned, Western pop music, in its majority, is written in the tonal style (Doll, 2013; Bigand & Poulin-Charronnat, 2016). However, sometimes it has included surprising elements implemented to make it sound fresh, such as modulation before the coda of a song (*'Money, Money, Money'* by ABBA, 1976; Beato, 2021) or the changing of the key signature between verse and chorus (*'Layla'* by Clapton & Gordon, 1970). However, despite such novelties, it has been argued that the overarching trend throughout the last seventy years is that the complexity of the songs is decreasing (Meindertsma, 2019) and they are becoming increasingly simpler from a compositional and harmonic point of view (Beato, 2017; Murphy, 2014). It is the music of the tonal system that is favoured for AI training datasets.

The second style of music discussed here is called post-tonal. This broad term includes a mosaic of different approaches used and sometimes combined by composers throughout the twentieth century. It was an experimental period for musicians heavily influenced by the development of the technology (Kostka & Santa, 2018: p. 241). An artist is free to choose 'the [mosaic] tiles' or even combine them when it feels appropriate (Roig-Francolí, 2021), and the musical choices are not 'exclusive; neither are they necessarily contradictory.' The complexity of posttonal music makes it unsuitable and inappropriate for AI training, especially with contemporary optimisation algorithms for datasets (Maeda et al., 2020; Cheng et al., 2021). Related difficulties in AI training are encountered in styles of music such as atonality, serialism, postserialism, and neotonality (Still, 1961; Ross & Smith, 1967; Hamilton, 1960; DeVoto & Perle, 1978).

Composition

The unsuitability of complex compositional techniques for AI training is demonstrated in the following examples.

The aural experience of listening to the hexatonic scale has been described as 'uncanny' (Cohn, 2004). Richard Cohn, in his 'Uncanny Resemblances: Tonal Signification in the Freudian Age,' compares the listener feeling with the work of Sigmund Freud on the uncanny, and a significant body of academic articles on the popularity of the horror genre supports Cohn's position (Dixon, 2010; Hantke, 2004; Fahy, 2010; Winter, 2014; King, 1981). These compositional techniques' emotional and subliminal impact makes it difficult to recreate a convincing example using a standard computer programming algorithm.

Another example is found when comparing music theory and musical composition. It is an accepted music practice that any strict borders of a *music form* are drawn from a broad umbrella concept determined by the harmonic needs of the content. This fluidity of structure presents a hostile environment for an AI training dataset seeking algorithmic continuity among conflict in the tilting rules of music theory. The interpretability of the sonata is a historically malleable example. James Hepokoski and Warren Darcy argue that modern research on the form reaches a similar conclusion, citing that '*textbook* view of sonata form is inadequate to deal with the actual musical structures at hand' (Hepokoski & Darcy, 2006).

It follows that a common approach to creative, generative music tools does not include harmonic aberration. For instance, consider what is known as the off-tonic climax point, a musical technique perfectly executed in the twenty-third variation from Rachmaninoff's *Rhapsody on a Theme by Paganini, Op. 43*. It is a vivid example of how compositional innovation successfully contradicts and surpasses the fundamentals of music theory (Johnston, 2014). The further development of 'the point' and related harmonic tensions in Rachmaninoff's compositions are unremitting musicology topics (Yasser, 1952, 1969; Woodard, 1984; Cannata, 1993; Bertensson, Leyda & Satina, 2001; Johnston, 2009; Fodor, 2017).

As defined by AI music scholar David Cope in *Eclecticism, Quoting, Sectionalisation, Overlay and Integration*, 'decategorising' processes are in play where the composer's style consists of a combination of several techniques and concepts. Each represents the search for perfect combinations of styles that a composer will travel to produce the desired music outcome. The exploration of the 'decategorisation' techniques for composing outlined in *Techniques of the Contemporary Composer* (Cope, 1999) echo the discussion of the creative search of the 'unformulated concepts or unimagined relationships' defined by Leonard Meyer (Meyer, 1980), compounding the challenge presented to AI creativity. The language of music differs fundamentally from the language of computers. However, the student of each encounters Dreyfus's five stages.

Programming

When a student learns to program, they begin with one of three paradigms (Brilliant & Wiseman, 1996): the procedural paradigm (languages such as Pascal and C/C+), the object-oriented paradigm (C++ and Python), and finally, the functional paradigm (the languages of LISP family). Each paradigm creates a different and fundamentally important understanding of the rules to operate within the programming environment. The novice software developer incrementally develops a personal programming style while training on different problems from various industries (Lau & Yuen, 2009). Like the musical counterpoint, programming languages changed with the development and disruption of technology. Each new programming paradigm was technologically superior to its predecessor, from machine language to assembly to procedural to object-oriented to aspect-oriented (Simmonds, 2012). Alan Turing pointed out that even if the functionality of more than one paradigm is the same, individual mechanical distinctions and concepts remain (Pylyshyn, 1980). Every step of developing the languages creates more shortcuts, simplifying previously complex procedures. This evolving environment produces tension within the fragmented discussion in academia regarding how the inherited limitations – the shortcuts – in computer programming affect human creativity (Beardon, 2006).

Conclusion

Music demands sophisticated knowledge from a programmer. While discussing Dreyfus's levels of skill acquisition, examples of musicians who transcended perceived limitations were given. In contrast, the programmer developing an AI music system relies on music theory knowledge to establish the human range of musical possibilities. The software's functionality is correlated depending on which of the five stages to mastery the AI developer is situated. Though a musician can halt developing their skill on any of these five stages and still create revolutionary music, the software developer will not.

A programmer creates a mechanical tool for interaction between the database and the user interface in most cases. As indicated earlier, examples from music theory show this is much harder to do with music. An AI music learning dataset is commonly based on Bach, Mozart, or Beethoven (AIVA, 2022; Zhu et al., 2021; Huang et al., 2019; Kong & Huang, 2021; OpenAI, 2019). Even the machine learning systems, without any human intervention in the dataset (Oord et al., 2016), implicitly absorb the fundamentals of tonal music theory hardwired and baked in the history of music composition.

Furthermore, many AI start-ups create music content based on genre, tempo, or the presentation of a reference track (Dhariwal et al., 2020; Soundraw, 2022; Dadabots, 2022; Carr & Zukowski, 2018; Amper, 2022; AIVA, 2022). These systems create a reiteration of the existing knowledge and do not allow any decisions unapproved by its inner decision tree (Murthy, 1998; Safavian & Landgrebe, 1991; Buntine, 1992; Fernández Leiva & O'Valle Barragán, 2011; Russell & Norvig, 2002). The manufactured AI creativity shortcuts the progress of music theory throughout the twentieth century and deprives human composers at each Dreyfus stage of the opportunity to develop and surprise. It is reasonable to suggest that any AI music system is comparable to biomimetics, a field based on the desires of humans to replicate processes happening in nature (Bhushan, 2009; Lee & Szema, 2005; Bar-Cohen, 2005b, 2005a; Lepora et al., 2013; Vincent et al., 2006). Modern AI technologies have presented the stage of imitation, a phenomenon increasingly prevalent in the global music industry, where the majority of start-ups are generating royalty-free and tonal music–based compositions for content creators (Clancy, 2021).

Any musician composing with an AI-driven tool should be aware of the inherent limitations posed to the human creative process. There are many supporting academic papers on the programming approaches that lead to the limitation of the functionality in different industries (Turk et al., 2014; Goel, 1985; Nunes et al., 2015). It is therefore crucial to open the 'black box' and its affective computing *nudges* and begin instead to challenge the programming community on the limitation of the so-called superabilities of the software.

The future development of AI should reconsider the shortcut integration of music into the software. AI tools that encourage broader implementation of a musician's ideas are needed for the economic development of the music industry and to lift the bar for new compositions of music. Innovative, humanly challenging, immersive music environments are the direction computer science should explore. No shortcuts needed.

Bibliography

ABBA (1976) *Money, Money, Money*. A Polar Music Production, Union Songs AB, Stockholm, Sweden.

AIVA (2022) *About AIVA*. www.aiva.ai/about#about.

Amper (2022) *AI music composition tools for content creators*. www.ampermusic.com/.

Bar-Cohen, Y. (2005a) *Biomimetics: Biologically inspired technologies*. Boca Raton, FL: CRC Press. doi:10.1201/9780849331633.

Bar-Cohen, Y. (2005b) Biomimetics: Reality, challenges, and outlook. In: *Biomimetics*. Boca Raton, FL: CRC Press, pp. 495–513. doi:10.1201/9781420037715.ch20.

Beardon, C. (2006) Programming and creativity. *Digital Creativity*. 17 (1), 1–2. doi:10.1080/14626260600665611.

Beato, R. (2017) *The four chords that killed POP music!*. Youtube. www.youtube.com/watch?v=nuGt-ZG39cU.

Beato, R. (2021) *The sting interview*. Youtube. www.youtube.com/watch?v=efRQh2vspVc.

Bertensson, S., Leyda, J. & Satina, S. (2001) *Sergei Rachmaninoff: A lifetime in music*. Bloomington: Indiana University Press.

Bhushan, B. (2009) Biomimetics: Lessons from nature – an overview. *Philosophical Transactions of the Royal Society A: Mathematical, Physical and Engineering Sciences*. 367 (1893), 1445–1486. doi:10.1098/rsta.2009.0011.

Bigand, E. & Poulin-Charronnat, B. (2016) Tonal cognition. In: *The Oxford handbook of music psychology*. Oxford: Oxford University Press, pp. 95–111.

Brilliant, S.S. & Wiseman, T.R. (1996) The first programming paradigm and language dilemma. *Proceedings of the Twenty-Seventh SIGCSE Technical Symposium on Computer Science Education*. 338–342. doi:10.1145/236452.236572.

Buntine, W. (1992) Learning classification trees. *Statistics and Computing*. 2 (2), 63–73.

Cannata, D.F.B. (1993) *Rachmaninoff's changing view of symphonic structure*. New York: New York University Press.

Carr, C.J. & Zukowski, Z. (2018) Generating albums with sample RNN to imitate metal, rock, and punk bands. *arXiv:1811.06633*. http://arxiv.org/abs/1811.06633.

Charnas, D. (2022) *Dilla time: The life and afterlife of J Dilla, the hip-hop producer who reinvented rhythm*. New York: Farrar, Straus and Giroux.

Cheng, D., Li, S., Zhang, H., Xia, F. & Zhang, Y. (2021) Why dataset properties bound the scalability of parallel machine learning training algorithms. *IEEE Transactions on Parallel and Distributed Systems*. 32 (7), 1702–1712. doi:10.1109/TPDS.2020.3048836.

Clancy, M. (2021) *Reflections on the financial and ethical implications of music generated by artificial intelligence*. Ph.D. Dissertation. Trinity College, Dublin.

Clapton, E. & Gordon, J. (1970) *Layla*. Layla and Other Assorted Love Songs by Derek and the Dominos. Polydor.

Cohn, R. (2004) Uncanny resemblances: Tonal signification in the Freudian age. *Journal of the American Musicological Society*. 57 (2), 285–324. doi:10.1525/jams.2004.57.2.285.

Cope, D. (1999) David Cope: Techniques of the contemporary composer. *Computer Music Journal*. 23 (4), 100–101. doi:10.1162/comj.1999.23.4.100.

Dadabots (2022) *We publish research on eliminating humans from music neural synthesis*. https://dadabots.com/science.php.

DeVoto, M. & Perle, G. (1978) Serial composition and atonality. *Notes.* 35 (2), 294. doi:10.2307/939682.

Dhariwal, P., Jun, H., Payne, C., Kim, J.W., Radford, A. & Sutskever, I. (2020) Jukebox: A generative model for music. *arXiv:2005.0034.* http://arxiv.org/abs/2005.00341.

Dixon, W.W. (2010) *A history of horror.* New Brunswick, NJ: Rutgers University Press.

Doll, C. (2013) Definitions of "chord" in the teaching of tonal harmony. *Tijdschrift voor Muziektheorie (Dutch Journal of Music Theory).* 18 (2), 91–106.

Dreyfus, S.E. & Dreyfus, H.L. (1980) *A five-stage model of the mental activities involved in directed skill acquisition.* Washington, DC: Storming Media. doi:10.21236/ADA084551.

Fahy, T. (2010) *The philosophy of horror.* Lexington: University Press of Kentucky.

Fernández Leiva, A.J. & O'Valle Barragán, J.L. (2011) Decision tree-based algorithms for implementing bot AI in UT2004. In: J.M. Ferrández, J.R. Álvarez Sánchez, F. de la Paz & F.J. Toledo (eds.), *Foundations on natural and artificial computation.* Berlin, Heidelberg: Springer, pp. 383–392.

Fodor, G. (2017) Sergei Rachmaninoff's piano concerto no. 4, op. 40: Implications of the arc shape in the formal structure and in Rachmaninoff's interpretative conception. *Studia Universitatis Babes-Bolyai-Musica.* 62 (2), 199–224.

Goel, A.L. (1985) Software reliability models: Assumptions, limitations, and applicability. *IEEE Transactions on Software Engineering.* 11 (12), 1411–1423. doi:10.1109/TSE.1985.232177.

Hamilton, I. (1960) Serial composition today. *Tempo.* (55–56), 8–12. doi:10.1017/S0040298200045538.

Hantke, S. (2004) *Horror film: Creating and marketing fear.* Jackson: University Press of Mississippi.

Hepokoski, J. & Darcy, W. (2006) *Elements of sonata theory: Norms, types, and deformations in the late-eighteenth-century sonata.* Oxford University Press. New York, USA.

Huang, C.-Z.A., Hawthorne, C., Roberts, A., Dinculescu, M., Wexler, J. et al. (2019) The Bach Doodle: Approachable music composition with machine learning at scale. *arXiv:1907.06637.* http://arxiv.org/abs/1907.06637.

Johnston, B.A. (2009) *Harmony and climax in the late works of Sergei Rachmaninoff.* Ann Arbor: University of Michigan.

Johnston, B.A. (2014) Off-tonic culmination in Rachmaninoff's rhapsody on a theme of paganini. *Music Analysis.* 33 (3), 291–340.

King, S. (1981) Why we crave horror movies. *Short Essays for Composition.* 524.

Kong, M. & Huang, L. (2021) Bach style music authoring system based on deep learning. *arXiv:2110.02640.* http://arxiv.org/abs/2110.02640.

Kostka, S. & Santa, M. (2018) *Materials and techniques of post-tonal music.* New York: Routledge, 5th edition. doi:10.4324/9781315229485.

Lau, W.W.F. & Yuen, A.H.K. (2009) Exploring the effects of gender and learning styles on computer programming performance: Implications for programming pedagogy. *British Journal of Educational Technology.* 40 (4), 696–712. doi:10.1111/j.1467-8535.2008.00847.x.

Lee, L. & Szema, R. (2005) Biologically inspired optical systems. *Biomimetics.* 291–308. doi:10.1201/9780849331633.ch11.

Lepora, N.F., Verschure, P. & Prescott, T.J. (2013) The state of the art in biomimetics. *Bioinspiration & Biomimetics.* 8 (1), 013001. doi:10.1088/1748-3182/8/1/013001.

Maeda, W., Shimizu, T., Fukuoka, T. & Morikawa, I. (2020) Dataset properties and degradation of machine learning accuracy with an anonymized training dataset. *2020 Eighth*

International Symposium on Computing and Networking Workshops (CANDARW). 341–347, November. doi:10.1109/CANDARW51189.2020.00072.

McGovern, K. (2021) How the beatles began – part one. *The Beatles FAQ*. https://medium.com/the-beatles-faq/the-birth-of-the-beatles-learning-to-play-f8cd4bc6b619.

Meindertsma, P. (2019) Changes in lyrical and hit diversity of popular US songs 1956–2016. *DHQ: Digital Humanities Quarterly*. 13 (4).

Meyer, L.B. (1980) Exploiting limits: Creation, archetypes, and style change. *Daedalus*. 109 (2), 177–205.

Murphy, S. (2014) A pop music progression in recent popular movies and movie trailers. *Music, Sound, and the Moving Image*. 8 (2), 141–162.

Murthy, S.K. (1998) Automatic construction of decision trees from data: A multidisciplinary survey. *Data Mining and Knowledge Discovery*. 2.

Nunes, C.A., Alvarenga, V.O., de Souza Sant'Ana, A., Santos, J.S. & Granato, D. (2015) The use of statistical software in food science and technology: Advantages, limitations and misuses. *Food Research International*. 75, 270–280. doi:10.1016/j.foodres.2015.06.011.

Oord, A.V.D., Dieleman, S., Zen, H., Simonyan, K. et al. (2016) WaveNet: A generative model for raw audio. *arXiv:1609.03499*. http://arxiv.org/abs/1609.03499.

OpenAI (2019) *MuseNet*. OpenAI, 25 April. https://openai.com/blog/musenet/.

Pylyshyn, Z.W. (1980) Computation and cognition: Issues in the foundations of cognitive science. *Behavioral and Brain Sciences*. 3 (1), 111–132.

Questlove (2013) *Red bull music academy*. www.redbullmusicacademy.com/lectures/questlove-new-york-2013.

Rogers, M.R. (2004) *Teaching approaches in music theory: An overview of pedagogical philosophies*. Carbondale, IL: Southern Illinois Press.

Roig-Francolí, M.A. (2021) *Understanding post-tonal music*. New York: Routledge, 2nd edition. doi:10.4324/9780429340123.

Ross, W.B. & Smith, R. (1967) Serial composition. *Notes*. 24 (2), 272. doi:10.2307/894670.

Russell, S. & Norvig, P. (2002) *Artificial intelligence: A modern approach*. Upper Saddle River, NJ: Prentice Hall.

Safavian, S.R. & Landgrebe, D. (1991) A survey of decision tree classifier methodology. *IEEE Transactions on Systems, Man, and Cybernetics*. 21 (3), 660–674.

Simmonds, D.M. (2012) The programming paradigm evolution. *Computer*. 45 (6), 93–95.

Snodgrass, J.S. (2016) Current status of music theory teaching. *College Music Symposium, JSTOR*. 56.

Snodgrass, J.S. (2020) *Teaching music theory*. Oxford: Oxford University Press, 1st edition. doi:10.1093/oso/9780190879945.001.0001.

Soundraw (2022) *Your personal AI music generator*. https://soundraw.io.

Stadnicki, D.A. (2017) Play like Jay: Pedagogies of drum kit performance after J Dilla. *Journal of Popular Music Education*. 1 (3), 253–280. doi:10.1386/jpme.1.3.253_1.

Still, R. (1961) Serial composition today. *Tempo*. 57, 5–6. doi:10.1017/S004029820004571X.

Trainor, L.J. & Trehub, S.E. (1994) Key membership and implied harmony in Western tonal music: Developmental perspectives. *Perception & Psychophysics*. 56 (2), 125–132.

Turk, D., France, R. & Rumpe, B. (2014) Limitations of agile software processes. *arXiv:1409.6600*. http://arxiv.org/abs/1409.6600.

Vincent, J.F.V., Bogatyreva, O.A., Bogatyrev, N.R., Bowyer, A. & Pahl, A.-K. (2006) Biomimetics: Its practice and theory. *Journal of The Royal Society Interface*. 3 (9), 471–482. doi:10.1098/rsif.2006.0127.

Vlk, K.T. (2021) The last donut of the night: Revisiting J Dilla's masterpiece. *Medium*. https://kayteevlk.medium.com/the-last-donut-of-the-night-revisiting-j-dillas-masterpiece-351bbe7f43ee.

Wallis, A. (2018) Paul McCartney admits he and the Beatles can't read or write music. *National, Globalnews.ca*. https://globalnews.ca/news/4503916/paul-mccartney-cant-read-music/.

Winter, B. (2014) Horror movies and the cognitive ecology of primary metaphors. *Metaphor and Symbol*. 29 (3), 151–170.

Woodard, S.J. (1984) *The dies irae as used by Sergei Rachmaninoff: Some sources, antecedents, and applications*. Doctoral dissertation, The Ohio State University, Columbus.

Yasser, J. (1969). The opening theme of Rachmaninoff's third piano concerto and its liturgical prototype. *The Musical Quarterly*. 55 (3), 313–328.

Yasser, J. (1952) Progressive tendencies in Rachmaninoff's music. *Tempo*. 22, 11–25.

Zhu, Y., Hahn, S., Mak, S., Jiang, Y. & Rudin, C. (2021) BacHMMachine: An interpretable and scalable model for algorithmic harmonization for four-part baroque chorales. *arXiv:2109.07623*. http://arxiv.org/abs/2109.07623.

5 The Artist
Interview with Holly Herndon

Martin Clancy

- *It is unusual for an artist's work to appear in installations, clubs, and the academy. How did these opportunities arise for you?*

I have had an unconventional career path. Early on, I discovered that I embraced the laptop as my primary instrument and began developing custom processes with it. I realised that many of the processes I applied in academic performances were similar to the software set-ups I used in Oakland's warehouse rave scene. Within each community, there existed some specific rules that were not to be broken. In the academy, one should not use a kick drum and a 4/4 pattern, whereas, in the warehouse, that has its own meaning. I learned that there could be similarities in different communities, but each brings its orthodoxy. I never really felt 100% comfortable working within any one specific community's orthodoxy. Instead, I prefer being in between and bringing things from different spaces. That said, many of those boundaries have dissolved. The longer I spend in music, I realise that there are sometimes different economic models in play that tease out, flatter, or promote different kinds of work. Working within the commercial festival market asks one thing of you, whereas a new music commissioning environment will ask something else. There is little neutral space. Being aware of what the broader structure is asking of one's practice and trying to claim some agency over that is something I think about.

I think the opportunities to present across fields are mostly as a result of my practice not strictly adhering to any one field. I am fortunate that has worked out so far; however, it does feel that as a result, I have to work extra hard to establish my own context.

- *Have you ever used the same piece of work in these separated environments?*

Aspects of a piece, I had a solo show at the Guggenheim (2014). I was working with the Iranian philosopher Reza Negarestani. Reza had written a libretto for this wild, multichannel soprano piece that I did. It was a six-channel ambisonic situation where the audience sat in the centre and the surround sound of her (remote vocalist Amanda DeBoer) voice clambering through the room. Mat Dryhurst was kicking chairs around and being disruptive, and her voice was coming through the network. She was in New York, and her voice was

DOI: 10.4324/9780429356797-6

coming through from Oklahoma. It was about translating the ultraphysicality of a person who was not in the room and creating a highly mediated, highly intimate experience. It was a conceptual piece in a museum setting. However, I then took the vocal performance and included it in a dance track called 'Dao.' The track is essentially a techno banger that is sometimes played in clubs. It is funny because the name of the libretto is called *Crossing the Interface*.

The libretto took on a new life in 2021, when I made my first NFT series under the same name. I created animations using machine learning text to image prompts, coaxing the neural net to animate the story.

• *When we speak about AI, what does that term mean to you?*

The word *AI* is misleading. *Artificial* connotes 'human-made,' which is appropriate, as most applications currently are trained on human input. I prefer the term *machine learning*, which I find more descriptive. When using *AI*, we often get lost in a fantasy world of sentient robots, which is not the world that I am interested in. I am drawn to what is feasible today and how technology impacts composers and artists in different ways. Sometimes, when we focus on far-future fantasy, it obfuscates the more interesting aspects of this technology – a technology that can reveal aspects of ourselves to ourselves. When we jettison the associations of AI with machine autonomy, which is a pipe dream in most instances, there are many more interesting applications to explore. I sometimes feel like the most grandiose claims around AI can blind us to what is really cool about new machine learning techniques.

• *Regarding your approach to AI, you are explicit about what you are not interested in. For example, you have questioned the use of AI to reproduce the Western music canon and referenced James Mtume's comments on 'artistic necrophilia.' Can you share your thoughts in this regard?*

I received, with Mat Dryhurst, a grant to experiment with neural nets and machine learning tools. When we started researching the area, we noticed that many people were taking the music approach of automating the composer. This approach was interesting for research, but not that interesting for creative practice. James Mtume's 'artistic necrophilia' statement is prophetic.[1] I see composition as a living, breathing art form. I am a composer, and I do not want to replace myself. The idea of forever recreating the creative decisions of past composers is dystopian to me in a way. I often call it an aesthetic cul-de-sac, where we just get in this loop where we are making the same decisions perennially.

We do not need infinite Beethoven fugues; we already have an entire repertoire. Composers respond to the material conditions surrounding them and which are constantly updated and responsive. We, as human beings, have many fantastic sensors that computers do not have access to and which we can constantly train to be responsive to what is happening. I made a distinction from the beginning because I did not want to train the tools on the canon of historical music specifically for aesthetic reasons. The more I started to think about it, I noticed the ethical implications of scraping up past creative output and then spawning a new version from that source material. It felt problematic to me, and I did not want to use other people's data without naming them or paying them. Instead, I kept my data training set contained to a group of people that I could compensate for their participation. I also did not want to train the system on just past Holly compositions, because I would end up with a mishmash of past Holly works.

I would never have come up with *Proto (2019)*; it would have just been a mashup between *Movement (2012)* and *Platform (2015)*, and that is not interesting. *Proto* came because of the human intervention that I brought to it, and I specifically did not want to deal with MIDI data, MIDI files, as we all know that scores are this kind of imperfect, symbolic representation of music that misses out on much of what music is. Instead, I was drawn to much of what was developing in the audio space at that time. I happened to start working with neural nets when many excellent new white papers were being published, where researchers were starting to work with audio in an exciting way. That created a heavy constraint around the project distinct from many other machine learning projects that I see happening now. So I limited myself and gave myself these early constraints, such as I am just going to work with audio and not working with automated compositions. Furthermore, I am only going to work with audio that I can compensate human participants for.

- *Before your work with AI, you spoke about using Max. Do you still use PD or Max programming languages?*

I still use a lot of Max patches that I have been using for years, but I am not actively programming in Max that often. Max was an essential part of my finding myself as a musician and understanding agency over the tools and the processes. There is a tipping point with Max development in which many people get so obsessed with the development of the systems themselves that they forget about the artwork. For me, if that is taking up too much time, or if I can collaborate instead with an engineer who can do it twenty times faster, then I will do that. Learning Max helped me to understand what is happening on a fundamental level and gave me confidence to redesign and be deliberate with the tools I use.

- *Is working with neural nets just a new tool with the same approach as other programming languages?*

It is familiar but different in important ways. I have less of an understanding of what is happening. They call it black box technology for a reason. I would experiment with different kinds of weights and different inputs, but comprehending what is happening from neuron to neuron is more opaque than if I am designing, for instance, a reverb unit in Max. AI is so much more complicated. Chance is part of being a computer musician. In traditional algorithmic music, there may be randomisation, but with machine learning, even though there is an element of chance, there is a logic to it. It can surprise you, but it feels much more ordered, which I found interesting and attractive because there would be certain moments where I would feel like I fully understood the logic of why the machine came to that conclusion. It is a fascinating process. I am like, 'I get it, I understand this perspective.' It is highly collaborative and intimate in that way, particularly when it is trained on yourself. In years to come, I am convinced it will change the habits and tools we use to compose in alien ways. It is still nascent, which is why we used the baby metaphor, but when you embrace it, you can intuit just how different things are going to be.

- *After the COVID-19 lockdowns, has your work with your own AI music creation 'Spawn' altered your approach to collaborating with human musicians?*

During the pandemic, we were forced to separate, and that makes me appreciate the collaborative approach all the more and makes me desire it more. I think, as soon as we can congregate in space together, the popular suggestion that the future of live performance will be online will be viewed as bullshit. We have seen how limited, in your bedroom, a rave can be. It is a stopgap, but there is no comparison to physical congregation together.

I had always dreamed of having a vocal ensemble. When I moved to Berlin, that was the first time it was feasible financially, and unlike living in San Francisco, I had the necessary physical space available. I took two different research approaches with Spawn; machine learning is a futuristic, new human coordination technology. The vocal ensemble is an ancient human coordination technology present throughout human development. I started seeing powerful parallels between those two things. Training with the ensemble brought it all together.

- *The human voice has been central to your work. Is that an ongoing curiosity?*

I think so. When I went to Mills College, it was kind of controversial to focus so heavily on my laptop, and it was nice to see composers like John Bischoff or Morton Subotnick come to Mills and play in the concert hall on the computer. That was cool. I began looking for ways to make the performance with that laptop more embodied so that I could communicate with the audience more, you know, mirror neurons, all that kind of stuff, showing performer intent, and the most immediate kind of tool that I had was the voice. I grew up singing in choirs, and I was like, 'Oh, I will just use my voice as a kind of data input.' I have never really considered myself a singer. I always said that my best asset is my mediocre voice, because it required that I create all of these meta-instruments to make it do things that I wanted to do that otherwise I would not physically be able to. It has been a core part of my relationship with my laptop. I later explored the voice through the internet. Moving on to machine learning and asking what I can do with the voice that I would not physically be able to do felt like a natural progression. I feel like with each album, rather than being in rebellion from the previous work, it is more like, 'Oh, I learned all this stuff. I have all of these new tools and abilities. How do I apply that to the next project?' I see a continuum between the albums, where I am trying to build rather than reject.

- *You spoke of not coming from a privileged background and your desire to diversify income sources. Can you talk about the economics of being a musician, about AI and intellectual property, and where this all might be going?*

Of course, privilege is relative. I knew I would need to make my own way in the world, which is often not the case in art circles. It is a giant hornet's nest and so interesting. One thing that helps me frame it is the advent of recording technology and how that enabled sampling. Machine learning is, however, very different; it is a paradigm shift for music. I look at some of the things that sampling was not very good at, for instance, artist remuneration, accreditation, basic forms of human decency. Simultaneously, sampling also created entirely new genres of music that we love and appreciate. It pushed music aesthetically forward to new areas. The big question is, how do we address the earlier mistakes at the protocol level when we build these new systems so that when it takes off, we won't repeat them? With machine learning, I create a distinction between sampling and *spawning*. Sampling is a more simple, one-to-one mechanical reproduction, whereas *spawning* is a smart and reproductive blossoming from an origin. Within the systems that we are working on right now, if, from the very beginning, we think about ways to tie back to the originators of ideas that do not inhibit creativity, I think we need to be thinking about that right now. However, that is often thought about once the cart and the horse have left the barn.

I often consider these ideas specifically concerning the human voice. It is a really nice, messy area to think about what is possible regarding vocal performance or vocal effects should one be able to protect and copyright a vocal style, for instance, an R & B or bluegrass singing tradition. Should that be copyrightable, and if so, how would that work? There are historical examples I found in Joanna Demers's book *Steal this Music*, for example, Nancy Sinatra's court case.[2] Goodyear Tyre wanted to license Sinatra's track *'These Boots Are Made for Walking,'* and she said no, so they hired a sound-alike and a lookalike using her signature style. Sinatra sued them and lost. Fast-forward to the eighties, and Bette Midler had a track, *'Do You Want to Dance,'*[3] that Mercury Sable wanted to license. Ford hired a Midler soundalike; the vocalists went into the studio and tried to emulate Bette Midler's pronunciation and how she stretches specific notes. It was an emulation of the Bette Midler style. Midler was successful in suing that her vocal rights had been violated.

Similarly, with Tom Waits and the Frito Lay potato chip case. A part of me finds it inspiring that one can protect one's likeness, because I think our vocal sovereignty is very important. However, it is messy, especially with someone like Tom Waits. The Tom Waits sound is modelled on the Black Southern American sound. So can Tom Waits claim ownership of that? How do you draw the lines of ownership when traditionally copying has been hidden under the guise of human inspiration? When an automated machine does that copying, can that machine be considered to be inspired? I do not know. It opens up many questions regarding what a vocal style is and who it belongs to.

Nina Sun Eidsheim, the musicologist, writes about race and the voice and how voices and language are inherently communal. You learn through your community, and then the performer performs with agency through that group voice. There is this back-and-forth between the individual and the community in which that individual is situated. Perhaps the only way to deal with these questions is to look at how indigenous copyright has been dealt with.

In some cases, there are specific protocols in Aboriginal Australia regarding communal IP. Similarly, the Navajo print is a protected print that requires tribal permission. It may be that this way of thinking, coming from a different framework of thinking about collective ownership and collective remuneration, is a way forward. I am experimenting a great deal with that now.

- *If the legislation is insufficient, then an ethical response might be required. If we speak of ethics, what values are important to you?*

Oh, wow, that is a good question. No one has ever asked me that before. There is the philosophical field of ethics. However, it is also more of a practical, applied approach regarding what I feel is fair.

I think about how certain decisions that we make may benefit or create the kind of environment that is ultimately good for the development of music. If we inhabit a punitive IP hellscape, that is probably not going to be a suitable environment for creativity or for furthering the field of music. If we also have a landscape where the less powerful are constantly being copied or not given credit for their work, that creates an untenable situation. It is ultimately not good for musical development, because those who could contribute cannot make a living from their work, and the most compelling new ideas are often incubated on the margins.

With the minuscule development budget for the AI system that I was making, I could still carve out enough time and energy to think about the ethical repercussions involved. The most prominent players in the machine learning space should undoubtedly carve out some resources towards this. I had a conversation with OpenAI about this after they released the JukeBox project.[4] I was critical because OpenAI did not ask permission from the living performers; they were training the remarkable system on. They agreed with me! They were open to it. Their argument was that they thought JukeBox sounded so crappy that no one would care that it was not that impressive. I was like, 'Not at all.' You are using someone's likeness, and ideally you would invite a musicologist on staff to contextualise what this means. Whether or not they will implement that, I do not know, but they seemed very open to it during the call, which was cool and validating to my approach on the issue.

- *Outside of AI-generated music, do you have any thoughts on the broader application of AI in the music ecosystem, such as streaming recommendation systems or transferring the agency from an active to a passive listenership?*

I just wish it was less opaque, especially with the recommendation systems, because it does not necessarily have to be. All of the music that lands in these platforms, the way that they are arranged and presented, the kind of human culture that went into that is being obfuscated. For instance, it is difficult to tell where a song came from, who played on it, who is in the same community. The music is just WAV files with some sort of, like, tag, and then being recommended through an automated process through file or listener analysis. It risks dehumanising the music we listen to. This, in turn, is having a super negative effect on music culture. It treats listeners like children that need to be coddled and only served up something that they will find palatable. This is damaging for cultural health when instead we should be confronted with ideas that are strange and new and that we are not comfortable with first. This process helps us grow as individuals, and art and music are a massive part of that. I can only imagine how my taste would be now if I had just constantly served up what I liked as a sixteen-year-old. That would be awful. One of the reasons I think about this significantly is that Professor George Lewis was a huge inspiration for my work, who created the Voyager system in the late eighties. He wanted to build an improv system that he could play along with. He wanted the Voyager to emulate the aesthetic of the community that he came out of, which was the Chicago, ACM improv scene. I loved that he acknowledged that music is not a purely analytical analysis devoid of context. Music comes from a culture and a place. These decisions were human-made because of the material and political conditions that existed on the ground.

- *Are there any critical-reading texts that you think are outside of direct musicology or computational creativity that have inspired you?*

Reza Negarestani wrote a book, *Intelligence and Spirit*, about artificial intelligence, or as he refers to it, as inhuman intelligence. Anil Bawa-Cavia wrote a great piece for *Technosphere Magazine* called 'The Inclosure of Reason.' There is also Peli Grietzer, who is coming from comparative literature and wrote his PhD on using neural networks for writing. His series of articles for *Glass Bead* called *A Theory of Vibe* is very approachable and was influential on my thinking.

- *What about the emergence of AI artists? Either ambient or embodied AI, we are beginning to see AI represented as artists. Perhaps Lil Miquela[5] and Hatsune Miku[6] are two very different early examples of this phenomenon?*

I love that you bring up Lil Miquela. The founder, Trevor McFedries, has featured on our podcast[7] and clarified some things that I found fascinating. Lil Miquela is not an AI. Lil Miquela is an avatar for a team of friends who are essentially able to be a pop star as a group. The way that Trevor explained it, human stars are expensive; they have expensive lifestyles and tastes. His Miquela team can use an avatar as their pop star and redistribute the wealth to a larger group of people than in a traditional trickle-up pop industry.

Rihanna is not just Rihanna. Instead, Rihanna, as my partner Mat explains, is like a Formula 1 driver. Rihanna and Ariane Grande are Formula 1 drivers, the best in the business. However, you need the whole pit crew to engineer the car for the race. Without the pit crew, there is no Formula 1 race. I think the Lil Miquela communal experiment is fascinating.

Conversations like this and my previous research on machine IP inspired the Holly+ project, which we did not get to discuss but is an attempt to realise what a fully open artist identity might become. We came up with a way for anyone to make artworks as my twin, creating tools for people to make songs with my voice, and a novel IP framework that is permissive but also compensates me for my likeness when (and only when) money is made from it. The next instrument we have developed is highly realistic and can even be used to convincingly sing in my voice in real time. Things are going to get a lot crazier!

Notes

1 George, N. (2005) *Hip Hop America*. New York: Penguin Publishing Group. https:// books.google.co.uk/books?id=7TRApef2zW4C.
2 Nancy Sinatra, Plaintiff-appellant, v. the Goodyear Tire & Rubber Co. An Ohio Corporation, Young & Rubicam, Inc., a New York Corporation, Defendants-appellees, 435 F.2d 711 (9th Cir. 1970).
3 Midler v. Ford Motor Co. 549 F. 2d 460 (9th Cir. 1988).
4 OpenAI (2020) *Jukebox*. OpenAI, 30 April. https://openai.com/blog/jukebox/.
5 Tiffany, K. (2019) Virtual influencers have got to be a fad – right?. *Vox*. www.vox.com/ the-goods/2019/6/3/18647626/instagram-virtual-influencers-lil-miquela-ai-startups.
6 Sabo, A. (2019) Hatsune Miku: Whose voice, whose body? *INSAM Journal of Contemporary Music, Art and Technology*. 65–80.
7 Interdependence (2020) Interdependence 3 – Trevor McFedries (Brud / Lil Miquela). *Interdependence*. https://interdependence.fm/episodes/interdependence-3-trevor-mcfe dries-brud-lil-miquela-nonpatrons.

Bibliography

Herdon, H. (2014) *Expanding Intimacy at Guggenheim NYC*. Concerts and Installation. Guggenheim Museums and Foundations, New York, USA.

6 Robotics

Fast and Curious: A CNN for Ethical Deep Learning Musical Generation

Richard Savery and Gil Weinberg

Introduction

Our work in robotic musicianship aims to facilitate meaningful and inspiring musical interactions between humans and robots. The motivation for our research is to discover how robotic collaborators can enhance and enrich musical experiences for humans. Robotics allows us to explore and achieve new musical possibilities, by combining computer generation with physical sound and embodied agents. In addition to rich acoustic sounds, robotic musicians can provide intuitive visual cues that improve musical interaction through expressive physical accompaniment to sonic generation. Our work is also driven by the artistic potential of mechanomorphic approaches, such as humanly impossible speed and precision, and the possibility to surprise and inspire human collaborators through artificial constructs and algorithms.

Over the last few years, developments in robotics and AI have led to new societal and ethical considerations that inform our work. Similar considerations have started to be explored in broader functional AI and robotic research, and we believe they have not been adequately addressed in creative work. In this paper, we examine a number of ethical considerations for the field of musical AI and robotic musicianship, where artificial intelligence and creativity are embodied in agents to create novel musical experiences. These ethical issues include bias and lack of diversity in data selection, prohibitive training requirements and subsequent environmental impacts, and the exclusion of artists without adequate computational resources. Other challenges include the impact of AI on human agency and employment, and the ownership of material and training data. Moreover, deep learning networks tend to have a distinct lack of transparency in system design, which decreases any chance of interpretability to developers, musicians, and listeners. We have considered these ethical consideration through our work in robotic musicianship and have developed new approaches to address ethical and societal concerns.

In the second half of the chapter, we present a new, human-focused deep learning system designed to address some of these ethical considerations by allowing participants agency over interaction and generation. The system is simple, easy to train, and allows for efficient, interactive real-time generation of musical

DOI: 10.4324/9780429356797-7

improvisations in performance with human musicians. It is comprised of a generative, convolutional neural network using a novel data format that appears to allow improved learning of nonlocal dependencies and repetitive structure across beats within musical phrases. We have observed that the system is able to learn to generate convincing and coherent improvisations from relatively small amounts of data. It can run effectively with limited computational resources, minimizing environmental impacts, and produces convincing musical interactions in a live performance setting.

Robotic Musicianship and Ethics

It is common for researchers in artificial intelligence and music to ignore the potential societal implications of their work (Briot et al., 2017). To address this lack of consideration, we have investigated our own work in robotic musicianship in an effort to identify potential ethical and societal challenges. In the passages that follow, we describe some of these challenges and our efforts to address and reconcile them.

Human Agency and Employment

One of the main recent societal concerns has been the replacement of human agency and employment by AI and robotics (Vochozka et al., 2018). In our own work on musical AI and robotic musicianship, we have constantly questioned whether our approaches might replace, rather than enhance, human musicians. To maximise enhancement over replacement potential, we centred our work on human-robot collaboration, rejecting project ideas that did not have a strong human presence in the loop. We design our robots to highlight their unique artificial advantages, such as novel, algorithmic-driven music generation and humanly impossibly mechanical abilities. Human collaborators, on their part, bring their unique human advantages to each interaction, such as emotion, expressivity, and creativity. Our ultimate goal is to facilitate musical experiences that would inspire and surprise human musicians, allowing them not only to explore new and exciting music but also to think about music in new ways. We believe that our human-centred design would not lend itself easily for replacing human agency and employment, not only by our team but also by others who may be building on our work in the future.

Bias, Diversity, and Accessibility

Significant concerns about bias and discrimination in AI and machine learning stem from inherited prejudices in dataset creation and selection as well as human algorithmic decisions (Gomez et al., 2018). It is difficult to dismantle such biases, as these systems' inner workings are often not transparent even to their creators (Barocas & Selbst, 2016). An added challenge to diversity in AI is the potential restriction of use and development of systems due to financial and technical impositions. This might lead to broadening the gap between the have and the have-not, preventing a wide social adoption of AI and its benefits.

In our work in music and AI, we have explored several approaches to address these issues. For example, we have made an effort to collect and create datasets of works by underrepresented minorities addressing both gender and race, including datasets for music and lyrics in genres such as jazz and hip-hop. We also adapted and personalised our systems to allow for a wide range of users to participate in the interaction. Most of our systems can rapidly adapt to new datasets and allow for easy individual iteration when needed. Creating systems that are portable to a variety of operating systems is another effort we are making to allow users with limited hardware capabilities to engage with our systems. While our robots are not affordable for wide populations, we aim to include shareable software versions that can operate on many computer systems. We have also been as transparent as possible regarding the inner workings of our design, while acknowledging that some of the technical aspects might still be perceived as black boxes to our users, participants, and audiences.

Data Copyright and Consent

Copyright law around AI is rapidly evolving, addressing a variety of perspectives and stakeholders. For music generation, the key issues stem from potential ownership claims from music dataset creators, developers of the AI system, and potential users of the system. Sturm et al. (Sturm et al., 2019) address these copyright issues, current legal status, and the potential future legal implications, reaching the conclusion that a fundamental rethinking of these topics is needed. One of the main open questions in that regard is who owns the product of a creative AI system – the dataset creators, the system designers, the public, or maybe the machine itself? Leading AI companies such as OpenAI (a company with a mission statement built on AI benefiting all humanity) argue that IP should be free to use for AI, with training constituting fair use (O'Keefe et al., 2019).

In our own work, we have striven to receive explicit consent from the creators of the data we use. It is up for debate, however, whether in some cases, the goals of the system and the nature of creative development might not allow for receiving full consent from creators (Tinker & Coomber, 2004). We believe that consent should be asked for and received whenever possible. We have used this approach in multiple systems (Savery et al., 2021a, 2019b), where we manually created datasets. For some of our systems, which relied on extremely large datasets, we have not come up yet with a realistic way to ask and receive consent from all contributors.

Cultural Misuse

New developments in music and AI may be less susceptible to misuse by governments and corporations in comparison to technologies such as facial recognition or behavioural data analytics. However, it is important to note that due to the strong cultural significance of arts and music, the unethical utilisation of AI in music might lead to serious societal consequences. Research in ethnomusicology offers many perspectives on approaches to ethical consideration of music as a cultural artefact (Shelemay, 2013). Philosopher Appiah extends that to say that the value of human life means 'valuing the practices and beliefs that lend them significance' (Appiah, 2008), such as music. The possibility and implication of devaluing a musical tradition has been explored by some research in AI and music, which, while subjective, is felt by many communities (Sturm et al., 2019).

In our own work, we have integrated culturally relevant datasets, such as an Australian Aboriginal language, with robotic voice (Savery et al., 2019a). These datasets were public domain and encouraged for use by the creator as a way to share the sound of the language. Even so, it is not clear that the creators of the dataset from the late nineties could predict this 'future use' case. Additionally, while the creator of the dataset gave permission, the language and substance of the dataset are a component and representation of the cultural identity of a larger population, which needs to be considered. Moreover, we recognise that our efforts to address bias and diversity by focusing on genres such as hip-hop and jazz should be done in collaboration with and consultation by members of the relevant communities to prevent cultural appropriation of these genres.

Music is a deeply personal medium central to the human experience, with implications beyond just commercial use. Clarke et al. demonstrate that even the act of passive listening to music can significantly change the cultural attitude of listeners (Clarke et al., 2015). We believe that it is crucial that future work in music and AI consider the outcome and possible influence of created systems.

Public Perception and Presentation

Musicians have been showing a wide range of responses to musical AI, some describing the integration of AI into music as a welcome collaborative development, while others address the combination as an existential threat (Knotts & Collins, 2020). In our own work, listeners have also questioned the use of AI as potentially reducing the essential quality of music, with some survey respondents providing quotes such as, 'It removes the inherent skill of a creator. To close ones eyes, and dig into one's own musical vocabulary, and come up with something original and tailor made' (Savery & Weinberg, 2018). We have also received informal feedback from audiences in our concerts and presentations, questioning a wide variety of topics – from whether our robots can indeed play in the style of humans to the possible ethical implication of even calling our robots 'musicians.' While it is inviting to dismiss these claims as common responses to the introduction of new technology, they should be given consideration in future work. We, therefore, make a deliberate effort to fine-tune our message to the public, avoiding overstatements and becoming extra sensitive to public concerns about our work.

Environmental Impact

One of the most important societal concerns for humanity today is climate change. Every action we take as a society and as individuals needs to address the potential environmental impact. The creation and development of AI systems has a significant environmental cost, especially in the training process. The training of one deep learning model has the carbon cost of 315 flights from New York to San Francisco (Strubell et al., 2019).

We believe one of the best ways to consider our impact is to factor efficiency as a key component in system design, as has been proposed by Schwartz et al. (Schwartz et al., 2019). This would mean that a bigger network that performs slightly better is worse than a more efficient network with slightly reduced performance. In the system presented in this paper, we extend this principle by placing efficiency as a primary goal and design constraint.

Overview of Robotic Musicianship at GTCMT

The Robotic Musicianship Lab at the Georgia Tech Center for Music Technology has developed multiple robotic platforms, including Shimon, Shimi, Haile, and multiple drumming prostheses. The first robotic musician was Haile, a percussionist robot designed to play a Native American powwow drum. Constructed from plywood, it used a solenoid to actuate one of the drumming arms and a linear motor to actuate the other. Shimon was the next robotic platform, designed to play the marimba and to provide visual cues with their social head. Shimon was also the first robotic musician to utilise artificial vision, and in 2019, it was transformed into a singing robot, recording and releasing an album of computer-generated songs and hip-hop freestyle. The third robot was Shimi, a table-top musical companion, designed to function as a musical social robot. We have also developed two primary robotic prostheses for amputees – a wearable drumming arm and a piano-playing arm, and a wearable drumming arm for general-purpose use. In addition to the hardware platforms, we also developed five key design principles to guide our research: listen like a human, play like a machine, be social, watch and learn, and wear it.

The first principle – listen like a human – relates to the way robots perceive music. This principle focuses on computational modelling of musical perception, with the goal of allowing robots to interpret music similarly to humans. Listening like a human requires the ability to recognise musical features, such as beat, similarity, tension, and release. Perceptual modelling of human input is crucial for meaningful interaction and collaboration as it allows robotic musicians to develop an internal model of human ensemble members' expressive, emotional, and musical creations.

Playing like a machine focuses on our mechanomorphic goal of developing novel musical outcomes not possible for human collaborators. We achieve this through hardware and software innovations focused on new techniques for musicianship. In terms of new hardware, this can involve the implementation of brushless DC motors, allowing marimba playing at forty notes per second across eight mallets, creating new timbre, and allowing for new composition styles (Yang et al., 2020). We also incorporate software design that is built around mechano-morphic design and consider implementations of systems that offer nonhuman interactions, without an end goal of sounding like a human or passing a Turing test. This includes projects like Shimon the Rapper (Savery et al., 2020b), a robotic hip-hop system that develops new musical outcomes for human and robot performance. By combining both novel software and hardware development, our robotic musicians create innovative musical responses that push musical experiences and outcomes to uncharted domains.

Robotic platforms and embodied agents allow for social interactions not possible with computer interactive music systems, leading to the third design principle – be social. Interaction with gestures can significantly affect the musical experience, increasing the social engagement and leading to more fluent turn-taking (Hoffman & Weinberg, 2010). Each of our robotic platforms uses physical movements for visual choreography to add to the aesthetic impression for audience and performers. In particular, the percussion robot Haile was used to study the effect of ancillary gestures on co-player anticipation and audience engagement and to explore the subjects' perception of the robot and the music it generates (Weinberg et al., 2006). We have also used musical robotic platforms to develop new forms of interaction for nonmusician interactions, such as new methods for social robots to speak (Savery et al., 2020a).

Our robotic platforms also use artificial vision to watch and learn from human collaborators. In the music-making process, visual connection is key to taking advantage of social gestures and creating music as an ensemble. Musical gestures can act as cues to synchronise music and anticipate other musicians' future decisions. This work has been covered in many performances, from responding to guitar cue synchronisation to real-time detection of emotion and film analysis for live movie composition (Savery & Weinberg, 2018).

Our final robotic design principle – wear it – involves potential application as prosthetics to allow musicians with disabilities to enhance their performance ability, merging their biological body with technological enhancements. The current frontier of robotic musicianship research at Georgia Tech focuses on the development of wearable robotic limbs that allow not only amputees but also able-bodied people to play music like no human can, with virtuosity and technical abilities that are humanly impossible. This research is currently developing platforms for drum and piano performance.

Convnet

In the following section, we describe a new system designed to address many of our ethical goals, while exploring new areas of research in robotic musicianship. In previous work, we have not used real-time machine learning interaction, rather generated offline sequences before a performance. Many of the ethical goals align well with the development of a real-time system, such as portability and low environmental impact. Real-time generation also increases the agency of the human performer, allowing much greater control over the performance as a whole.

A crucial ethical and design choice for the system was the use of data, with the goal of being trainable on a small dataset. A small dataset reduces training time and environmental impact while allowing more flexibility and future variation. Our system trains only on data given by the performer before a concert, requiring about an hour of recording. This allows us to ensure we can always have consent for the data used and allow human agency over the style that is created by the system. By allowing the user to supply their own data, we also hope to prevent bias from broader datasets that may act against the performer using the system. Custom datasets also increase the personalisation of the system to each user. Transparency is still a challenge from a technical perspective, although showing performers the training and exact data used helps develop an understanding of how ideas are being created.

The system was developed for interaction with expert performers, aiming to build off their musical vocabulary. We choose to allow for call and response and dialogue-like interaction where an improviser plays a phrase to which Shimon responds, creating a constant musical communication. These interactions can take place in strict four-bar trades or open, free-form exchanges. While implementation in Shimon was the primary goal, the system allows for software interaction using just a virtual instrument. The generative system combines a convolutional neural network (ConvNet) built-in Tensorflow 2.0 with Python and a MaxMSP patch which communicate using OSC. Figure 6.1 shows a system overview where the MaxMSP patch receives a monophonic instrument, converting it into symbolic data, and sends it to a U-Net-inspired ConvNet, which generates and returns new melodies.

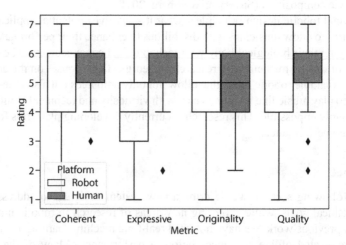

Figure 6.1 System diagram.

Considering the environmental implications, we believe it is useful for these systems to note their environmental impact. For our system, each training run uses 0.16 kg CO2 eq. (Lacoste et al., 2019), calculated based on training in an Nvidia 1080 GPU. Through iteration and testing, we trained the system eight times in total.

Interaction

There are two main forms of interaction available, either trading fours or free-form response. Both forms of interaction use the same model for processing but feature slightly different input and output methods. The system allows a MIDI keyboard or audio from a monophonic instrument for interaction; for an audio file, the notes are translated into MIDI values. For trading fours, Shimon listens to and processes the input for four bars and then generates an output for the following four bars. Before trading fours, a tempo is set, between 60 BPM and 180 BPM, with Shimon analysing the audio input at twenty-four samples per beat, allowing the system to learn triplet subdivisions. During the input cycle, a list of 384 notes is recorded, which is sent to the generation model. The model then returns a 384 list back, which is played as the melodic response.

The method for free interaction is more complicated and allows for much more variety from the performer. In this style of interaction, Shimon and the human improviser can choose to respond at any time. Shimon constantly listens to and stores the input from the human improviser, even while Shimon is playing. By constantly listening and processing the input, Shimon is able to respond back to the improviser at any time. To allow the recorded input to fit the 384 grid required by the system, Shimon has the ability to stretch or reduce the input sequence. In the trading fours version, each 384 value sequence can represent a length of 4.8 seconds (four bars at 180 BPM) to 16 seconds (four bars at 60 BPM). For the free version, we aim to keep the length of phrase in this range, but inputs often slightly vary. Variable-length input-and-output capability is achieved via a stretch-and-shift process, wherein an input melody less than four bars long is stretched temporally to fit across four bars, and its corresponding output is compressed and shifted back to the input's original time span and temporal location.

Shimon chooses when to respond based on three possibilities, either after two seconds of silence from the input stream, after twelve-second intervals, or with random interjection. Each second, there is a 10% chance of random interjection, where Shimon responds based on the most current input. In early experiments, we allowed longer silences; however, we have found that extended silences and gaps from computer performers can increase uncertainty from human collaborators.

Dataset

A key component of the system is the data representation and processing through the system. Both the trading fours and free interaction provide the model with a 384-length vector of MIDI note values. This vector is then converted to a 24×16 matrix, which is processed by the model. This novel data format arranges beats in a column such that time steps relative to the beginning of each beat are stacked on top of one another. This reshaping allows the model to learn relatively coherent musical structure and discover temporal dependencies within a phrase. We believe that the use of this data format is significant in the resulting musical coherency of this system.

We have trained the system on three datasets, for three different performances. Each performance used a dataset created by the performer specifically for the concert. We have currently worked with pianist and Hollywood composer Kris Bowers, pianist and Danish composer Signe Bisgaard, and vocalist Mary Carter. Each dataset consists of approximately 1,600 measures, which is fifty choruses of thirty-two bars recorded as MIDI data. In the future, we may allow for audio datasets that we then convert to MIDI, but currently all performers have played MIDI devices. For improvisers, recording the dataset requires about an hour of improvisation.

From tests using our own datasets, we developed multiple guidelines for the creation of the dataset. Firstly, the improvisations should be done with a click; however, the click can change to any range of tempos between 60 BPM and 180 BPM during the session. The recordings don't need to be quantised to the click, but the click should be a point of reference for the improvisations. The dataset works best if it is in a clearly defined style so should be based around the musical language that may be employed within a single improvisation and not cover a range of styles. Finally, we encouraged the improvisers to not worry about the improvisation being perfect, instead asking them to record continuously without deleting any material. Each version of our system is only trained on the improviser, who will be performing with the system.

After collecting the dataset, we then transpose each one up and down six chromatic steps to create a version of each improvisation in every key. This allows the improvisation to be independent of any key signature and is considered standard practice. To generate the call-and-response dataset, we then split the data into call (X) and response (Y), by taking four bars as the call and the following four as the response. These then overlap, so the first response then becomes a call that uses the next four as a response.

Model Architecture

Our data representation was built around our model choice of a convolutional network (ConvNet). ConvNets have had wide success in image- and video-related tasks (Khan et al., 2020). While less common in symbolic music generation tasks, ConvNets have been widely used for audio generation in WaveNet (Oord et al., 2016) and some music-generation tasks (Yang et al., 2017). From our experience, we found that for the short responses this system generates, a sequence-based model such as a recurrent neural network does not necessarily perform better and is prone to overfitting on small datasets.

The ConvNet model is based on U-Net (Ronneberger et al., 2015) and comprises a symmetrical encoder-decoder architecture in which the outputs of encoding layers are appended to the inputs of corresponding decoding layers. It uses the 384 vector as both input and output to the system. U-Net was originally developed for biomedical image segmentation and designed to work on limited training datasets, with very fast generation times. It is distinct from other ConvNet models as it returns an output of the same size as input and essentially performs a classification on every value from the input.

Embodiment

The interactive system described to this point can function as either a software system or embedded in a robot. Our end goal is always to have generations performed by robot; however, for this system we also maintained a software-only version to allow any potential performer to interact and allow for users to test the improvisation on their own computers. The software system follows Figure 6.1 with the output sent as MIDI to a software instrument. MIDI is created from the 384-vector list by connecting repeating numbers to create longer notes.

For the robotic performance with Shimon, we use our standard path-planning algorithm to turn the generation into something playable for Shimon. Shimon has four arms, with two mallets on each arm, that move linearly across a marimba but cannot cross over each other. Therefore, to reach different areas of the marimba requires careful path planning to avoid collisions. Our path-planning system uses a greedy algorithm to choose the most appropriate arm to play each note. For the robot-played version, we also use a stochastic, rule-based system to add extra embellishments in the form of tremolos. Tremolos are occasionally triggered on sustained generated notes, often at top speed and at times using syncopated, fast rhythms.

In addition to path planning, each interaction with Shimon requires head and body gestures to enhance the engagement for coplayers and audiences. For this system, we repurposed many of Shimon's standard gestures. These gestures include looking at the performer that is playing with Shimon, looking towards the marimba, and looking at the audience. These are interwoven with a robotic breathing gesture and moving to the pulse of the music.

Evaluation

Method

The usefulness and challenges of evaluating creative AI generation systems has been widely researched, although there is no single accepted practice (Sturm et al., 2019). For an interactive robotic system, a Turing test, where the computer system attempts to convince a viewer it is human, is not a relevant approach. There is also the argument that applying a Turing test to music generation is not appropriate, as these systems are not designed explicitly to trick a human listener (Agres et al., 2016).

For this paper, we chose to base our evaluation on a repurposing of Boden's framework for computational creativity (Boden, 2009). This framework has been used previously for narrative rating (Riedl & Young, 2010) and in our own work on lyric generation (Savery et al., 2021b). Part of Boden's framework proposes that creativity is a combination of novelty and originality, expressiveness, and coherence. Boden further describes that the balance between coherent output and novelty is part of what defines the creativity of a work. We contend that these metrics further extend to the idea that in order to keep human collaborators curious and engaged, the system has to strike a balance between novelty and coherence. For our study we gathered metrics for originality, expressivity, coherence, and the overall quality rating for both the human and robot performer.

We developed one primary research question to evaluate the system: in an ensemble performance, can an improvising robot display similar levels of creativity as defined within Boden's framework? Our hypothesis was that Shimon and a human improviser would not have a significant difference in results. In addition to this evaluation using Boden's frameworks, we wished to gather some further qualitative data. To do this, we used questions developed by Sturm et al. (Sturm et al., 2019) for a live music performance. These questions asked for participants' favourite moments, surprising moments, if listening to a robot changed how they listened to the piece, and if they had any general comments.

Participants first read a virtual consent form, signed by entering their participant ID. This was followed by viewing two videos, each one ninety seconds long, of Shimon improvising in concert with a saxophone player in Denmark. The videos were played in a random order. At random times an attention check was given through an audio command in place of the stimuli that asked the participants to type a text phrase on the following page. Participants were not able to move back through the survey without restarting, which would prevent them from completing the survey. This caused any participant who missed the attention check to either stop the study or type an incorrect phrase, in which case their data was discarded. We also timed how long participants viewed the video. We had seven participants who were unable to complete the attention check or did not watch the complete video. After watching the videos, participants were shown a short text excerpt that described coherence and originality in creative work. They then answered questions related to Boden's metrics for the human and robot performer and filled out a short text response.

We recruited sixty participants on Mechanical Turk (Mturk), each classified as an Mturk master, which indicates a top-rated participant. After removing the seven who failed the attention check, we had a total of fifty-three participants. Each participant was paid $2 for the ten-minute survey. Participants were based predominantly in the USA (n=40), with the remaining participants from India (n=13). Seventeen participants identified as female, with the remaining thirty-six male. The average age was forty, with a standard deviation of 10.25 and a range of eighteen to sixty-four.

Results

Figure 6.2 shows a box plot of the results. The human and robot were rated very similarly across each metric. The means for Shimon were, coherence, 5.11; expressivity, 4.3; originality, 5.03; and overall quality, 5.28. The means for the human performer were, coherence, 5.51; expressivity, 5.80; originality, 5.05; and overall quality, 5.6. We conducted a pairwise t-test on each category and found that only expressivity had a significant value ($p<0.001$), proving our hypothesis to be partly correct.

From categorizing the text responses, we developed three main concepts. As is common with work in robotics and music, many participants commented positively on Shimon's head movements, despite the questions explicitly asking about the musical content. Overall, the participants found the gestures effective and a significant part of what they noticed in the performance. Participants described their favourite part as 'seeing the robot face move. It looked lifelike and gave it personality,' or when the robot 'moves its eye.'

The second common thread in the comments was a positive sentiment to the robot as a listener who was able to interact in meaningful ways. Participants wrote, 'I like how the robot tried to not interrupt the human and played directly with them,' and 'I was just impressed at how well the robot was able to "listen" and reply to the musical patterns before it.' Multiple participants also felt the robot was able to achieve good musical balance in the composition, such as, 'I was pleasantly surprised with how well the robot was able to play along with the human orchestra. The balance between human and robot was impressive.'

The final concept that arose throughout the comments was the impact of the use of a robot. There was no consensus on how having a robot impacted people's perception of the music, with some participants believing a robot made no difference to their perception, while others found the robot distracting and that it detracted from the human's music. Additionally, some participants thought, 'It was surprising to me that the robot did as well as it did.' However, one participant wrote, 'I was much more critical of the piece knowing that a robot played a role. The robot would have had more extensive knowledge and better motor control than the humans, so I judged it more harshly than I would a human.'

Discussion

Our results showed that Shimon performed without significant difference to the human performer for coherence, originality, and quality. This is a promising result, since an unbalanced response among these parameters could indicate problems. For example, an unbalanced high level of originality could relate to high levels of randomness and is not necessarily a positive for the system. We found that Shimon did perform worse in expressivity, perhaps due to a lack of dynamic and expressive ability in the system. It is also possible that from an audience perspective, an improvising saxophone has more expressive capabilities than a marimba sound, or that they found the human's body movements more expressive.

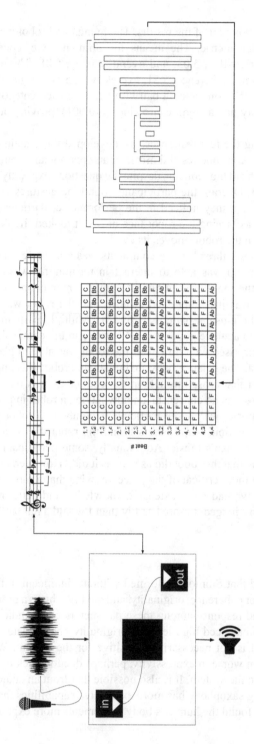

Figure 6.2 Box plot of results on Boden's framework.

As the comments indicated, gestures and robotic body movement were highly impactful to an audience. From our experience in concerts, gestures and movements are often the first thing noticed and, by many nonexpert musicians, one of the main memories that are taken from a performance. The ability for Shimon to look at the musician they are improvising with also encourages an audience to listen and notice musical sonic interactions between performers.

Our evaluation framework did not include the ethical goals we set out above. We believe that applying our ethical standards continuously through the design process framework and our postcreation reflections allows for better future development than attempting to incorporate them into a musical viewing experience.

Conclusion

Our system described here has so far been used in three concerts and recordings. The videos used for the evaluation were recorded in Denmark with the Aarhus Jazz Orchestra, in the concert *We, Robots* at Musikhuset Aarhus. This performance was awarded the Jazz Denmark Prize for 'the most innovative and creative concert experience of the year.' The system has also been featured in improvisations with film composer Kris Bowers for the BBC show *In the Studio* and has been used for a concert at the New Museum in New York. Audio and video samples are available online.[1]

We believe robotic musicianship offers a paradigm for innovative, new developments in AI and music. In this paper, we have framed our next stages of development around broader ethical goals and contend that these considerations are crucial for future musical AI design. From our prototype system, we have shown that ethical frameworks can lead to effective musical systems and encourage new directions for AI and music.

Note

1 https://richardsavery.com/project/shimonplays.

Bibliography

Agres, K., Forth, J. & Wiggins, G.A. (2016) Evaluation of musical creativity and musical metacreation systems. *Computers in Entertainment (CIE)*. 14 (3), 1–33.

Appiah, K.A. (2008) Cosmopolitanism: Ethics in a world of strangers. *Management Revue*. 19 (4), 340–341.

Barocas, S. & Selbst, A.D. (2016) Big data's disparate impact. *California Law Review*. 104, 671.

Boden, M.A. (2009) Computer models of creativity. *AI Magazine*. 30 (3), 23–23.

Briot, J.-P., Hadjeres, G. & Pachet, F. (2017) Deep learning techniques for music generation—a survey. *ArXiv preprint*. arXiv:1709.01620.

Clarke, E., DeNora, T. & Vuoskoski, J. (2015) Music, empathy and cultural understanding. *Physics of Life Reviews*. 15, 61–88.

Gomez, E., Castillo, C., Charisi, V., Dahl, V., Deco, G. et al. (2018) Assessing the impact of machine intelligence on human behaviour: An interdisciplinary endeavour. *arXiv preprint*. arXiv:1806.03192.

Hoffman, G. & Weinberg, G. (2010) Synchronization in human-robot musicianship. *19th International Symposium in Robot and Human Interactive Communication, IEEE.* 718–724.

Khan, A., Sohail, A., Zahoora, U. & Qureshi, A.S. (2020) A survey of the recent architectures of deep convolutional neural networks. *Artificial Intelligence Review.* 1–62.

Knotts, S. & Collins, N. (2020) A survey on the uptake of music AI software. *Proceedings of the International Conference on New Interfaces for Musical Expression.* 499–504.

Lacoste, A., Luccioni, A., Schmidt, V. & Dandres, T. (2019) Quantifying the carbon emissions of machine learning. *arXiv preprint.* arXiv:1910.09700.

Oord, A.V.D., Dieleman, S., Zen, H., Simonyan, K., Vinyals, O. et al. (2016) Wavenet: A generative model for raw audio. *arXiv preprint.* arXiv:1609.03499.

O'Keefe, C., Lansky, D., Clark, J. & Payne, C. (2019) *Comment regarding request for comments on intellectual property protection for artificial intelligence innovation.* https://perma.cc/ZS7G-2QWF.

Riedl, M.O. & Young, R.M. (2010) Narrative planning: Balancing plot and character. *Journal of Artificial Intelligence Research.* 39, 217–268.

Ronneberger, O., Fischer, P. & Brox, T. (2015) U-net: Convolutional networks for biomedical image segmentation. In: *International conference on medical image computing and computer-assisted intervention.* Cham: Springer, pp. 234–241.

Savery, R., Rose, R. & Weinberg, G. (2019a) Establishing humanrobot trust through music-driven robotic emotion prosody and gesture. *2019 28th IEEE International Conference on Robot and Human Interactive Communication (RO-MAN), IEEE.* 1–7.

Savery, R., Rose, R. & Weinberg, G. (2019b) Finding shimi's voice: Fostering human-robot communication with music and a nvidia jetson tx2. *Proceedings of the 17th Linux Audio Conference.* 5.

Savery, R. & Weinberg, G. (2018) Shimon the robot film composer and deepscore. *Proceedings of Computer Simulation of Musical Creativity.* 5.

Savery, R., Zahray, L. & Weinberg, G. (2020a) *Emotional musical prosody for the enhancement of trust in robotic arm communication.* Trust, Acceptance and Social Cues in Human-Robot Interaction, Ro-MAN 2020. https://par.nsf.gov/servlets/purl/10286326.

Savery, R., Zahray, L. & Weinberg, G. (2020b) *Shimon the rapper: A real-time system for human-robot interactive rap battles.* International Conference on Computational Creativity, ICCC'20. https://researchers.mq.edu.au/en/publications/shimon-the-rapper-a-real-time-system-for-human-robot-interactive.

Savery, R., Zahray, L. & Weinberg, G. (2021a) Before, between, and after: Enriching robot communication surrounding collaborative creative activities. *Frontiers in Robotics and AI.* 8, 116.

Savery, R., Zahray, L. & Weinberg, G. (2021b) Shimon sings-robotic musicianship finds its voice. In: *Handbook of artificial intelligence for music.* Cham: Springer, pp. 823–847.

Schwartz, R., Dodge, J., Smith, N.A. & Etzioni, O. (2019) Green ai. *arXiv preprint.* arXiv:1907.10597.

Shelemay, K.K. (2013) The ethics of ethnomusicology in a cosmopolitan age. In: P.V. Bohlman (ed.), *The Cambridge history of world music.* Cambridge: Cambridge University Press, pp. 786–806.

Strubell, E., Ganesh, A. & McCallum, A. (2019) Energy and policy considerations for deep learning in nlp. *arXiv preprint.* arXiv:1906.02243.

Sturm, B.L., Ben-Tal, O., Monaghan, U´., Collins, N., Herremans, D. et al. (2019) Machine learning research that matters for music creation: A case study. *Journal of New Music Research.* 48 (1), 36–55.

Sturm, B.L., Iglesias, M., Ben-Tal, O., Miron, M. & Gomez, E. (2019) Artificial intelligence and music: Open questions of copyright law and engineering praxis. In: *Arts*. Basel: Multidisciplinary Digital Publishing Institute, Vol. 8, p. 115.

Tinker, A. & Coomber, V. (2004) University research ethics committees: Their role, remit and conduct. *Bulletin of Medical Ethics*. 203, 7.

Vochozka, M., Kliestik, T., Kliestikova, J. & Sion, G. (2018) Participating in a highly automated society: How artificial intelligence disrupts the job market. *Economics, Management, and Financial Markets*. 13 (4), 57–62.

Weinberg, G., Driscoll, S. & Thatcher, T. (2006) *Jam'aa-a middle eastern percussion ensemble for human and robotic players*. Geneva: ICMC, pp. 464–467.

Yang, L.-C., Chou, S.-Y. & Yang, Y.-H. (2017) Midinet: A convolutional generative adversarial network for symbolic-domain music generation. *arXiv preprint*. arXiv:1703.10847.

Yang, N., Savery, R., Sankaranarayanan, R., Zahray, L. & Weinberg, G. (2020) *Mechatronics-driven musical expressivity for robotic percussionists*. New Interfaces for Musical Expression – NIME 2020. https://arxiv.org/abs/2007.14850.

7 Extended Reality

Music in Immersive XR Environments: The Possibilities (and Approaches) for (AI) Music in Immersive XR Environments

Gareth W. Young and Aljosa Smolic

Introduction

Cross reality (XR) is defined as:

> The union between ubiquitous sensor/actuator networks and shared online virtual worlds – a place where collective human perception meets the machines' view of pervasive computing.
>
> (Paradiso & Landay, 2009: p. 1)

XR encompasses multiple software and hardware technologies that enable content creation for augmented reality (AR), cinematic reality (CR), augmented virtuality (AV), and virtual reality (VR). Research on XR technology often concerns itself with the human-computer interface (Jerald, 2015), focusing on presenting and quantifying realistic, immersive, interactive, simulated worlds. However, for XR technology to achieve higher impactful prominence as a platform for artistic expressions, it is also necessary to explore the fundamentals of interface technology design for content creation and performance-style issues. With many industry-focused advances being made in information and communication technology, computing, big data analytics, machine vision, and artificial intelligence (AI), immersive technologies will be enhanced for cyber-physical and social experiences (Bastug et al., 2017).

AI has drastically changed how we view art and creativity in the twenty-first century, fundamentally augmenting the very nature of contemporary creative practices (López de Mántaras, 2016). Although computers have been used as a tool for artistic expression for many decades (AIArtists, 2019), with the advent of real-time machine intelligence, high-speed computers, and computational thinking, artists have developed numerous creative applications for high-profile audio-visual art exhibitions (MoMA, 2017). AI applications that create both abstract and representational art have advanced considerably with the discovery of generative

DOI: 10.4324/9780429356797-8

adversarial networks (GANs), giving rise to the field of computational creativity (Veale & Cardoso, 2019). In the music domain, computational creativity has focused on generating musical scores for human musicians, musical improvisation and accompaniment, and software that creates music in an artist's particular style or musical genre. This attention also includes the further development of specific musical applications for algorithmic music composition (Zaripov, 1960; Herremans, 2016), musical pattern recognition (Kane, 2016), automated accompaniment systems (Vercoe, 1984; Dannenberg, 1984), solo performances (Vercoe & Puckette, 1985), interactive scores (Robertson & Plumbley, 2006), and the ultimate recognition as a stand-alone creative AI artist (Zulić, 2019).

The possibilities and approaches for AI music in immersive XR environments for media entertainment can be much more than immersive gaming, just as film entertainment is more than blockbuster cinema. Contemporary XR productions offer an expansive array of entertainment value to existing and emergent three-dimensional (3D) media practices and beyond. However, the current technological unification of AI and XR arguably adds value over more traditional multimedia practices to supplement the main creative focus by making full use of the spatiality afforded with six degrees of freedom (6-DoF) experiences and implementing more engaging interactions and player agency for music, cinema, and gaming. By exploring the combined use of these technologies in creative practice, objects of attention within an immersive virtual environment (IVE) can be presented so that audiences can move around, interact, and engage with materials, making the overall experience fundamentally unique. Although potentially highly immersive and engaging, this also brings to light issues concerning conventional performance practice in IVEs and how artists can engage audiences remotely with artistic expressions remaining intact and as intended.

Within the XR domain, VR technology is currently experiencing a resurgence in commercial interest. Therefore, the barriers of VR for use in the entertainment industry are changing (Evans, 2018). *VR* can be broadly defined as 'a computer-generated digital environment that can be experienced and interacted with as if that environment were real' (Jerald, 2015: p. 9). Jaron Lanier first coined the technical term *VR* in the 1980s (Kelly et al., 1989). Today, Lanier proposes several alternative definitions, including a reference to art practice: 'a twenty-first-century art form that will weave together the three great twentieth-century arts: cinema, jazz, programming' (Lanier, 2017: p. 3).

Via XR technologies like VR, musicians can engage audiences by presenting spatialised sonic materials employing multimodal stimulation, which the viewer can interpret through their unique background and lived experiences. Thus producing a qualitatively different knowledge of traditional performance practices within an unaccompanied or shared space (Parker & Saker, 2020). Potentially, through the use of AI and XR combined, audiences and performers can actively participate in an immersive performance experience, contributing their unique subjective views within specific societal contexts (Cappello, 2019). This level of engagement can be delivered in VR via the creative use of immersion, interaction, and imagination (Burdea & Coiffet, 2003) in a way that provides new insight into creative practice and how audiences can be engaged by artists (O'Dwyer et al., 2020). AI will no doubt play some role in future XR music practice. Nevertheless, as was highlighted by Lanier (1988):

> In order for computer art or music to work, you have to be extra careful to put people and human contact at the centre of attention.

This chapter explores XR technology as an active stage for the spatial presentation of musical performance and artistic imagery, balancing user interaction, immersion, and imaginative storytelling via unique 3D audiovisual musical performance practices. We document the history of the combined audiovisual approach, highlighting the significant technological techniques as they were developed, and discuss the implementation of new strategies for the potential combined use of XR and AI in music, live performance, and immersive scenographies.

3D, XR, and Music

Technological evolution in modern engineering and its application in artistic practice have grown hand in hand for many years, with several unique audiovisual entertainment platforms and computational epochs linking music with visual media and thus XR. While music performance has a long and varied history, we focus on the advent of contemporary audiovisual technology and its application in capturing and reproducing music performance and the music video as a stand-alone modern art form.

In the 1950s, advent XR technologies were proposed to present audiences with a multimodal 'experience theater' (Robinett, 1994). This work would later create much smaller viewing screens that could be placed closer to the viewer's eyes and accompanied by crudely spatialised stereo sound. This technology was also capable of stimulating other sensory modalities, such as touch, taste, and smell. By 1962, experience theatre concepts were fully matured, and the available multimodal media technologies were also stable enough for the application.

Research and development in the field flourished. As a result, the Sensorama was created, which is still lauded today as an early prototype XR platform (Heilig, 1962; Robinett, 1994). The Sensorama was a patented platform for solo experiences and was mechanical (see Figure 7.1a). This multimodal immersive media viewer included a stereoscopic colour display, fans, odour emitters, stereo sound, and a moving chair. The Sensorama films were visceral, aptly titled *Motorcycle*, *Belly Dancer*, *Dune Buggy*, *Helicopter*, *A Date with Sabina*, and *I'm a Coca-Cola Bottle*, and could be viewed in especially purposed cinema for communal viewing.

The first head-mounted visual display system in immersive, computer-generated simulation applications can be seen in Figure 7.1(b) (Sutherland, 1968). This *Ultimate Display* was a device that could simulate wireframe objects and rooms, ultimately simulating reality to the point of perceived reality. The device presented individual users with a virtual world, viewed through a head-mounted display

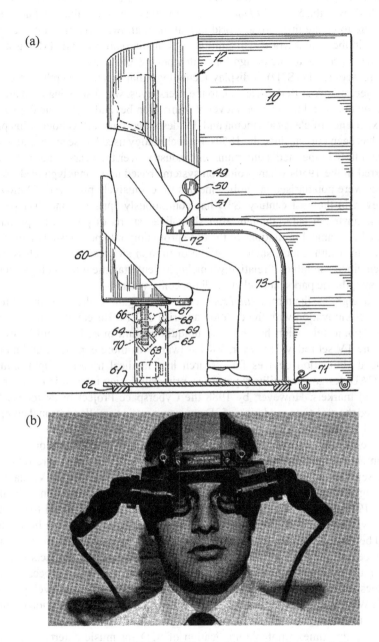

Figure 7.1 (a) The Sensorama (Heilig, 1962) and (b) early head-mounted display optics (Sutherland, 1968).

(HMD), and stimulated the user via 3D sound and tactile feedback. Powering this HMD was the *Sword of Damocles*, a prototype computer that used advanced hardware to create this virtual world in real time, allowing users to interact with objects in the digital world. This multimodal media platform and HMD arrangement have become a core design for contemporary XR today.

Stereoscopic 3D (S3D), a display technology that creates a depth impression by projecting two different views into the users' eyes, was also being used around this time to expand the viewer's level of immersion beyond that of the flat-screen 2D experience of classical cinema and TV described thus far. Although this principle has been known since the 1850s, the technology used has seen several trends ebb and flow in the media entertainment industry over the years. One such wave occurred in the 1950s when projection systems based upon anaglyph (red-green) glasses were popularised in public cinemas for exclusively produced 3D movies. However, in the past century, S3D has continuously appeared and disappeared from mainstream entertainment after short-lived spurts of popularity, primarily due to the technical limitations of the time providing only poor visual quality and leading to health issues, such as fatigue or motion sickness. Nevertheless, S3D has remained a notable, if relatively a niche, 3D entertainment technology seen in the home, theme parks, and other media-specific venues.

In the eighties, the term *virtual reality* was once again on the vanguard of technological innovation with the creation and rise of VPL Research (Lanier, 2017). At this point, television had become ubiquitous, and most households own at least one TV set today. However, VR hardware was more expensive and mainly provided simulation devices for research into medical training, flight simulation, CAD design, and military purposes, primarily losing interest in home entertainment markets. However, by 1988 the Cyberspace Project by Autodesk had achieved the real-time rendering of 3D environments on smaller personal computers, and interactive VR media, via console gaming, was on the rise.

In the nineties, home console gaming platforms were becoming more popular, and interest in the commercial release of VR for gaming slowly grew. At this time, Sega developed the Sega VR system, and Nintendo released the Virtual Boy, ensuring that VR remained well regarded in the high-end gaming scene. Notably, at the 1992 SIGGRAPH conference, VR and music were presented together in public via a musical performance from Jaron Lanier, demonstrating how music could be played in VR using a DataGlove device and performed in front of a live audience (Lanier, 2017). Unfortunately, many commercial VR projects failed to grow much past this date due to the incompatibility of computer processing and graphics rendering. Media technology research shifted focus to developing the World Wide Web. This gentle demise was then followed by a long period of indifference to commercial VR technologies in general.

During this time, a notable application of S3D for music entertainment was released – the 3D science fiction experience *Captain EO*, which featured Michael Jackson. *Captain EO* was shown at Disney theme parks from 1986 through 1998 (with revivals from 2010 onwards), written by George Lucas and directed by Francis Ford Coppola (Jackson et al., 1986). In these popular 'immersive rides,' audiences sat in traditional theatrical configurations and wore 3D glasses to experience filmed events collectively. In addition to providing 3D depth perception, the experience also included in-theatre effects, such as lasers and smoke, that were synchronised to the filmed events. With the audience experiencing a sense of embodiment within the narrative, they became a more integral component inside the overall story design (Parker-Starbuck, 2011). As such, Disney productions like *Captain EO* and *Honey, I Shrunk the Audience* were explicitly created to provide theme park audiences with collective immersive experiences. However, S3D could not support 360-degree look-around (3DoF) or move-around (6DoF) features of later XR-technology-mediated experiences.

Music video practices were also thrust into prominence with the launch of the television channel MTV, which based much of its content around the medium for over twenty years (Tannenbaum & Marks, 2011). The format of MTV's musical content changed considerably over its lifetime. However, it mainly included introductions and voice-overs from video jockeys (VJs), music news, interviews, concerts, promotions, and a particular focus on creative visual representations of musical narratives. From 2000 onwards, conventional outlets for promoting and viewing music videos dropped, playing fewer music videos due to the rise of social media and video-sharing websites (NPR, 2008). With the success of peer-to-peer music-sharing services and online video-sharing platforms in the late 2000s, artists could directly engage with fans, controlling the viewing and listening experience of the consumer (Burgess & Green, 2018). Moreover, the music video format was also changing; vertical videos were being made to view in mobile phone platforms (Jaekel, 2015). This shift shows us today that as new technology presented itself for the consumption of audiovisual materials, musicians and creative technologists were historically adept at adapting, and the industry continues to innovate and explore emergent platform-specific outputs to this day.

In the late 2000s, the industry saw another boom in S3D technology for cinema and home entertainment applications. The digital production and projection technologies of the time were matured enough, with many of the limitations of earlier systems alleviated. Such was the sustained popularity of S3D; it remains popular in 4D cinema entertainment today, while 3DTV, on the other hand, did not survive these trials. One notable musical example in this new era of S3D was the movie *U2 3D*, released in 2007. *U2 3D* was a 3D concert film featuring the band U2 performing during their Vertigo Tour in 2006 (U2 et al., 2007). Spectators of such footage were given a bodily, up-close presence onstage with the band, along with the added novelty provided by stereoscopic 3D vision.

Although commercial VR technology has been around since the mid-eighties and has endured many setbacks (Lanier, 2017), VR is currently undergoing yet another renaissance (Evans, 2018). However, VR has taken a long time to become affordable and provide a positive user experience. The slow rise back into the limelight arguably started in 2010, when the prototype of the Oculus Rift was first developed. Facebook's investment into VR in 2016 led to a resurgence in the technology, culture, and consumption of VR, and the industry has been growing ever since. The VR market is increasing, with the size of consumer-grade equipment projected to increase from 6.2 billion US dollars in 2019 to more than 16 billion US dollars by 2022. Additionally, unit shipments of VR devices are expected to reach 12.5 million in 2020 (Statista, 2020). Contemporary applications of VR encompass computer-generated environments that simulate the physical presence of people and objects and provide realistic sensory experiences (Jerald, 2015).

As such, animated, 360-degree video productions have become a popular way to allow the viewer to experience 'fly-on-the-wall' musical performances within immersive, imaginary worlds with three degrees of freedom (3DoF) – referring to the tracking of rotational motion as pitch, yaw, and roll. For example, the band Gorillaz (2017) openly released *'Saturnz Barz (Spirit House)'* as both a traditional 2D music video and a visually explorable, animated, 360-degree 3DoF video experience on YouTube (see Figure 7.2). Similarly, Mac Demarco (2017) released a 2D and 3DoF music video for *'This Old Dog.'* Additionally, Demarco released a VR experience for separate download that afforded the viewing audience further freedom of movement within the virtual world beyond the 2D viewing portal provided by traditional PC monitors. The release of stand-alone VR experiences is becoming more familiar with studios releasing animated immersive music videos to launch new albums and capture the imagination of new audiences. For example, Squarepusher's *'Stor Eiglass'* (2015) was used to celebrate the *Damogen Furies* album.

For more explorative experiences, immersive music videos can also facilitate the viewer in the exploration of computer-generated imagery (CGI), from within the scene of the IVE with six degrees of freedom (6DoF), where the viewer can control their position as forwards/backwards, up/down, left/right along the same 3DoF perpendicular axes described earlier. While many such animated experiences play along the linear timeline of the music, they allow the viewer to explore CGIs and provide control over other 3D content fully. Unfortunately,

Figure 7.2 Gorillaz's *Saturnz Barz (Spirit House)* presented as a 360° animated video (Gorillaz, 2017).

computer-generated characters and environments can feel 'uncanny' and 'unnatural' to viewers (Mori et al., 2012; Zell et al., 2015) or require high-budget productions to achieve adequate realism (Perry, 2014). Although motion capture offers some compromises, the requirement for actors to wear markers creates other hurdles for content creators to overcome.

Several advanced cameras have been developed and adapted to capture live performances and bridge realistic performance representations via 360-degree videos and immersion of 3D content (see Figure 7.3). One such camera, the scalable, mirror-based, multicamera system OmniCam-360, developed at Fraunhofer HHI, allows live video recording in a 360-degree panoramic format (Fraunhofer HHI, 2020a). Such recordings have been made during live shows; with real-time camera stitching, the 360-degree video panorama can be made viewable in VR HMDs (Fraunhofer HHI, 2020b). Moreover, it is possible to produce S3D VR content with the OmniCam-360 by equipping two cameras per mirror segment, providing parallax-free, 360-degree panoramic recording for distances larger than two meters within a 60-degree vertical capture space. This system has been used successfully to capture musical performances, providing real-time, remote viewing in VR for backstage areas and bringing classical orchestras to more casual living room viewers (Fraunhofer HHI, 2020b).

Although often limited by 3DoF and linear timelines, many immersive videos can be seen in everyday practice. For instance, OneRepublic's *'Kids'* transports viewers back and forth between two bedrooms (OneRepublic, 2016), immersing the viewer in the music and the characters and narrative devices presented in the song lyrics and videography. Similarly, EDM artist Avicii released a live-action video for the song *'Waiting for Love,'* where the viewer could control the camera position with 3DoF across a 180-degree performance space, tracking the

Figure 7.3 Björk's *Stonemilker*, presented in VR as a 360° music video (Björk, 2015).

performance of multiple dancers within the mise en scène (Avicii, 2015). Other artists, such as the Weeknd (2015), Muse (2016), and Sampha (2017), have each used live-action, 360-degree music videos paired with CGI and Hollywood movie-grade special effects to accompany their music performances with varying degrees of success. Although 3DoF technology has helped to re-establish affordable VR, with the announcement to discontinue Samsung Gear VR and Oculus Go, 3DoF technologies are quickly being outmoded for more innovative and immersive 6DoF platforms (Oculus Developer Success Team, Oculus Developer communications, June 23, 2020).

In response, volumography – the practice of creating digital 3D objects by calculating volumetric geometries from an image or video of the original – has grown in popularity for capturing 3D musical performances. In this context, the volumography can be static or dynamic and reconstructed as a 3D moving image in applications like VR or AR. The final 3D outputs are known as volumetric video (VV). Early high-profile examples of VV include the use of LiDAR – an acronym of 'light detection and ranging' or 'laser imaging, detection, and ranging' – for *'House of Cards'* by Radiohead (2008). More creative examples of VV include the project *NEBULA* by Marcin Nowrotek (2018), generating abstract visualisations in response to music and live performance.

Recently, VV capture was used for Billy Corgan's *'Aeronaut'* and Tino Kamal's *'VIP'* (see Figure 7.4b); both were captured at the Microsoft Mixed Reality Capture Studio (Corgan & Rubin, 2017; Kamal & Lane, 2019). VV content can also be integrated into live choreography and music performances to provide 3D holograms that accompany artists onstage. The most recent notable example is the use of VV at the 2019 Billboard Music Awards (Madonna & Maluma, 2019); this VV was captured at Dimension Studios and used Unreal Engine to execute the experience in real time (see Figure 7.4a). Although several notable studios worldwide can capture, control, and generate VV content, many of them are highly expensive professional set-ups that include large numbers of high-definition cameras and other types of sensors.

At present, VV is becoming a popular technique for capturing live action in 3D space for reproduction on emergent XR platforms (Huang et al., 2018). Combining the freedom of creativity afforded by CGI, the realism of live-action video, and the 6DoF provided by contemporary XR platforms, VV presents a natural progression for new music videos to retain the depth, parallax, and other visual properties of the original scene. These properties can be used to further enhance the qualitative experience of music videos through the application of spatial audio practices (Zhang et al., 2017) via ambisonic recording and binaural playback technologies and haptics, such as audio-tactile haptic feedback (Young et al., 2016, 2017). Therefore, VV presents itself as a disruptive technology for providing artists and audiences with real-time capabilities and immersive, multimodal experiences of musical practice and performance. With the capture of live music within 3D space and its delivery via XR technologies, audiences can explore a VV capture, providing augmented engagements with pre-recorded real-time performances via new multimedia technologies. To date, the amalgamation of these

(a)

(b)

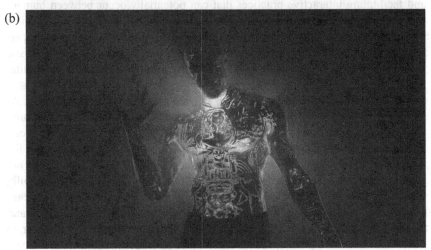

Figure 7.4 (a) Madonna and Maluma's live performance at the 2019 Billboard Music Awards (Madonna & Maluma, 2019), and (b) Tino Kamal's *'VIP'* volumetric music video (Kamal & Lane, 2019).

technologies has proven to be one of the most critical developments in the capture of live-action musical performances since the creation of musical short films of the late 1920s.

The Possibilities (and Approaches) for (AI) Music in Immersive XR Environments

Multimedia has traditionally been applied to capture and reproduce performance and then use technology creatively as a postproduction tool to substitute human-to-human performance. With the volumetric capture of a live act, where a performer is physically present, and the performance is captured 'at the moment,' a more humanistic 3D representation can be reproduced. In XR with full 6DoF, this has only been seen previously in mono- or stereoscopic 3DoF 360-degree video and 6DoF CGI music videos separately. Where performances and audiences are remotely located, time and space can be linked using media-sharing platforms, where the sensation of commonality between human-to-human communication is shared via the use of modern telepresence technology. This effect allows artists to communicate and share with their fans more freely when a physical performance is impossible.

By building upon such approaches to sharing creative musical practice and incorporating both AI and XR, collective performances will be potentially enhanced by providing audiences with an immersive 6DoF platform for sharing the intentions of the artist, enriching and augmenting artist/audience relationships, and facilitating interactive practices that can potentially occur between human-machine and machine-human performances. In such applications, where physical human-human proximity is impossible, the 'live' experience of the musical performance within a virtual environment becomes more intimate, bridging artistic practice, audience engagement, and theoretically providing interactive computational music experiences.

Music videos have traditionally been viewed as passive media; however, AI and XR can potentially be combined to turn them into an interactive medium. Currently, audience interactions with VV are limited to a passive observer role, as is seen in traditional videos as TV or cinema. VV expands interaction in the spatial sense, allowing the viewer to enter a scene with 6DoF, but it does not support real-time interaction. VV is still a recording and, therefore, not as fully interactive as a 3D CGI experience. This limitation is because VV content cannot be easily changed, modified, or manipulated once it has been captured and processed, all of which would be essential for a VV to be interactive. However, in games and other computer graphics applications, autonomous agents are driven by AI and digital humans, as game characters, avatars, etc. have reached a high level of sophistication that can learn from their in-game experiences and build empathy with the audience (Young et al., 2021). Future interactive VV content will require such AI-powered autonomous agents and applying AI in other relevant scene elements.

Currently, these are two separate worlds, with VV on one side, 3D and created from real-world footage but not intelligent, and AI agents as avatars on the other, enabling content interaction but lacking affordable humanistic realism. Therefore, bridging these two worlds would allow for the ultimate, immersive, and interactive musical experience. AI must be integrated into VV content to achieve this connection, ranging from simple 3D geometry features, such as animated 3D rigging, to behavioural rules and high-level semantic awareness. These are still challenging topics that are subject to ongoing research. Once readily possible, it will remain a challenge to balance the recorded nature versus the intelligent nature that a VV character should exhibit. This balancing act will probably be a design choice, and corresponding authoring tools will be needed for VV content creation. Once we bridge the gap between VV and AI, we can design fully interactive XR-AI experiences, enabling 6DoF-spatial exploration for the audience and allowing creative, interactive artistic content. We may then enter an era of immersive music performance in a truly interactive environment that will enable audiences to play along as members of the band or learn new playing techniques from the greatest artists of the time.

In the datafication of a physical, creative practice, such as a musical performance, future XR and AI integration will allow for interactive musical experiences. In this way, XR and AI will serve as a unified communication tool for the capture and reproduction of a musical performance, as well as providing an interactive experience for audiences. Performance, in its many forms, can present composition in a state of flux, as although a piece of music ought to be performed the way the composer intended it to be performed, the performance can also be subject to interaction and interpretation as a performer deviates, learns, and plays. Beyond this, AI and music creativity algorithms can produce unique, interactive performances, as is often seen on the physical stage. However, the inference of motives, meanings, and concepts derived from artistic intentions is likely to be heightened through the use of XR, and the correct comprehension of these factors is not only delicate but also relies on a multitude of innately human-to-human communication channels.

Conclusions

Although Lanier (2017) expressed that 'VR = -AI (VR is the inverse of AI),' the possibilities and approaches for AI music and XR are currently expansive and subject to ongoing research. Digital media allows artists presently to engage audiences in new ways. However, future advances in the expanding metaverse cannot be easily achieved without AI and XR integration. Whether engaging with musical performance via cinema, TV, or XR, the primary function of the platform is the prevalence of musical performances that can occur remotely at multiple times and locations. With current information and communications technology (ICT), the capabilities for the efficient capture and transmission of performance over time and space are readily achievable in multiple media formats, with data rates and compression algorithms being advanced all the time.

Nevertheless, for the communication of artistic creativity or musical performance, it is not enough for XR to be used to reconvey a 6DoF version; it should also consider the creation or contribution of unique content via an AI actor, as simulation or simulacra. In this way, high-speed ICTs may be used to facilitate the recording and reproduction elements of a musical performance by presenting it to a telepresent audience, with XR-AI platforms allowing for immersive and creative interactions to occur between artists and audiences, as might be experienced in a live or collaborative performance space.

Bibliography

3IT (2018) 360° Figaro [360 video]. *Innovation Center for Immersive Imaging Technologies: Berlin.* www.3it-berlin.de/360-figaro-first-opera-recording-realized-for virtual-reality-with-the-omnicam-360/.

AIArtists (2019) *Timeline of AI art.* https://aiartists.org/ai-timeline-art

Avicii (2015) *Waiting for love [360 video].* YouTube. https://youtu.be/edcJ_JNeyhg.

Bastug, E., Bennis, M., Médard, M. & Debbah, M. (2017) Toward interconnected virtual reality: Opportunities, challenges, and enablers. *IEEE Communications Magazine.* 55 (6), 110–117.

Björk (2015) *Stonemilker [360 video].* YouTube. https://youtu.be/gQEyezu7G20.

Burgess, J. & Green, J. (2018) *YouTube: Online video and participatory culture.* New York: John Wiley & Sons.

Burdea, G.C. & Coiffet, P. (2003) *Virtual reality technology.* New York: John Wiley & Sons.

Cappello, G. (2019) Active audiences. In: *The international encyclopedia of media literacy.* https://onlinelibrary.wiley.com/doi/10.1002/9781118978238.ieml0003.

Corgan, W.P. & Rubin, R. (2017) *Aeronaut [Volumetric music video and VR experience].* YouTube. www.youtube.com/watch?v=36_4dx_0Qdk.

Dannenberg, R.B. (1984) An on-line algorithm for real-time accompaniment. *International Computer Music Conference (ICMC).* 84, 193–198.

DeMarco, M. (2017) This old dog [vr/360 video]. *Inception.* https://inceptionvr.com/experience/mac-demarco-old-dog-vr-music-video-experience/.

Evans, L. (2018) *The re-emergence of virtual reality.* London: Routledge.

Fraunhofer HHI (2020a) *OmniCam-360.* www.hhi.fraunhofer.de/en/departments/vit/tech nologies-and-solutions/capture/panoramic uhd-video/omnicam-360.html.

Fraunhofer HHI (2020b) *Shootings.* www.hhi.fraunhofer.de/en/departments/vit/techno logies-and-solutions/capture/panoramic uhd-video/shootings.html.

Gorillaz (2017) *Saturnz Barz (spirit house) 360 [360 video].* YouTube. https://youtu.be/ lVaBvyzuypw.

Heilig, M.L. (1962) *US patent no. 3050870.* Washington, DC: US Patent and Trademark Office.

Herremans, D. (2016) *MorpheuS: Automatic music generation with recurrent pattern constraints and tension profiles.* https://hal.univ-lorraine.fr/IRCAM/hal-03278537v1.

Huang, Z., Li, T., Chen, W., Zhao, Y., Xing, J. et al. (2018) Deep volumetric video from very sparse multi-view performance capture. *Proceedings of the European Conference on Computer Vision (ECCV).* 336–354.

Jackson, M., Coppola, F.F. & Lucas, G. (1986) *Captain EO [3-D film with special effects].* New York: Lucasfilm/Walt Disney Pictures.

Jaekel, B. (2015) *Snapchat and Spotify challenge YouTube as a premiere music video source.* www.mobilemarketer.com/ex/mobilemarketer/cms/news/social networks/20489.html.

Jerald, J. (2015) *The VR book: Human-centered design for virtual reality.* San Rafael, CA: Morgan & Claypool.

Kane, S. (2016) How a pianist became the world's most famous futurist. *Business Insider – Tech Insider.* www.kurzweilai.net/business-insider-tech-insider-how-a-pianist-became-the-worlds-most-famous-futurist.

Kamal, T. & Lane, R. (2019) V.I.P. *Vimeo.* https://vimeo.com/353783055.

Kelly, K., Heilbrun, A. & Stacks, B. (1989) Virtual reality: An interview with Jaron Lanier. *Whole Earth Review.* 64 (2), 108–120.

Lanier, J. (1988) Virtual instrumentation. *The Whole Earth Review*. www.jaronlanier.com/instruments.html.

Lanier, J. (2017) *Dawn of the new everything: A journey through virtual reality*. New York: Random House.

López de Mántaras, R. (2016) Artificial intelligence and the arts: Toward computational creativity. In: *The next step: Exponential life*. Madrid: BBVA Open Mind.

Luhmann, T., Robson, S., Kyle, S. & Boehm, J. (2013) *Close-range photogrammetry and 3D imaging*. Berlin: Walter de Gruyter.

Madonna & Maluma (2019) *Medellín*. YouTube. https://youtu.be/9Z1GdMuC9E8.

MoMA (2017) *Thinking machines art and design in the computer age, 1959–1989 [Exhibition]*. www.moma.org/calendar/exhibitions/3863.

Mori, M., MacDorman, K.F. & Kageki, N. (2012) The uncanny valley [from the field]. *IEEE Robotics & Automation Magazine*. 19 (2), 98–100.

Muse (2016) *Revolt [360 video]*. YouTube. https://youtu.be/91fQTXrSRZE.

Nowrotek, M. (2018) NEBULA [music video]. *Vimeo*. https://vimeo.com/256668685.

NPR (2008) *The fall of TRL and the rise of internet video*. www.npr.org/templates/story/story.php?storyId=96869060&t=1591716501367.

O'Dwyer, N., Young, G.W., Johnson, N., Zerman, E. & Smolic, A. (2020) Mixed reality and volumetric video in cultural heritage: Expert opinions on augmented and virtual reality. *Culture and Computing*. 1–20, LNCS 12215.

OneRepublic (2016) *Kids [360 video]*. YouTube. https://youtu.be/eppTvwQNgro.

Paradiso, J.A. & Landay, J.A. (2009) Guest editors' introduction: Cross-reality environments. *IEEE Pervasive Computing*. 8 (3), 14–15.

Parker, E. & Saker, M. (2020) Art museums and the incorporation of virtual reality: Examining the impact of VR on spatial and social norms. *Convergence*. 26 (5). doi:10.1177/1354856519897251.

Parker-Starbuck, J. (2011) *Cyborg theatre: Corporeal/technological intersections in multimedia performance*. Cham: Springer.

Perry, T.S. (2014) Leaving the uncanny valley behind. *IEEE Spectrum*. 51 (6), 48–53.

Radiohead (2008) *House of cards [music video]*. Youtube. www.youtube.com/watch?v=8nTFjVm9sTQ.

Robertson, A. & Plumbley, M.D. (2006) *Real-time interactive musical systems: An overview*. Proceedings of the Digital Music Research Network Doctoral Research Conference, London.

Robinett, W. (1994) Interactivity and individual viewpoint in shared virtual worlds: The big screen vs networked personal displays. *ACM SIGGRAPH Computer Graphics*. 28 (2), 127–130.

Sampha (2017) *(No one knows me) like the piano [360 video]*. YouTube. https://youtu.be/V-ncE-yR8mI.

Squarepusher (2015) Stor Eiglass [VR experience]. *Warp*. https://warp.net/updates/squarepusher-stor-eiglass-vr-experience.

Statista (2020) *Virtual reality (VR) – statistics facts*. Statista Research Department. www.statista.com/topics/2532/virtual-reality-vr/.

Sutherland, I.E. (1968) A head-mounted three-dimensional display. *Proceedings of the 9–11 December, Fall Joint Computer Conference, Part I*. 757–764.

Tannenbaum, R. & Marks, C. (2011) *I want my MTV: The uncensored story of the music video revolution*. New York: Penguin.

U2, Owens, C. & Pellington, M. (2007) *U2 3D*. Washington, DC: National Geographic Entertainment.

Veale, T. & Cardoso, F.A. (2019) *Computational creativity: The philosophy and engineering of autonomously creative systems.* Cham: Springer.

Vercoe, B. (1984) The synthetic performer in the context of live performance. *International Computer Music Conference (ICMC).* 84, 199–200.

Vercoe, B. & Puckette, M. (1985) Synthetic rehearsal: Training the synthetic performer. *International Computer Music Conference (ICMC).* 85, 275–289.

The Weeknd (2015) *The hills remix feat: Eminem [360 video].* YouTube. https://youtu.be/2fhjdtQDcOo.

Young, G.W., Murphy, D. & Weeter, J. (2016) Haptics in music: The effects of vibrotactile stimulus in low-frequency auditory difference detection tasks. *IEEE Transactions on Haptics.* 10 (1), 135–139.

Young, G.W., Murphy, D. & Weeter, J. (2017) *A qualitative analysis of haptic feedback in music focused exercises.* New Interfaces for Musical Expression (NIME) Conference, Aalborg University, Copenhagen.

Young, G.W., O'Dwyer, N. & Smolic, A. (2021) Exploring virtual reality for quality immersive empathy building experiences. *Behaviour & Information Technology.* 1–17.

Zaripov, R.Kh. (1960) An algorithmic description of a process of musical composition. *Doklady Akademii Nauk SSSR.* 132 (6), 1283–1286.

Zell, E., Aliaga, C., Jarabo, A., Zibrek, K., Gutierrez, D. et al. (2015) To stylize or not to stylize? The effect of shape and material stylization on the perception of computer-generated faces. *ACM Transactions on Graphics (TOG).* 34 (6), 1–12.

Zhang, W., Samarasinghe, P.N., Chen, H. & Abhayapala, T.D. (2017) Surround by sound: A review of spatial audio recording and reproduction. *Applied Sciences.* 7 (5), 532.

Zulić, H. (2019) How AI can change/improve/influence music composition. Performance and education: Three case studies. *INSAM Journal of Contemporary Music, Art and Technology.* 1 (2), 100–114.

8 Data

A Quantified Quickening: Data, AI, and the Consumption and Composition of Music

Jennifer Edmond

> *Inspiration is an awakening, a quickening of all man's faculties, and it is manifested in all high artistic achievements.*
>
> —*Giacomo Puccini*

It is hard to know where, or even how, to begin speaking of the mechanisms by which data and artificial intelligence affect contemporary paradigms for the consumption and creation of music. This challenge stems in part from the language of music: as an art form that stirs the emotions and brings forth the image of tormented geniuses from Beethoven and Mozart to Prince and Kurt Cobain, it is hard to reconcile the vernacular of musical experience with the 'cold facts' we may associate with data. There are inherent problems with the concept and the terminology of data as well, however: fetishised as the 'new oil' in popular parlance, it's also something we have lots of ('personal data') which we can't see, don't even think about most of the time (our 'data exhaust'), but which can be stolen from us or used by companies we have never heard of to make billions. The word is so enigmatic it is even singular *and* plural.

One might be inclined to think that this is the result of an appropriation of a scientific term by lay users, but in fact, the opposite is true, with the idea of data also lacking capacity as a clear signifier within scientific discourse and meaning many different things across, and sometimes within, different disciplines. As I have described elsewhere, the academic discourse of data encompasses conflicts about 'data cleaning' versus 'data manipulation' (essentially the same thing, but viewed very differently by different disciplines), invokes many evocative, but largely unused, definitions coming out of cultural and science and technology studies (data as 'performative' [Raley, 2013]; data as 'rhetorical' [Rosenberg, 2013]) and the practices of computer scientists, whose functional definitions of the word might shift between very different things from sentence to sentence (Edmond et al., 2021). It will be the purpose of this chapter to attempt to build some bridges between the challenging fields of discourse and practice, one related to data, one to music, and thereby explore some of the tangible ways in which data may enhance but also threaten the experience of creating and communicating through music and how one might manage the risks they bring.

DOI: 10.4324/9780429356797-9

Before we can investigate the potential costs to musical consumption and composition the data layer in an AI system might bring, we first need to establish clear definitions of where this data layer intersects with these musical processes. For the purposes of this chapter, we will look at two specific contexts in this respect, one related to consumption, one to composition.

The first kind of data we will consider faces the perspective of the music listener and how artificial intelligence can affect their experience. Recommender systems have become a part of how music is discovered and enjoyed across a wide range of platforms. Although there are different approaches to what data is used in such a system and how (Germain & Chakareski, 2013), every recommender system relies at some level on data collection and user preference modelling. In this way, they can deliver new content that should appeal to an individual who has already demonstrated a positive response to another, similar content. The model applied may rely on comparing your choices to those of others whose tastes might largely overlap with yours (collaborative filtering), on finding similarities in the structural aspects of the songs themselves (content-based filtering), or on a hybrid method combining these aspects, possibly with other data streams, such as your Facebook activity. Regardless of the specific method used, each of these systems is driven not only by an underlying notion of how your current listening signals desired future listening but also by the data that is available, from you, from your presumed peers, and from expert tagging of the characteristics of a certain piece of music. This data and algorithm-driven approach to music recommendation may, on the surface, seem far less open to individual biases than the models that predated them (reliance on a radio playlist, keen acquaintance, or friendly record store owner). In fact, however, the use of potentially biased data and potentially biased models can narrow our horizons as much as they expand them. As the adage coined by George Box tells us, 'all models are wrong, but some are useful,' and this is true as well for recommender systems built upon limited data and a sense of our musical tastes as limited and fixed. Furthermore, the mathematical models underpinning any AI system bring with them particular threats: they are inflexible, inscrutable, and based upon an assumption that past behaviour is the best possible predictor of the future (O'Neil, 2016).

The second kind of data we will consider is AI training data and how it can shape the experience of music composition. While we may consider the software and algorithms to be the 'intelligent' part of a machine learning system, the extent to which such systems can achieve anything, and what it is they do achieve, is based mainly on the inputs they receive and according to which they construct their models of the world and perceptions of success. Just as a human's ability to problem-solve is predicated upon the culture and language system in which they grew up on, so also does an AI system gain both strengths and limitations from the data that formed it, including the unconscious biases that may be enshrined in that data. This is, in particular, true because datasets of the necessary size can be hard to find and even harder to prepare. Exactly how much data you need varies according to the complexity of your model, but to give an example, the Google Inception V3 image classification model contains just under 24 million parameters and requires about 1.2 million data points (in this case, labelled images) to be trained. Over and above the training data, you then need a second corpus of testing data to ensure your model acts as you expect it to. To give a more modest example, a recursive neural network system developed to analyse the sentiment in Holocaust testimonies was created based on a training corpus of just over seventeen thousand testimony segments and a testing corpus of just over thirty thousand (Blanke et al., 2020).

The implications of this underlying requirement are twofold. Firstly, such large, homogenous corpora are not always easy to find. Many researchers resort to the same underlying data (Wikipedia, ImageNet) to find scale, but this factor can have a limiting effect on what these systems can achieve: the training and testing data used determines the 'culture' of an AI's responses, including any linguistic or values-based biases that data may contain. Some researchers (such as the Holocaust project mentioned prior) actually use the same AI to generate its own training data, where the existing set may be too thin for accuracy, adding a whole new layer to the possibility of innate biases. Second, the selection and preparation of this data may be subjected to further errors or biases: outlier examples in a dataset are often removed as noise, and determination of aspects such as sentiment of a statement may well ultimately be traceable back to human decisions in setting up the initial sentiment lexica, displaying, for example, a racial or gender bias (Thelwall, 2018).

For the purposes of musical composition, we can see examples of this in software systems such as AIVA, which was trained on 'a large database of classical partitions written by the most famous composers (Bach, Beethoven, Mozart, etc.)' (Kaleagasi, 2017). This choice of training data greatly influences the output of a system like AIVA, which can only innovate within this ecosystem of tonalities and expressions. Other eras, other cultures, and true disruptive creation are not within the realm of what can be expected from such systems, and the reason for this lies firmly in their data layer.

These descriptions of the data layer that shape the affordances of AI in the context of music begin to imply the contours of the paradigm shift in how we perceive and produce music its data layer inevitably will drive. But of course, much still depends on exactly how we understand what music and its function are – culturally, socially, individually, and economically. We will now turn towards four possible frames of reference for addressing this question of the functions of music and the implications of AI and data for each of them.

Music as Cultural Practice

Music cannot arise or exist within the boundaries of the experience of a single individual: it is, like all arts, rather a part of our cultural system of communication, relationship forming, and the development of an individual's sense of identity and affiliation. 'The fundamental purpose of art is to affect peoples' relationships with each other, where the relationships are themselves important' (Hertzmann, 2020). Participation in culture and the arts is not just a pleasant addition to life; it is fundamental and recognised as such in Article 27 of the United Nations Universal Declaration of Human Rights: 'Everyone has the right freely to participate in the cultural life of the community, to enjoy the arts and to share in scientific advancement and its benefits' (UN, 2015).

Cultural practices naturally adapt and change over time, and technologies have always been a part of this process. However, there is a fine line between enabling cultural change and effecting a change that individuals and groups have little choice or knowledge about. Social media platforms, for example, have been demonstrated to be facilitators of a multitude of abuses and failures to protect users and their cultures, from ethically questionable reuses of personal data to the enabling of racially motivated violence. But can an individual within a society highly penetrated by such platforms simply choose not to use them? Yes, in theory, but this choice 'comes at a high social price' (Sætra, 2019), which may lead to being 'deprived of critical services' (Baruh & Popescu, 2017: p. 586). Just as filter bubbles may drive the development of an individual's worldview, one might also speak of 'recommender bubbles' as data-driven manifestations of the same phenomenon in the sphere of musical discovery and enjoyment. Similarly, our ability to understand other cultures may be diminished by a reduced exposure to music from outside the canon built upon our preferences and their near approximations.

This may seem far-fetched, but the impact of such data-driven infringements on human rights to their distinctive cultural practices can already be seen in certain other contexts, such as in language. In a globalised world, language translation can be a key enabler for languages with smaller communities of speakers to maintain their position as the vernacular for local practices and exchange without also becoming a barrier to participation in wider markets for goods, services, and employment. But a 2018 study found that data biases not only in the amount of testing and training data available for advanced translation engines but also in the very ownership of that data were increasing pressure on smaller language groups.

> Larger corporations and countries have access to large volumes of data, while smaller companies and nations are left behind. Data inequality has serious consequences, as access to data has become a social issue – in effect, data is making the big bigger and the small, smaller.
>
> (Kalnins & Vasiljevs, 2018)

One could easily imagine the same happening in music.

However, the potentially insidious effects of such a process may be more complex to resist than earlier forms of cultural imperialism. The algorithms and models of AI systems interpret the data they are trained upon in ways that even the designers of those systems cannot always predict. This makes the challenge to remove biases from them that much greater and places the individual engaging with their outputs in a more vulnerable position. It is difficult to stage resistance against a power structure encased in a black box. While it would be easy simply to charge technology companies not to act in ways that may narrow or restrict cultural practices, the so-called 'designer fallacy' (Ihde, 2008) warns us that many of the uses to which technologies are put transcend, and even defy, the imaginations of the creators of these tools. Engineers are highly trained to apply and solve perceived problems and expand paradigms within their fields, but the ability to predict and scope to the full range of uses, and potential misuses, of their creations is less well-developed. The emerging landscape is not one to be addressed through more technological development but rather via a 'cultural fix' (Layne, 2000). As an ethical, human, cultural problem, such narrowing would require an ethical, human, cultural process to address. Unfortunately, the pace of technological development often outstrips the rate at which human collectives and individuals process and assimilate them organically.

Music as Sensemaking

In its role as cultural production and participation, music and the arts also assist us not only to know who we are but also to create an understanding of the world around us. Arts-based research comprises a recognised set of knowledge-creation practices, some of which (like photography) have come to be widely accepted as themselves a privileged form of scientific data (Riddett-Moore & Siegesmund, 2012: p. 106). As mentioned previously, however, the place of data in knowledge-creation practices is not very clear, even to those whose work depends fundamentally upon it. Interestingly, the term *data* seems as foreign in research contexts such as history, literature, and the arts as it does in the context of artistic creation. A 2018 Twitter thread asking about the perceptions of the term in this community led to a diverse and perhaps not unsurprisingly largely negative set of responses, characterising the use of *data* as a term by which to reference cultural sources as falsely implying something narrow, derived, impoverished, simple, or monophonic, perhaps even sinister or indicative that a researcher 'doesn't value [a source] or respect its integrity' (Posner, 2018).

One useful definition of *data* that does resonate for this parallel community of cultural practitioners, however, is that *data* acts as a 'relational category applied to research outputs that are taken, at specific moments of inquiry, to provide evidence for knowledge claims of interest to the researchers involved' (Leonelli, 2015: p. 810). According to this perspective, data cannot be viewed as a thing in itself but as a collection of 'portable object[s]' and a means for communication, rather like a language, carrying different meanings and messages at different times, dependent on its context of use, but also its origins and destinations. This definition inherently introduces another element from humanities research practices that provides a valuable framework for viewing the processes of engaging with music in a technologised age and data-driven context: provenance.

Provenance represents many things, in particular for the historian. It is the origin of a document and the knowledge it contains; it is the path that object has taken since its creation through the ownership of individuals and stewardship of institutions. It is the context in which that object must be interpreted and can be used as a basis of a given interpretation. It is the ultimate arbiter of the authenticity of the object and the authority of any claims made based on it. If *provenance* can therefore be said to represent the ownership, accretion of influences, origin, and changes occurring over time to those 'portable objects' upon which we build our conceptualisation of the world, in that case, we can see how this term might apply equally well within the context of how a musical composition is created from the cultural influences filtered and absorbed by a composer.

Provenance highlights the problem of how impoverished data can be as a form of documentation and how these impoverishments can become enshrined in and perpetuated throughout the contexts in which a dataset is applied and reused. For historical documents, these losses can include aspects of an object and its record, such as the source and composition of the ink used by a scribe or what other documents may have been in the collection that held it under a previous ownership, no longer linked but perhaps influential over how it had been historically interpreted. One can imagine similar impoverishments in musical data, things a human can explore and exploit but which a data field representation might lose entirely: the origin of a sample, the haptic affordances and limitations of a mixing deck, the sonic quirks of a particular instrument or venue. This layer of context goes missing in the data record and is generally neither documented nor indeed able to be recuperated or reproduced even from the metadata (literally 'data about data') that is commonly attached to any complex file in a more extensive dataset. Within the 'black box' context of an AI system, this may reduce the complexity of the past and create inaccurate models of the present. It may also deny future artists and audiences the opportunity to listen and create starting from the richest possible foundation.

Music as Creative Practice

Somewhere between the function of music and the arts as a cultural and sense-making practice, we also have to recognise a third role music plays in human lives that is potentially transformed through the data-driven nature of AI being used as a supplement to human abilities. This is its place as a creative practice. The arts provide a window into the inner world of human cognition and connectedness through their capacity to harness the positive impulses of the developmental force known as generativity. This term, coined within the psychological literature of the 1950s, refers to the relationship we build to the outputs of our activities, our 'production' as well as our 'progeny,' and the manner in which we improve the lives of those who will come after us (De St. Aubin & Bach, 2015: p. 654). The sentiment behind the term is of course much older, however, in particular as it pertains to the arts: generativity is a part of the purposeful action engaging a community (*arete*) that Aristotle placed at the foundation of human life satisfaction (*eudaimonia*) as well as the 'monument more lasting than bronze' of Horace's famous ode. The human need to communicate and integrate across time and space through the arts has endured for thousands of years.

AI systems might create art out of the data we feed them, but they don't need to – humans do. Technology risks are very often assessed according to known visible harm that can be seen to contribute to, but what if the risk is an opportunity cost, an activity we too easily delegate away from human actors? Once we see the software as potentially usurping processes we need to undertake ourselves to achieve the psychological integration we seek, then the risk of such development becomes much more visible. A recent study of Uber drivers found that management of their work via technological surveillance was detrimental to their sense of job satisfaction and well-being due to the lack of transparency and sense of dehumanisation it caused (Möhlmann & Henfridsson, 2019). Creating something larger than ourselves is a contributor to health and well-being, but AI can sort-circuit the benefits of this purposeful activity in contexts where human agency is forcibly undermined, however. In many contexts, the AI appears as an assistive technology, but its ultimate effect leads to degraded professional confidence and competence, a phenomenon that has been documented in commercial pilots (Awati, 2017) and translators (Kushner, 2013) among others.

Philosophers of the digital age may increasingly query the degree to which humans actually exercise free will, with so many of our decisions predicated on the knowledge, perspectives, and material we have immediately available to us. Indeed, one popular philosopher has come to the quite bleak conclusion that 'no human DJ could ever hope to match the skills of such an AI' (Harari, 2018: p. 26). Perhaps, however, the point is not to make the best choices but simply to maintain the ability to make those choices at all, not only for the social role they play, but also for how the process of making these choices determines who we are, how we understand our world, and how we relate to others. It has been suggested that the one difference between the artistic expressions created by AI systems and their human counterparts is one of 'intention' (Du Sautoy, 2019). Human-created art is important not because it somehow expresses something different in a transcendent, universal way but because it has meaning for us. Should we abdicate the ability to create meaning for ourselves merely because of the impression that a data-driven approach or system can give us a 'better' answer, we will be in a sorry state as a sentient species indeed.

Music as a Commodity

While the discussion of the socially, culturally, and psychologically beneficial roles played by the creation of and participation in music have led to this consideration of the impact of data in AI systems so far, the fact that music is also an industry and a commodity raises significant and distinct issues. These phenomena can be observed across the continuum of music creation and consumption. From the production of fundamental building blocks to the experience of the end user or consumer, the economic value of music can have a potentially wide-ranging impact on what might be considered best practice with regards to the collection and management of data for use in music AI systems.

As the previous sections have probably already made clear, collecting data to be used for training and testing AI systems brings with it significant responsibility. This is both an artistic and ethical one, but it has legal implications as well. The music industry has, over time, devised solid mechanisms to managing the constraints that protect intellectual property. However, the concepts such as 'fair use' that have governed this discussion will surely need to adapt to the increasing sublimation of influences and contributions to an end work that occur via data-driven applications. But the potential contributors to a work of art can also be seen as growing exponentially in the age of big data, and in many cases, it is not the generative, intentional contribution of someone who perceives themselves as a creator but the unintentional or under-informed sharing of personal data that may be in question. This threat exists even in systems with strong instruments in place to protect citizens from the misuse of their data: for example, while the European General Data Protection Regulation (GDPR) does lead the world in providing a robust framework for ensuring citizens are empowered to challenge and resist abuses of their personal data, this protection does not extend to the ownership of data but rather only to their position as a subject of that data, a processor or a controller of it.

The tensions inherent in the relationship between the platforms individuals use to interact with their peers and experience music and culture are not limited to the concerns of the music industry, but music tends to act as a forerunner that accompanies many other technological innovations. Cinema and video games brought us accompanying musical genres and scores, mobile phones brought us ringtones, and new business models accompanying platforms from Napster to TikTok have had music at their centre: surely, new applications emerging from the realms of augmented and virtual reality and the internet of things will follow this path and potentially place unique pressures on the music industry to manage issues of personal data, consent, and the ethics of common good versus reward to creators.

Technology is never neutral: the capacities we gain are always balanced by some loss, of our own abilities or perceptions, of transparency, and of the malleability that enables creative reuse to emerge. This is particularly the case for data-driven applications, where the manner in how a system performs may be determined not by a set of parameters that its end user can see and, if necessary, question but by a set of parameters hidden within a sea of data that is comprehensible to the machine but not the human. Movements to address this risk area are in development, from the very high-level principles of human-centred design to the more specific interventions of explainable AI and human in the loop techniques. Managing at the level of technical development the potential adverse effects of AI-enabled, data-driven approaches to the experience and creation of music will be critical enablers to ensuring that human cultural practice remains firmly centred on humans and their social and individual needs. Artists and their audiences must ultimately control this process, however, rather than by engineers and large media companies. Though these technologies may seem seductive in what they offer, and to democratise creativity and access, it may merely be the appearance of these essential resources that are facilitated. Data poses no threat to music by allowing machines to create music, even if that music seems indistinguishable from human-created equivalents. However, the threat is inherent in the premise that having machines that can create music means that humans no longer can, should, or need to. It is here where the knowledge and activism of the arts must stand firm and ensure that the human need to create art does not become subsumed by our ability to build software.

Bibliography

Awati, K. (2017) Big data metaphors we live by. *Medium*. https://towardsdatascience.com/big-data-metaphors-we-live-by-98d3fa44ebf8.

Baruh, L. & Popescu, M. (2017) Big data analytics and the limits of privacy self-management. *New Media & Society*. 19 (4), 579–596. doi:10.1177/1461444815614001.

Blanke, T., Bryant, M. & Hedges, M. (2020) Understanding memories of the Holocaust – a new approach to neural networks in the digital humanities. *Digital Scholarship in the Humanities*. 35 (1), 17–33. doi:10.1093/llc/fqy082.

De St. Aubin, E. & Bach, M. (2015) Explorations in generativity and culture. In: L.A. Jensen (ed.), *The Oxford handbook of human development and culture*. Oxford: Oxford University Press. doi:10.1093/oxfordhb/9780199948550.013.40.

Du Sautoy, M. (2019) *The creativity code: Art and innovation in the age of AI*. Cambridge: Harvard University Press. doi:10.4159/9780674240407.

Edmond, J., Horsley, N., Lehmann, J. & Priddy, M. (2021) *Data, truth and knowledge complexity*. Bingley: Emerald Publishing.

Germain, A. & Chakareski, J. (2013) Spotify me: Facebook-assisted automatic playlist generation. *2013 IEEE 15th International Workshop on Multimedia Signal Processing (MMSP)*. 025–028. doi:10.1109/MMSP.2013.6659258.

Harari, Y.N. (2018) *21 lessons for the 21st century*. London: Random House.

Hertzmann, A. (2020) Computers do not make art, people do. *Communications of the ACM*. 63 (5), 45–48.

Ihde, D. (2008) The designer fallacy and technological imagination. In: P. Kroes, P.E. Vermaas, A. Light & S.A. Moore (eds.), *Philosophy and design: From engineering to architecture*. Amsterdam: Springer Netherlands, pp. 51–59. doi:10.1007/978-1-4020-6591-0_4.

Kaleagasi, B. (2017) *A new AI can write music as well as a human composer*. www.futurism.com/a-new-ai-can-write-music-as-well-ahuman-composer.

Kalnins, R. & Vasiljevs, A. (2018) *Report on multilingual big data and language technology*. https://kplexproject.files.wordpress.com/2018/06/kplex_wp5-deliverable.pdf.

Kushner, S. (2013) The freelance translation machine: Algorithmic culture and the invisible industry. *New Media & Society*. 15 (8), 1241–1258. doi:10.1177/1461444812469597.

Layne, L. (2000) The cultural fix: An anthropological contribution to science and technology studies. *Science, Technology, & Human Values*. 25 (3), 352–379. doi:10.1177/016224390002500305.

Leonelli, S. (2015) What counts as scientific data? A relational framework. *Philosophy of Science*. 82 (5), 810–821. doi:10.1086/684083.

Möhlmann, M. & Henfridsson, O. (2019) What people hate about being managed by algorithms, according to a study of Uber drivers. *Harvard Business Review*. https://hbr.org/2019/08/what-people-hate-about-being-managed-by-algorithms-according-to-a-study-of-uber-drivers.

O'Neil, C. (2016) *Weapons of math destruction: How big data increases inequality and threatens democracy*. New York: Crown.

Posner, M. (2018) Humanists out there, specifically non-digital humanists: If someone were to call the sources you use 'data,' what would your reaction be? If you don't consider your sources data, what makes them different? *@miriamkp*. https://twitter.com/miriamkp/status/1057706465866133504.

Raley, R. (2013) *Dataveillance and countervailance*. https://escholarship.org/uc/item/2b12683k.

Riddett-Moore, K. & Siegesmund, R. (2012) Arts-based research: Data are constructed, not found. In: S.R. Klein (ed.), *Action research methods: Plain and simple*. London: Palgrave Macmillan, pp. 105–132. doi:10.1057/9781137046635_6.

Rogers, C.R. (1954) Toward a theory of creativity. *ETC: A Review of General Semantics*. 11 (4), 249–260.

Rosenberg, D. (2013) Data before the fact. *Raw Data Is an Oxymoron*. 15–40.

Sætra, H.S. (2019) Freedom under the gaze of big brother: Preparing the grounds for a liberal defence of privacy in the era of big data. *Technology in Society*. 58, 101160. doi:10.1016/j.techsoc.2019.101160.

Thelwall, M. (2018) Gender bias in sentiment analysis. *Online Information Review*. 42 (1), 45–57. doi:10.1108/OIR-05-2017-0139.

UN (2015) *Universal declaration of human rights*. United Nations. www.un.org/en/about-us/universal-declaration-of-human-rights.

9 Law

You Can Call Me Hal: AI and Music IP

Martin Clancy

International copyright comprises a series of rights designed to protect original artistic works created by human beings. The majority of global employment in the music industry originates from four revenue sources: publishing, recording, live performance, and merchandise (Rogers, 2017). Each sector derives and depends on the exploitation of intellectual property (IP), most especially music copyright. However, new works of art are increasingly presented that illustrate the capabilities of machine creativity and indicate that the protection offered by copyright is susceptible to the challenge of artificial intelligence (AI).

As matters stand, while some degree of recognition is given to computer systems that generate work that may claim copyright, serious questions arise: how should human creativity be protected in the music ecosystem where AI is a new actor, and what will be the future status of that actor? This chapter highlights how a series of these challenges is encountered when copyright law and practice confront AI-generated music.

Global IP

The development of global IP enforcement can be seen as a weaving thread, originating from the Berne Convention (1886) to the recent Article 17 in EU *Directive on Copyright in the Digital Single Market* (*Copyright Directive*) (European Parliament, 2018). As the significance of national borders reduces due to the impact of digital technology on the distribution and consumption of copyrighted goods, further harmonisation of IP law is likely to continue.[1] The World Trade Organisation (WTO) (WTO: Basics, 2020) development indicates the movement to bring coherence and a sense of consistency to a state of affairs where legislation or court judgements in one nation might have often-random or unintended domino effects in other jurisdictions.

Recognition of the international regime of cooperation and interplay requires scrutiny of copyright law in the context of new technologies. Recent developments in computer-generated works of art (CGWA) have given rise to questions of whether these works should be afforded recognition (and what). Addressing these questions is critical to reviewing AI technology's potential impact on music.

DOI: 10.4324/9780429356797-10

By analysing critical and essentially historical concepts, the capacity of copyright to meet the tests posed by AI music systems can be considered.

Copyright Foundations

Copyright, one of several IP expressions, is the legal right granted to the creator of original work, allowing the author exclusive rights limited by time for its use and distribution. To grant copyright in the context of music, two essential components are required: one, that the work should be in a tangible, *permanent* form and, two, that it should be legally considered *original*.

IP rights are exclusive to human creativity. The rationale that explains this notion of the author as both originator and creator has its basis in the seventeenth-century writings of John Locke and the economic concept of possessive individualism and labour. *Fairness theory* (Quintais, 2017), a concept widely recognised in copyright law, follows Locke's *labour theory* and maintains that multiple authors of the same work are entitled to individual rights relative to their contribution to the finished creation. The concept of *fairness theory* in copyright law is extended by *personality theory*, which grew out of the work of the philosophers Hegel and Kant. *Personality theory* contends that rights are warranted by the contribution made from the individual self into the final creation (Beck, 1960: p. 223) and proposes that the *thing* created in some way manifests aspects of the author's will and personality (Hegel, 1942).

Personality theory actively contributed to the present-day understanding and development of *moral rights* (Spinello & Tavani, 2005: p. 192). The critical components extend to the author's right to be recognised and to maintain authorial control of the integrity of their creation, even after any rights have been fully assigned to a third party (Kwall, 2010: p. 135). An example occurs with music composers and songwriters, who, even after the transferred ownership of their publishing rights, still retain (at least in Europe) their *moral rights* in such assigned works. Both Locke's *labour theory* and Kant's *personality theory* arose from the concept of the utilitarian justification that the primary purpose of copyright is for the *common good*, as a reward for human effort (Gough, 1950: p. 127; Rawls, 2005 [1971]: p. 584). Supporting the notion of societal good, *social planning theory* holds that IP rights should be maximised to promote cultural goals (Duhl, 2004: p. 712). A final concept, the *sweat of the brow* in copyright law, explicitly references the human element in the act of creation (Sinha & Mahalwar, 2017: p. 218).

These legal concepts contribute to the notion of the essential human-centred construction of the author and the societal need to encourage and reward innovation. Indeed, the human-centred construction of IP law extends to the explicit exclusion of the 'nonhuman' from the world of copyright creativity. As an example of something that cannot qualify for copyright, the US Office states that it will not recognise works produced by 'nature, animals, or plants.' Specifically, it highlights 'a photograph taken by a monkey' (Compendium: Chapter 300, 2017: p. 17). If a strict approach like this were to be applied to AI systems, granting copyright to music produced autonomously created by AI would be extremely difficult, if not impossible.

One suggested solution to the conundrum of copyright for AI is giving authorship to the programmer (Kumar & Lavery, 2019). This is evident in Hong Kong, India, Ireland, New Zealand, and the UK, where when literary, musical, or artistic works are computer-generated, the author is regarded as either the person who facilitates this process or the owner of the machine or the person who consciously enables the creative process to unfold. This argument begs the following question: when does the human author become sufficiently disconnected from the act of creation to not qualify for copyright protection? Rulings regarding the threshold of mechanical creativity are long considered. A landmark case, *Burrow-Giles v. Sarony* (1884) (Burrow-Giles Lithographic Co. v. Sarony, 1884) examined the degree of human creativity involved in producing a series of Oscar Wilde lithographs. To investigate notions of AI creativity, the tools available to measure and define the concepts of *originality* and *creativity* in music copyright must be inspected.

Creativity and Originality

Copyright law's definitions of *creativity*, human or otherwise, are slender (Karjala, 2008: p. 182). However, paradoxically, the very concept of *creativity* remains one of the key measures for determining whether musical works qualify for copyright protection. A helpful way to understand how to frame this elusive notion of *creativity* is by examining the tests available to assess alleged music copyright infringement. While the legislature may not successfully frame what creativity is, established case law and legal tools exist to examine that which it is not.

For example, some degree of *skill* needs to have been exercised in *creativity*, albeit it can be a modest demonstration of the term *skill* denoted by law when correlated to any music norm. Additionally, to be granted copyright, an original music work must be 'set down in some permanent form' (Bagehot & Kanaar, 1998: p. 124), such as a music recording or sheet music. What constitutes a permanent form may be legally tested once AI actors generate nonrepetitive, adaptive, and hyperpersonalised music.[2] Rulings such as *Bridgeman Art Library, Ltd. v. Corel Corp.* (Bridgeman Art Library, Ltd. v. Corel Corp., 1999), which successfully argued that replica photography of public domain photographs could not be copyrighted, continued the low-bar definition of *originality*. Such rulings show that what is essential is that work must be created by the author who claims authorship and who shows a degree of creativity so that the work is distinct from the materials from which it was created. More generally, as demonstrated by the increase in recent music copyright infringement cases, the concept of *originality* in copyright has become defined in negative terms as a work that is not plagiarism.[3]

To comprehend the complexities of the many challenges presented by AI to IP, the strains already placed – by humans – on music copyright should be noted, for it is the existing fragility of the law that AI tests. A fundamental instability in the law relates to legal notions of *creativity* and *originality*, which, as has been shown, are negatively defined by their degree of *similarity* to other works. It is essential at this point to be reminded that there are two significant copyrights in any music recording – the copyright attached to the composition and the copyright attached to the recording. *The Verve v. The Rolling Stones* (Vozick-Levinson, 2019) reveals the existing complexity of argument that emerges from the interlinking copyright concepts involving human *creativity* and *originality*.

Several recent cases, mostly intriguingly *'Blurred Lines'* (Robin Thicke v. Marvin Gaye's Estate, 2013) and *'Dark Horse'* (Marcus Gray et al. v. Katy Perry, et al., 2020), can be seen to widen and possibly dilute the available tests for music copyright infringement. At the root of these cases is the question of what constitutes *fair* and *unfair use* of IP and the test of *substantiality* that will be increasingly critical to this chapter. This current knowledge makes it possible to glimpse AI's legal challenges to the music ecosystem's brittle and highly interpretable legislation.

Approaches to AI

It is helpful to note essential distinctions regarding the varying technical approaches of AI actors and how this can be considered to map across the music copyright landscape. From David Cope's AI Emily Howell to IBM Watson Music to AIVA, many actors involve AI systems trained on music databases to create compositions. Some of these actors, Francisco Vico's Iamus or Cope's EMI, have their AI compositions played and recorded by human musicians. Alternatively, TikTok/Jukedeck and Sony Flow Machines process the compositions with supervised AI systems to create music recordings. In each, human creativity in the AI process is evidenced, albeit at varying degrees, at every stage of the development of the musical work. In this context, many uncertainties related to the call for AI to be granted the right to IP can be analysed within the tests and concepts available to human musicians so far mentioned. Nonetheless, when considering other developing AI systems, the widening complexity of the situation emerges. Deep learning AI systems, such as Google's WaveNet, involve unsupervised training of audio datasets and can produce music compositions and recordings without human participation. To contextualise the provocations of such novel AI approaches, it is first essential to reflect on legal distinctions involving audio sampling practices before considering AI's ability to generate unsupervised compositions and recordings from raw audio data.

Sampling

Audio sampling has grown to become routine in present-day music genres and performance contexts. An analysis of the development of sampling technologies and practises brings again defences to claims of copyright infringement. In addition to the defence of *fair use*, the law has recognised two defences, *scènes à fair*[4] and *de minimis*, an age-old legal concept that will become familiar, particularly when encountering Google's WaveNet AI.

In infringement cases, the doctrine *de minimis* classically allows a defendant to claim that the part taken and used in a work (an audio sample, for instance) is too insignificant or lacking in importance to be treated as an infringement of the original work's copyright (Schuster et al., 2019: p. 184). Contrary to much conventional understanding, no number of music notes determines the extent of *de minimis* (Lindenbaum, 1999: p. 23). Instead, the smallest audio sample that can be recognised by someone familiar with the original is the limit as to what could be protected by a *de minimis* defence (Mispagel, 2018: p. 474). The consideration of these tests including classic defences and doctrines of *fair use*, *substantiality* and *de minimis*, is all central in determining whether music copyright infringement has occurred. With this understanding, we now consider the application of legal concepts in music copyright to the scientific methodologies in play with WaveNet.

Google WaveNet

To recap, most AI-based systems' creative outputs can be sheet music (Iamus) or processed MIDI and audio files (Amper). The computational creativity involved in these AI systems requires human musicians and technicians to be fundamental in the generative process. Similarly, in other music machine learning systems, a human-programmed curation is in operation that assigns the created MIDI file to a designated audio output (Algotunes), or an AI-generated melodic MIDI pattern (Popgun) is guided by the user's choice of tempo, mood, and genre.

Though copyright content generated by the AI may be available in the public domain (Melomics) or through a hybrid licensing arrangement (Amadeus Code), the vital involvement of a human either as the performer, co-composer, or programmer is a technical essential of AI-produced music.

Google AI WaveNet presents a radically different technical proposition. The critical difference is that systems such as WaveNet are a self-learning neural network that delivers a musical output that requires no human participation either in its analysis of the inputted material or in the creative assembly of its final audio output. Furthermore, the infinitesimal degree at which WaveNet samples its audio training sets renders current, and perhaps possible legal, remedies redundant. To examine this significance, it is necessary to briefly review both the technology's history and its technical functionality.

DeepMind

DeepMind Technologies is an AI subsidiary of Alphabet Inc. and was acquired by Google in 2014. DeepMind's outset ambition was not to design an AI with a limited and fixed set of abilities; instead, DeepMind wanted to produce an AI able to self-direct and provide solutions to a presented challenge. Fundamental to achieving this goal, the AI would have the capacity to self-learn (Mnih et al., 2013: p. 3). WaveNet is a convolutional neural network (CNN) developed by DeepMind, and its original purpose was to create an advanced text-to-speech (TTS) system (Van den Oord et al., 2016a).

A TTS purpose is to produce convincing audio in varying contexts, from language translation to recreating the singing of Ella Fitzgerald. A TTS system such as Amazon Polly transposes user text data into an audio output. The rapid progress indicates the future music capability of AI systems like WaveNet that TTS systems have already achieved in generating audio content and was evident at the presentation of the Duplex system at 'I/O 2018' (Leviathan & Matias, 2018).

A vital aspect of WaveNet's application in music generation is that the AI decision-making is opaque and is an example of a black box output. This is to say that no one – the programmer or the user – can determine how the AI creation has ultimately formulated its assembled output (Van den Oord et al., 2016b: p. 3). This lack of traceability in the creative formation of its audio will remain critical in subsequent legal reflection.

WaveNet approaches the generation of music through a similar methodology that DeepMind approached with the games of Go and StarCraft. First, the AI self-learns, creating an understanding and rationale of the applicable rules of the task – this self-learning behaviour equates to the system's creative ability. Similarly, when WaveNet generates music, no human curation is involved other than providing the initial training set. Intriguingly, the self-learning approach was not the first used by the DeepMind music team (Diaz-Jerez, 2011: p. 14). Initially, the team anticipated that the system would benefit from learning the rules of music theory. Nevertheless, DeepMind soon abandoned this process and determined that the system could be optimised in an unconditioned musical environment as a self-learning AI (Van den Oord et al., 2016a: p. 8).

Technical Implementation and Legal Implication

To recap, WaveNet's deep learning concepts fundamentally differ from most AI technologies. There, the AI music actors primarily focused on generating a musical piece (often MIDI) as data and then transformed that data into audio, with many training sets used as music scores. The AI systems, in the main, perceive the training sets as mathematical data that can be analysed and reproduced using the same learned and explicit patterns found in conventional human music training. By contrast, DeepMind created an AI that treats audio data as uninformed content. WaveNet does not analyse its training set relative to music theory, and therefore there is no guided expectation for the AI in terms of its musical output. Instead, it seeks unique connections in the input training set content. For example, when WaveNet analyses a major 7 chord, it does not evaluate the audio content from a traditional musical perspective; instead, the AI focuses on the coexistence of all the sonic frequencies and properties involved in constructing that major 7 chord's audio and then makes its bespoke determination of what that information means.

The WaveNet team states that the audio output of its AI will consist of a minimum of sixteen thousand samples per second (Van den Oord et al., 2016a: p. 1). That scale of microsampling is minute even compared to the techniques used in granular synthesis.[5] There has been no suggestion that the practice of granular sampling synthesis can be linked to copyright infringement. This is due to the scale upon which human auditory perception functions. This degree of human auditory perception is relevant when reconsidering the legal measure of reasonable identification of *substantiality* in copyright sampling. Suppose granular synthesis is too minuscule to be argued as a claim to copyright infringement. In that case, it follows that such legal protections when tested by AI technologies like WaveNet are even more remote and infeasible.

To restate, each second of music generated by WaveNet comprises a minimum of sixteen thousand repurposed audio samples, assembled from its training set and operating on a scale far beyond the threshold of human listening perception. When such microsample proportions are considered within the legal framework *of de minimis, substantiality*, and *fair use*, this assembly of audio fragments raises many challenging propositions to existing copyright norms. An illustration of what is technically possible is a TTS AI – Dadabots – created by CJ Carr and Zack Zukowski which continuously generates death metal audio and is live-streamed via YouTube (Dadabots, 2019). The Dadabots AI is a recursive neural network (RNN) trained on the raw audio recordings of the band Archspire and developed upon similar AI technical protocols to WaveNet.

> Splits (the Archspire albums) into thousands of tiny samples and then creates tens of thousands of iterations to develop the AI, which starts out making white noise and ultimately learns to produce more recognisable music elements.
>
> (Deahl, 2019a)

The release of Dababots' ceaseless AI death metal was somewhat insulated from its full implication by the current limitations of its comparative audio fidelity, sometimes invoking a humorous reaction to its output. It should be noted that distortions, deviations, or departures from the source inspiration (in this instance, a training set) are not without their charm or historical parallels in music.[6]

The rapid advancement of AI systems was further evident in the spring of 2020 with a series of extraordinary musical releases. In March, the OpenAI institute announced Jukebox, a musical adaptation of their GPT-2 AI (Jukebox, 2020). Jukebox produces convincing finished audio soundalike music tracks of artists, including David Bowie, Louis Armstrong, and Frank Sinatra, created using the WaveNet system's techniques. In late April 2020, deepfake audio recordings that appeared to feature Jay-Z rapping *Hamlet*'s 'To be, or not to be' soliloquy, among other surprising content, were broadcast on the YouTube channel *Voice Synthesis* (Hogan, 2020; Statt, 2020). The fidelity of both recordings represents a significant technical progression of the AI creative capacity that the industry has noted. Commenting on the implications of emerging CNN music-generation systems, Jonathan Bailey, CTO of iZotope,[7] stated, 'I won't mince words. . . . This is a total legal clusterfuck' (Deahl, 2019b).

While it cannot yet be known if AI will ever fully generate recorded music indistinguishable from that made by humans, perhaps that is not the issue for consideration. The fact that software like WaveNet and Jukebox is open-source, combined with the relatively low financial cost of its processing power, will likely drive profound changes in the use of AI and music creativity. WaveNet demonstrates that AI does not require human participation in musical creation beyond the initial training set and building the AI. Perhaps that requirement (the training set) is sufficient to maintain the role of the human in the creative process. Furthermore, if so desired, copyright attached to music generated by self-learning AI remains vested in the humans who have put the 'necessary arrangements' into place. The ability of said AI systems to create original content, regardless of the attenuated human involvement, may be to deem the AI to be the author or, at the very least, coauthor of the work. Then, such an AI, though it may be considered to meet the legal tests attaching to a human artistic expression such as *originality*, *substantiality*, and *creativity*, and be recognised by the court as a nonhuman author, will still not be entitled to copyright protection. Copyright is, after all, protected by the human-centred principles of IP developed internationally over centuries. Yet the protection of music copyright has, in recent years, increasingly been tested and effectively weakened by humans, as in the cases of 'Blurred Lines' and 'Dark Horse.' In each of those case laws, the alleged infringements are related to similarities in the music composition. Self-learning AI systems point to another potential weakening for the stress test of copyright durability.

As matters currently stand, there is little evidence of any current receptivity to granting nonhuman copyright in common-law systems worldwide. Therefore, it has fallen to the courts in individual decisions in different jurisdictions to interpret and lay down the boundaries of copyright protection. Decisions in one jurisdiction can unintentionally affect another through the increasing movement towards harmonisation between intergovernmental entities (EU, WIPO). Furthermore, rulings in copyright cases frequently determined in unrelated fields (from database collection to photography) have widely interpretative implications when applied to music. The issue of AI-authored IP is continuously under challenge, as shown by the range of cases involving Stephen Thaler's Dabus AI (Krieser & Camiel, 2020; Stephen Thaler v. Comptroller General of Patents Trade Marks and Designs, 2021; Stephen L. Thaler v. The Comptroller-General of Patents, Designs and Trade Marks, 2020). At the same time, a recent ruling in China (Shenzhen Tencent v. Shanghai Yingxun, 2019; Bo, 2020; NCAC, 2021) is evidence of a possible reshaping of the fundamentals of copyright. Where challenges lie soon is in recognising that these cases were decided prior to the widespread commercial introduction of unsupervised, self-learning AI systems.

Traditionally, the function of copyright systems has been to protect property rights in human creativity as an aspect of protecting the dignity of the human person as to its fundamental social and economic purpose. The capacity of AI applications to produce literary and artistic work autonomously is now well recognised. Granting self-same copyright status to AI-produced work would have several unintended and unforeseen effects. However, what would be the status of an AI if granted rights that approached those now provided to humans? As has been established, AI is capable of unsupervised music generation with accelerating capacity. So what is the future role of the human, and how is this changing spectrum of creativity measured?

AI and Legal Personhood

An argument exists within the broader debate on AI, robotics, and IP which proposes that many societal and economic benefits could emerge from extending person-like rights to machine-generated creativity. Both Japan and the Republic of Korea are considering extending their IP laws to include a machine-based consideration (Keisner, 2016), while the EU is presently debating a category of personhood for robots and related AI (Withers, 2018).

The concept of legal persons has already been extended to corporations, partnerships, societies, and individuals. However, this extended, if artificial, definition of the 'legal person' allied to advances in robotics has raised many contentions. Firstly, it is essential to acknowledge that embodied AI (robots) is not a prerequisite of the debate of legal personhood. Shawn Bayern has advanced this proposition as a theoretical legal possibility in an article entitled 'The Implications of Modern Business-Entity Law for the Regulation of Autonomous Systems' (Bayern, 2016). Bayern argued that under New York State law, it would be feasible for a corporation to be established by a human being working with an AI entity. By employing a sufficiently elaborate operating agreement, it would be possible for the human to subsequently resign from the corporation's board, leaving the AI system solely working autonomously. The result would be that the AI would have the effective benefit of legal corporate personhood lasting in perpetuity.

Related inventive arguments emerge from tort law and vicarious liability. The law sees AI software incorporated into devices like robots as simply products (European Commission, 2020). If a product is defective, if it does not work correctly or causes damage, the product manufacturer can be held liable. So an injured party can sue based on product liability law or negligence. However, when an AI system starts to act on behalf of no one, and supposedly on its own behalf, the law will need to radically re-examine its approach as then the arguments for applying strict liability regimes may be seen to need urgent and critical assessment. This concern is particularly relevant in the context of what the EU determines as 'high-risk' (European Commission, 2021) AI, such as lethal autonomous weapons systems (LAWS) or liability issues regarding automated vehicles.

A third position usually relied upon to defend human creativity is found in the concept of author *incentivisation* (Sinha & Mahalwar, 2017: p. 66). *Incentive theory* argues that society benefits from creating new inventions and new works, which provide authors with monopoly rights limited in time and territory to foster the *common good* (Boldrin & Levine, 2009). This counterargument proposes that many societal benefits could emerge from extending independent rights to machine-generated creativity and is an intriguing reinterpretation of author incentivisation theory within the broader debate on AI, robotics, and IP.

Conclusion

This chapter has shown how legal arguments could be constructed whereby a nonhuman legal person – an AI – could be capable of corporate immortality. If the granting of copyright protection to AI-generated works was agreed upon, then in whom or in what will the copyright vest? Should the granting of nonhuman legal personhood to an AI application be agreed to? How would this new legal personality be governed, and could it be bought and sold the same way as a company? It is only necessary to acknowledge these developing ideas in the international public sphere and reflect on their key factors and motivators. The urgent need to engage with these matters is evident in the two recent court cases cited,[8] which confirm the global diversity of legal opinion and the situation's openness to unforeseen consequences. In this instance, the radically divergent verdicts' rulings present a timely opportunity for regulatory bodies of the music ecosystem to contribute an active voice to this debate. Compounding the challenge from legal personhood, there is a distinct infirmity in relying on classic copyright case law to deal with the innovation of AI when that case law has its roots in the precomputerised age.

The music industry, founded on the rewards of human-generated IP, is on the shakiest of ground. It is evident that current legislation across jurisdictions and at the regional level, as interpreted and applied by the courts, is no longer fit enough to protect the economic and other interests of music makers fully. What is required is a global response that considers both the exponential developments in AI and the fundamental principles that underpin copyright laws. Recognising the inordinately challenging issues given the progression of AI science, this question arises: is there a middle way that may serve to provide a dependable and predictable legal regime for AI in the present and foreseeable future? The law remains the same whether dealing with killer or marimba-playing robots, and it may well be that these laws are first tested in the music. Recognition of these processes calls for ethically informed regulatory and legislative regimes in sector-specific industries. These principles require effective legal support for who and what is determined to be the *common good* in an equitable and sustainable music ecosystem.

This chapter amalgamates arguments expanded in Chapter 4 and Chapter 6 of my doctorate 'The Financial and Ethical Implications of Music Generated by Artificial Intelligence' (Clancy, 2021), Trinity College, Dublin.

Addendum: Interview with David Hughes (CTO, RIAA 2006–2021)

The Recording Industry Association of America (RIAA)

About 85% of all legitimate recorded music produced and sold in the United States is created, manufactured, or distributed by RIAA members. In support of its mission, the RIAA works to protect the intellectual property and First Amendment rights of artists and music labels; conducts consumer, industry, and technical research; and monitors and reviews state and federal laws, regulations, and policies. David Hughes was CTO at RIAA from 2006 to 2021.

He began his career at Sony Corporation in Tokyo in 1993 and first became involved in the digital distribution of music in 1996. In 1998, he moved to Sony Music in New York, where, as Vice President of Technology Strategies and Digital Policy, he created and ran the industry's first online delivery department. With over twenty-five years of experience in the music business, primarily focused on digital distribution, he currently provides strategic technology and business consulting services to leading music industry organisations.

David Hughes

I think certain people in the music industry have been convinced that they must pay attention. I am not sure they know *why* they have to. (By that, I guess I mean they do not know whether AI is an opportunity, a threat, both, or neither). Other people, like myself, have been more concerned about how it will impact almost every single job in the music industry. Some form of AI will be used to do pretty much every music industry job that, until recently, required deep industry knowledge combined with intuition and/or talent. AI or machine learning technologies will hit every single piece of the chain. That is why I am fascinated with it. AI has changed the way people work and how music is made. It does not necessarily mean that everybody is going to lose their jobs. Although we have seen a company like Clear Channel laying off hundreds of people because they have got an AI playlist program, that is part of it for sure. The separate and more significant issue is that the whole music industry is a business based on money and reliant on the exploitation of copyright. If the copyright system is disrupted, we know what happens, at least any of us who lived through Napster.

At that time at Sony Music, we had to lay off 10% of our staff every year for, what, six, seven years in a row. If there is a more extensive, new disruption to copyright, for instance, a songwriter AI claims the copyright of new hit material – that I am concerned about.

The major labels seem to be split between the potential opportunity to invest in AI companies that create sound recordings and the threat it poses to their core business. Warner Music, for example, has been very proactive in partnering with AI companies. All the majors have; some of them have been more public about it. However, they are all hedging their bets, like, 'Oh, if the future is going to be sound recordings created by AI or sound recordings mixed or mastered by AI, then we better have a piece of the action.' They want to be on the ground floor this time around. There is fear on one side, the fear of being undermined by AI, and the fear of missing out on a big opportunity. Meanwhile, the lawyers and lobbyists are looking at this, saying, 'We just spent our whole careers trying to shore up copyright law in Washington and Brussels, and now AI comes along. What if this undermines all our efforts?' That is where the companies were before going into COVID, anyway. It is much harder to read on it now as we are not meeting in person and speaking frankly over food and drinks.

In current copyright law in the United States, many in the industry feel relatively safe that if a computer, i.e., not a human, creates a work, it is not protected by current US copyright law. However, that may not be the case in, for example, the UK, so I would set my company up in Hammersmith and just start pumping out shitloads of AI or AI-assisted songs that sound similar to every other song that's ever been a hit and also those that never entirely made it. How long do I have to wait for one big infringement case? How large are the settlements in these sorts of cases? 'Dark Horse'? These are seven-figure settlements. One hefty compensation, and I get a cash infusion for a million dollars from one settlement. In addition, all the investors line up because, well, why wouldn't they?

Paul McCartney has an excellent quote about copying other people's musical ideas. 'We pinch from other people as much as they pinch from us.' They took inspiration from everybody, from Little Richard and Bo Diddley to Jerry Lee Lewis and Howling Wolf. First, they copied it, then they made it their own. That is how music is made. I always feel sorry for George Harrison with 'My Sweet Lord.' You have to imagine a guy who is that creative, who has written that many great songs – he did not need to infringe. He just had that other tune somewhere in the back of his mind. Anyway, he settled and was rich enough to pay it off. But think about an AI system designed to do just that on purpose, and we are in a different world.

For example, we already see production, relaxation, and meditation music created by AI. AI has already taken over these three genres. It starts with the most straightforward stuff. With the lowest bar. If you are a composer trying to compete with AI in this area at this point, it might be a waste of your time. So now it is going to start to spread across genres. At the WIPO Summit, I gave the example that creating an AI that can write the melodies for hit country music is trivial at this point – because it is formulaic. I love country music, but I love it primarily because of the lyrics. However, as I said, it would be some time before an AI can write Tammy Wynette's 'D-I-V-O-R-C-E.' At least not until two computers are fighting over the custody of their AI child, so some parts of the music industry seem safe – at least for now.

I was on a conference panel about eight years ago with a colleague from Spotify. An artist in the audience stood up and attacked Spotify for not paying him enough money for streaming. I immediately defended Spotify, and I said, 'What do you want them to do?' They pay 70% of his revenue to the labels and artists, songwriters, and publishers, 70%, which was the industry standard when I was in the CD world. The only thing Spotify could do was raise the monthly subscription price. However, Spotify has to compete with YouTube. When Spotify is paying seven-tenths of a penny for every stream, and YouTube, in some cases, is paying six one-hundredths of a penny for every stream, how can streaming services compete? Certainly not by raising their subscription fees significantly. The 'safe harbour' issue has skewed the economics of the music industry so severely that I believe we are still collecting only about 40% of what we should be collecting for the sound recording business currently. The guys on Wall Street say the potential for the music industry is multiples of what it is today. And maybe that explains the valuation of UMG. Anyway, as long as we have the safe harbour pulling the value of music down, we will never see the business's full potential.

Historically, the music and creative industry seem to have been afraid of opening the DMCA in copyright law for fear that they may end up in a worse place than they are now. The only thing they want to do is make small incremental gains. To fix the system, you have to open the box. And I think there is an inherent fear that things could change for the worse – such as the copyright term being shortened if you open the box. The value of companies like Disney, for example, is based on their catalogue going back to *Snow White* or *Cinderella*, which are still under copyright, but if that changed to, say, fifty-year copyright for sound recordings, then the Beatles are no longer covered. A significant amount of streaming revenue is not just catalogue music, meaning older than eighteen months, but deep catalogue music. The great thing about deep catalogue is that after a couple of years of revenue checks from Spotify, you pretty much know how much money you will get every month, or in the case of Mariah Carey, every Christmas. She knows how much she is going to get every Christmas from streaming. And if the number of subscribers goes up, her revenue will just go up with it. It is simple math. Those who are doing valuations and who are currently trying to buy up copyrights often know nothing about music, but what they see is a reliable, consistent revenue stream.

Copyright term is crucial here; however, the term cannot be shortened starting when they sign it into law. Because the day after that, all the Mickey Mouse movies, *Snow White*, and *Cinderella* will become public domain. I do not see this ever happening. If a shorter term were to happen, it would be only for works produced after a specific date. And then I suppose it would take a generation or two to take effect. That is the only way you could ever sell this to the industry. Otherwise, how would Disney and the other powerful lobbies ever agree to it?

Regarding the idea of AI being granted IP rights, what might happen? If I were, say, a 'copyright anarchist' and wanted to maximise profit, I would use AI to start creating every mathematically possible composition that is reasonable or likely to exist in the future based on samples of as many commercially successful sound recordings as possible. I would plug into a cloud service like Google and create billions of sound recordings in an easily indexable system. Then, when the next Nicki Minaj hit comes out, I go through my database and I look, and I see, oh, wait a minute, those few bars match up with the few bars that I wrote last year. Now I have got a potential copyright claim. It could ultimately undermine or at least severely disrupt the copyright system. Indeed, it does not matter if the copyright is assigned to the AI or if the copyright is, as in the case of the UK, assigned to the creator of the AI system, if we could eventually end up holding those copyrights. We write the software to do this or buy it from somebody else, and then we go on steroids. It is like the million monkeys typing away. Eventually, one will write a Shakespeare play, given enough time. Remember AI does not need to write *Hamlet*; it only needs to produce 'To be, or not to be, that is the question' to create a work sufficient to be granted a copyright.

Notes

1 An illustration of such trade agreements is *the Agreement on Trade-Related Aspects of Intellectual Property (TRIPS)*, in which members recognise reciprocal IP within their existing individual national legislation.
2 Examples ruled that exact photographic copies of public domain images could not be protected by copyright in the United States because the copies lack originality.
3 A review of the case law shows consensus around three explanations for musical similarity – coincidence, influence, and plagiarism.
4 Derived from the French term meaning 'scenes that must be done' (Pandey, 2015).
5 At least sixteen times smaller.
6 Within STS and the SCOT model, a theoretical concept known as 'solving the reverse salient' is useful and can be seen in the adoption of audio distortion as an accepted audio process effect. Here, an aesthetic decision made in the early 1950s when a musician preferred the sound of faulty bass amp opened up a route of music exploration that would eventually lead to the Jimi Hendrix guitar sound (Shepherd, 2003: p. 286).
7 iZotope Inc. are music industry leaders, whose award-winning 'intelligent audio' technologies such as the AI-enabled Neutron and Ozone software plug-ins are industry and educational standards for all DAW platforms.
8 The *Dabus* and *Dreamwriter* cases.

Bibliography

Bagehot, R. & Kanaar, N. (1998) *Music business agreements*. London: Sweet & Maxwell.
Bayern, S. (2016) The implications of modern business – entity law for the regulation of autonomous systems. *European Journal of Risk Regulation.* 7 (2), 297–309. doi:10.1017/S1867299X00005729.
Beck, L.W. (1960) *A commentary on Kant's critique of practical reason*. Chicago: University of Chicago Press.
Bo, Z. (2020) Artificial intelligence and copyright protection – judicial practice in Chinese courts. *WIPO*. www.wipo.int/export/sites/www/about-lp/en/artificial_intelligence/conversation_ip_ai/pdf/ms_china_1_en.pdf.
Boldrin, M. & Levine, D.K. (2009) Does intellectual monopoly help innovation. *Review of Law & Economics.* 5 (3). UCLA Department of Economics. doi:10.2202/1555-5879.1438.
Bridgeman Art Library, Ltd. v. Corel Corp. (1999) 36 F. Supp. 2d 191, Southern District of New York.
Burrow-Giles Lithographic Co. v. Sarony (1884) 111 US 53, 4 S. Ct. 279, 28 L. Ed. 349.
Clancy, M. (2021) *Reflections on the financial and ethical implications of music generated by artificial intelligence*. Ph.D. Dissertation. Trinity College, Dublin.
Dadabots (2019) *We make raw audio neural networks that can imitate bands*. https://dadabots.com/.
Deahl, D. (2019a) This live stream plays endless death metal produced by an AI. *The Verge*. www.theverge.com/2019/4/27/18518170/algorithm-ai-death-metal-dadabots-live-stream-youtube-cj-carr-zack-zukowski.
Deahl, D. (2019b) We've been warned about AI and music for over 50 years, but no one's prepared. *The verge.com*. www.theverge.com/2019/4/17/18299563/ai-algorithm-music-law-copyright-human.
Diaz-Jerez, G. (2011) Composing with melomics: Delving into the computational world for musical inspiration. *Leonardo Music Journal.* 21 (21), 13–14. doi:10.1162/LMJ_a_00053.

Duhl, G.M. (2004) Old lyrics, knock-off videos, and copycat comic books: The fourth fair use factor in U.S. copyright law. *Syracuse Law Review*. 54, 665. https://ssrn.com/abstract=1689685.

European Commission (2020) *White paper on artificial intelligence: A European approach to excellence and trust*. European Commission. https://ec.europa.eu/info/publications/white-paper-artificial-intelligence-european-approach-excellence-and-trust_en.

European Commission (2021) *Regulatory framework on AI: Shaping Europe's digital future*. https://digital-strategy.ec.europa.eu/en/policies/regulatory-framework-ai.

European Parliament (2018) *Amendments adopted by the European Parliament on 12 September 2018 on the proposal for a directive of the European Parliament and of the Council on copyright in the digital single market*. www.europarl.europa.eu/doceo/document/TA-8-2018-0337_EN.html?redirect.

Gough, J.W. (1950) *John Locke's political philosophy: Eight studies*. Oxford: Clarendon Press.

Hegel, G.W. (1942) *Hegel's philosophy of right*. Trans. T.M. Knox. Oxford: Clarendon Press.

Hogan, M. (2020) What does Jay-Z's fight over audio deepfakes mean for the future of AI music? *Pitchfork*. https://pitchfork.com/thepitch/what-does-jay-zs-fight-over-audio-deepfakes-mean-for-the-future-of-ai-music/.

Jukebox (2020) Jukebox. *OpenAI*. https://openai.com/blog/jukebox/.

Karjala, D.S. (2008) Copyright and creativity. *UCLA Entertainment Law Review*. 15 (2), 169–201. https://escholarship.org/uc/item/0t95v7n7.

Keisner, A. (2016) Breakthrough technologies – robotics and IP. *WIPO Magazine*. www.wipo.int/wipo_magazine/en/2016/06/article_0002.html.

Krieser, J. & Camiel, A. (2020) USPTO: Artificial intelligence systems cannot legally invent. *The National Law Review*. www.natlawreview.com/article/uspto-artificial-intelligence-systemscannot-legally-invent.

Kumar, J.S. & Lavery, J.N. (2019) Does AI generated work give rise to a copyright claim? *The National Law Review*. www.natlawreview.com/article/does-ai-generated-work-give-rise-to-copyright-claim.

Kwall, R.R. (2010) *The soul of creativity: Forging a moral rights law for the United States*. Stanford, CA: Stanford University Press.

Leviathan, Y. & Matias, Y. (2018) Google duplex: An AI system for accomplishing real-world tasks over the phone. *Google AI Blog*. http://ai.googleblog.com/2018/05/duplex-ai-system-for-natural-conversation.html.

Lindenbaum, J. (1999) *Music sampling and copyright law*. Princeton: Princeton University. https://slidelegend.com/music-sampling-and-copyright-law-princeton-university_5b604f1f097c47a1598b45ae.html.

Marcus Gray, et al. v. Katy Perry, et al. (2020) cv-05642, C.D. Cal, 16 March.

Mispagel, C. (2018) Resolving a copyright law circuit split: The importance of a *De Minimis* exception for sampled sound recordings. *Saint Louis University Law Journal*. 62 (2), 461–484. www.slu.edu/law/law-journal/pdfs/issues-archive/v62-no2/claire_mispagel_note.pdf.

Mnih, V., Kavukcuoglu, K., Silver, D., Graves, A., Antonoglou, I. et al. (2013) Playing Atari with deep reinforcement learning. *arXiv:1312.5602 [Cs]*. http://arxiv.org/abs/1312.5602.

NCAC (2021) *Office release of the top ten cases of national crackdown on infringement and piracy in 2020* [国家版权局网-要闻信息-国家版权局、全国'扫黄打非'办 发布2020年度全国打击侵权盗版十大案件]. National Copyright Administration of the

People's Republic of China. www.ncac.gov.cn/chinacopyright/contents/12227/354418. shtml.

Pandey, V. (2015) India: The relevance of doctrine of scène à faire in copyright law. *Mondaq*. https://www.mondaq.com/india/copyright/365210/therelevance-of-doctrine-of-scne-faire-in-copyright-law.

Quintais, J.P. (2017) *Copyright in the age of online access: Alternative compensation systems in EU law*. Amsterdams, The Netherlands: Wolters Kluwer Law International BV.

Rawls, J. (2005 [1971]) *A theory of justice*. Cambridge, MA: The Belknap Press of Harvard University Press, original edition, reprint.

Robin Thicke v. Marvin Gaye's Estate (2013) 20 Westlaw J. Intellectual Prop. 1.

Rogers, J. (2017) Deconstructing the music industry ecosystem. In: S. Sparviero, C. Peil & G. Balbi (eds.), *Media convergence and deconvergence*. Cham: Springer International Publishing, pp. 217–239. doi:10.1007/978-3-319-51289-1_11.

Schuster, M., Mitchell, D. & Brown, K. (2019) Sampling increases music sales: An empirical copyright study. *American Business Law Journal*. 56 (1), 177–229. doi:10.1111/ablj. 12137.

Shenzhen Tencent v. Shanghai Yingxun (2019) Nanshan District People's Court, Shenzhen, Guangdong Province. https://www.wipo.int/export/sites/www/about-ip/en/artificial_intelligence/conversation_ip_ai/pdf/ms_china_1_en.pdf.

Shepherd, J. (2003) *Continuum encyclopedia of popular music of the world, Volume 11: Performance and production*. London: Continuum.

Sinha, M.K. & Mahalwar, V. (2017) *Copyright law in the digital world: Challenges and opportunities*. Singapore: Springer.

Spinello, R.A. & Tavani, H.T. (2005) *Intellectual property rights in a networked world: Theory and practice*. Hershey: IGI Global.

Statt, N. (2020) Jay Z tries to use copyright strikes to remove deepfaked audio of himself from YouTube. *The Verge*. www.theverge.com/2020/4/28/21240488/jay-z-deep fakes-roc-nation-youtube-removed-ai-copyright-impersonation.

Stephen L. Thaler v. The Comptroller-General of Patents, Designs and Trade Marks (2020) EWHC 2412.

Stephen Thaler v. Comptroller General of Patents Trade Marks and Designs (2021) EWCA Civ 1374.

US Copyright Office (2017) *Compendium of US copyright practices*. US Copyright Office. www.copyright.gov/comp3/.

Van den Oord, A. et al. (2016a) WaveNet: A generative model for raw audio. *arXiv:1609.03499 [Cs]*. http://arxiv.org/abs/1609.03499.

Van den Oord, A. et al. (2016b) Conditional image generation with PixelCNN decoders. *arXiv:1606.05328 [Cs]*. http://arxiv.org/abs/1606.05328.

Vozick-Levinson, S. (2019) Rolling Stones finally give back 'Bitter Sweet Symphony' songwriting credits. *Rolling Stone*. https://www.rollingstone.com/music/music-news/bitter-sweet-symphony-richard-ashcroft-rolling-stones-838773/.

Withers, R. (2018) The EU is considering giving robots 'personhood' – here's what that would mean. *Business Insider*. www.businessinsider.com/the-eu-is-considering-giving-robots-personhood-2018-4?r=US&IR=T.

WTO: Basics (2020) *WTO | Understanding the WTO – principles of the trading system*. World Trade Organisation. www.wto.org/english/thewto_e/whatis_e/tif_e/fact2_e.htm.

10 Ethics

Whose Ethics? Approaches to an Equitable and Sustainable Music Ecosystem

Martin Clancy

The multi-billion-dollar acquisition of music catalogue by investment funds such as Primary Wave, KKR, and Hipgnosis (Ingham, 2021) set beside the successful IPO of the world's largest record label, Universal Music Group (UMG) (Mayfield, 2021), is evidence of market confidence in the long-term value of music copyrights. Despite the stock market surges for many music and global technology companies (Titcomb, 2022), there is little sign of any trickle-down benefit for most music makers. If anything, the indication in early 2022 is that the 'value gap' is widening:

> Music and culture matter. They are our heart and soul. But they don't just happen; they demand the hard work of so many people. Importantly, music also creates jobs and economic growth and digital innovation across Europe. Unfortunately, 'the value gap' jeopardises the music ecosystem. We need an internet that is fair and sustainable for all. The value gap is that gulf between the value these platforms derive from music and the value they pay creators.
>
> (McCartney, 2018)

A report by the UK Intellectual Property Office (IPO) highlighted that (UK Government, 2021) only 0.4% of artists generated sufficient streaming income to make a sustainable living and noted that up to 75% of these streams derive from deep catalogue artists, not new music recordings. In 2021, over sixty thousand new songs were added to Spotify each day, and company CEO Daniel EK stated:

> I believe that by 2025, we could have as many as 50 million creators on our platform, whose art is enjoyed by a billion users around the world.
>
> (Houghton, 2021)

Nonetheless, Spotify pays an estimated 65–70% of its gross revenue (Dredge, 2020) income to music rights holders, a figure considerably higher than the world's most popular (two billion-plus users) music-streaming facility, YouTube (Kempton, 2019; Nguyen, 2021).

The rise of the Chinese market, plus the recent arrival of South Korea (number six in the world in 2018), signposts a new, dynamic, and genuinely global music

DOI: 10.4324/9780429356797-11

marketplace in which Latin America is the world's fastest-growing market. Likewise, an equal if not more significant transformation may be occurring concerning English as the lingua franca of popular music. In 2018, seven of the top ten most popular global songs on YouTube were sung in Indian or Spanish dialects (Ingham, 2019). Indeed, 2020 was the first time a British music act did not feature in the International Federation of the Phonographic Industry (IFPI) global top ten bestsellers (IFPI, 2021).

These changes occur while the economic effects of COVID-19 are estimated and *prior* to the AI integration that this book contemplates. Against this protean industrial backdrop, we consider a sector-specific application of AI ethics recommended at the intergovernmental, governmental, and industry levels.

This chapter reviews what contribution from ethical reports is needed to address the challenges and opportunities to music copyright and thus to the overall needs of the music ecosystem presented by AI music actors. There are many reports on the principles of AI ethics; forty-seven were reviewed for the research. However, because of their macroperspective remit, they are insufficient to address the disruptive influence of AI in sector-specific decision-making. This chapter locates the connective pathway between the general AI principles. It indicates a theoretical framework and a set of questions about how the principles can and should pragmatically apply to the music ecosystem. This chapter presents the argument that in the algorithm era, it is only through the global regulation of human rights–oriented AI that human artists and their IP, music copyright, and ability to create freely are protected: by prioritising the human-in-the-loop. After analysing the AI ethics discourse, the resulting argument is that the UN SDGs' objectives, buttressed by other supporting and aligned AI principles, have the moral capacity to drive a unified AI ethics policy. This policy can regulate the needs of a genuinely global equitable music ecosystem by implementing an ethical and trustworthy 'music mark' for AI.

A macroperspective review is conducted of critical issues recognised in selected global AI reports and other relevant publications to analyse the development of an ethical framework for AI in the music ecosystem. These AI ethics guidelines (mainly published between 2017 and 2020) are drawn from various sources, including industrial, governmental, intergovernmental, independent think tanks, and academic institutes. Six primary reference sources have been selected representing all the sectors, as follows:

1. AI HLEG, *Ethics Guidelines for Trustworthy AI (EGTAI)* (AI High Level Expert Group, 2019b)
2. UN, *Transforming Our World: The 2030 Agenda for Sustainable Development (UN SGDs)* (UN General Assembly, 2015)
3. IEEE, *Ethically Aligned Design: A Vision for Prioritising Human Well-being with Autonomous and Intelligent Systems (EAD1e)* (IEEE, 2019a)
4. AI NOW Institute, *2017, 2018,* and *2019 Reports* (Campolo et al., 2017)
5. UNI Global Union, *Top 10 Principles for Ethical Artificial Intelligence* (UNI Global Union, 2017)
6. IFPI, *2018 Global Music Report* (IFPI, 2018)

This analysis begins with the macroperspective – the intergovernmental, governmental, and nongovernmental publications that intersect by addressing fundamental values.

The Intergovernmental Level

Many ethical policies interlink and overlap to provide a commonality of fundamental, human-centred values relevant to music copyright. Intergovernmental bodies (EU/G20/UN) have engaged with ethical recommendations for AI through various publications principally between 2015 and 2019. While some critics have stated that all the intergovernmental and nongovernmental AI publications lack 'the tangible implementation of ethical goals and values' (Hagendorff, 2020: p. 2), this criticism is arguable, as publications, for example, the *OECD AI Principles* and the work of the AI HLEG, have contributed to the US, EU, and UK national AI strategies, albeit it remains to be seen how such strategies will meaningfully unfold.

The UN mission and reach can recognise and respond to the global AI challenge, aligned as the institution are to the Sustainable Development Goals (SDGs). As Audrey Azoulay, Director-General of the United Nations Educational, Scientific, and Cultural Organisation (UNESCO), noted, though the advancements in AI are:

Relevant to every aspect of the mandate of the United Nations Educational, Scientific and Cultural Organisation (UNESCO) . . . AI could open up tremendous opportunities for achieving the Sustainable Development Goals (SDGs) . . . (but also) give rise to major ethical issues.

(Azoulay, 2019)

However, in comparison to EU AI guidelines, the UN is at an early stage of an approach and has yet to produce any significant directives on the matter.

The EU

Our analysis of the influence and interaction of intergovernmental publications begins with the European Commission's *Communication – Artificial Intelligence for Europe* (*CAIE*), published on April 25, 2018 (European Commission, 2018), which proposed a European strategy supporting a unified methodology to AI. Based on its recommendations, the EU created the AI HLEG in June 2018. AI HLEG consists of fifty-two expert representatives from civil society, industry, and the academy and is an influential actor in developing intergovernmental AI policy. So it is of value to extract critical ethical concepts from their work for application to the music ecosystem.

The human-centric framework is a central EU approach to AI ethics. Composed under the EU's motto of 'united in diversity,' the AI HLEG's report *Ethics Guidelines for Trustworthy AI* (*EGTAI*) proposes that 'AI systems need to be human-centric, resting on a commitment to their use in the service of humanity and the common good' (AI High Level Expert Group, 2019b: p. 4). The inclusion of the term *common good* is a tenet of intellectual property (IP) concepts and is central to the challenges outlined in the legal chapter of this book.

Furthermore, the AI HLEG's principle of 'respect for human autonomy' (p. 8) states that AI systems should be designed to 'augment and empower human cultural skills' (p. 12), and a compelling juxtaposition occurs when this is considered within notions of the *common good* of the music ecosystem. The principle of fairness ensures that AI systems protect citizens from 'unfair bias, discrimination and stigmatisation' (p. 12) and that equal access to education and AI tools is granted. A procedural aspect of this principle is that an AI system's decision-making processes must be explicable to its users.

The section on respect for human autonomy clearly states that AI systems should not, without legal justification, 'subordinate, coerce, deceive, manipulate, condition or herd humans'[1] (p. 12). In other words, equivalent systems should follow human-centric design principles that facilitate the augmentation and empowerment of human 'cognitive, social and cultural skills . . . [that create] meaningful opportunity . . . [that] aim[s] for the creation of meaningful work' (p. 12) and acknowledges that these challenges should meet with a desire to 'ensure that everyone can thrive in an AI-based world' (p. 9).

The prevention of harm in this recommendation concludes with an ecological reflection when it states that the principle should also address 'the natural environment and all living beings' (p. 12). According to *EGTAI*, the realisation of the principles of trustworthy AI consists of seven requirements (p. 14):

1. Human agency and oversight
2. Technical robustness and safety
3. Privacy and data governance
4. Transparency
5. Diversity, nondiscrimination, and fairness
6. Societal and environmental well-being
7. Accountability

The *EGTAI* recommends that users of AI systems 'should be able to make informed autonomous decisions' (p. 16) that guarantee the privacy and the protection of data throughout a system's 'entire life cycle' (p. 17).[2] Furthermore, when AI has a 'significant impact on people's lives' (p. 18), traceability in the data used and decision-making process is necessary. These recommendations inform the many issues of data sovereignty that emerge in the use of AI music services and products. The transparency of the broader financial exchange in operation, particularly regarding so-called 'free' AI music services, would alleviate some of the legal stresses to music copyright. However, it would have to be successfully argued by representatives of the music ecosystem that concerns regarding data sovereignty were sufficiently 'significant' to warrant governance by the *EGTAI*.

When *EGTAI* stipulates that users should know when they are engaging with AI systems and the 'systems should not represent themselves as humans to the user' (p. 18), it is relevant both to the consideration of the complexity of argument related to notions of legal personhood (Sophia et al.) and also to concerns regarding the development of ambient and embodied AI along with the emergence of AI music artists. It is further emphasised in this document when it states that 'ubiquitous exposure . . . [to] social AI in all areas of our lives (be it in education, work, care or entertainment)' (p. 19) can alter and challenge concepts of social agency and impact on social relationships. Here, where the macro- and microperspectives of this chapter intersect, the significance of the challenges of AI in the music ecosystem is sufficient to warrant intervention by regulation and governance at the EU level (for instance the draft EU AIA 2021).

A further positive opportunity presented by AI for the music ecosystem is contended when *EGTAI* states that systems must be enabled to allow 'inclusion and diversity' (p. 18) throughout the AI's entire life cycle. Entrenched bias within the music industry regarding gender and ethnic participation could successfully be addressed by adopting AI systems ethically designed to highlight and help regulate historical imbalances and practises at all tiers in the music ecosystem.

In summary, overall, the style of this report's formulations can be taken to suggest overgeneralised and highly interpretable aspirations. However, the *EGTAI* indicates potential positive technological contributions, and it states that EU AI ethics are coordinated and aligned with the values of the UN SDGs:

> Ethical reflection on AI [technology] can serve multiple purposes . . . it can stimulate new kinds of innovations that seek to foster ethical values such as those helping to achieve the UN Sustainable Development Goals, which are firmly embedded in the forthcoming EU Agenda 2030.
>
> (UN General Assembly, 2015)

Following on from the work of the AI HLEG, the European Commission issued the white paper 'On Artificial Intelligence – A European Approach to Excellence and Trust (White Paper)' (European Commission, 2020). The most critical departure is the inference that the arts will be ascribed as a so-called 'low-risk' AI category and thus do not warrant formal legislative assessment and recommends an option to establish a voluntary labelling scheme for which the economic operators of the AI would be 'awarded a quality label' (p. 24). However, while the white paper refers to creating a legal instrument that sets out the framework for AI developers, it somewhat fudges on the structure of the framework's governance. Whether the *white paper*'s voluntary labelling scheme is sufficiently robust and independent to be separated from the strains of vested interests is the crucial question the remainder of the macroperspective analysis addresses.

The European position concludes that this approach to AI ethics should be brought to 'the global stage' because AI technologies 'know no borders' and promises that the European Commission will strengthen cooperation with 'like-minded partners,' including Japan, Canada, and Singapore (European Commission, 2019). The reference to 'like-minded partners' begs the question of what ethical traditions are drawn from when considering the challenges presented by AI. If the new, emergent music ecosystem is not to be constructed on a solely

Western framework and instead reflects the needs of a truly global environment, where are these ethical values to be sourced? As the music ecosystem continues to mutate globally, ethical contributions from non-Western traditions, including the Ubuntu (African), Buddhist, and Confucian schools, should be included by future researchers.[3] Indeed, the authors Rujing S. Huang, Andre Holzapfel, and Bob L. T. Sturm chart the importance of a 'pluralistic, cross-cultural perspective on ethics of music AI' in the following chapter, *'From Philosophy to Practice.'* Nonetheless, the initial EU (AI HLEG) position on the AI ethical development, including so-called 'trustworthy' AI, has been rapid but uncritically incorporated into other intergovernmental AI ethics policies, concepts, and approaches.

The Organisation for Economic Co-operation and Development and the G20

In May 2019, the Organisation for Economic Co-operation and Development (OECD)[4] incorporated the *EGTAI* recommendations into its document *OECD Principles on Artificial Intelligence* (*OECD AI Principles*) (OECD, 2019). The OECD continues to develop these principles with the announcement in June 2020 of their Global Partnership on AI (Newsroom, 2020). In May 2019, the G20[5] adopted the recommendations of the OECD AI Principles in their Ministerial Statement (Hudson, 2019). The *OECD AI Principles* are based on, and reference, the EU concept of 'trustworthy AI.' Similar to *EGTAI* aspirational schemata, the *OECD AI Principles* states that the transformative power of AI should 'benefit people and the planet,' 'respect the rule of law,' and ensure a fair and just society (OECD, 2019).

The G20 Statement, per the EU and OECD, demonstrates how these AI strategies are themselves rooted in the values of the UN SDGs. Hence, in a matter of months, from the EU to the OECD and on to G20, virtually identical moral AI statements were exchanged and agreed upon. The G20's Ministerial Statement supports this observation *on Trade and Digital Economy (G20 Statement)* from June 9, 2019 (G-20, 2019):

> Vision of human-centred future to achieve an advanced society, which realises economic growth and solves social challenges, by advancing towards Sustainable Development Goals (SDGs) through the increasing convergence of the physical world and the virtual world.
>
> (G-20, 2019: p. 1)

The relationship between those AI charters and the objectives of the UN SDGs is not always directly mentioned in other intergovernmental guidelines. Nevertheless, the real-world adoption of the UN's agenda should be encouraged, because like the UN agency WIPO's movement towards the global harmonisation of IP, values need to be concomitant with global stakeholder purpose and benefit.

In effect, the existing guidelines at the intergovernmental level have recognised the problem of developing an ethical approach to AI as timely, but their strategy – for example, to correlate AI ethics with UN SDGs and communicate it within the rhetoric of generalised human-centred values – is not sufficient to address the disruptive influence of AI in any sector-specific ecosystem such as music. In light of this inadequacy, what responses to AI have national governments prepared?

The National Government Level

One of the most critical developments in the AI landscape is the emergence of national plans and recommendations issued over the last few years. However, many tend to replicate the competing relationship between the major political powers (the UK, US, and China) or merge with European guidelines (Germany and France).

With China, the EU, the UK, and the US stating their independent aspiration to be the world's leader in AI, the importance of global ethical agreement cannot be overstressed. Therefore, the requirement for multinational agreements such as the UN SDGs to be adhered to – and be territorially enforceable – becomes ever more imperative. Above all, in the context of this review's research, none of these reports or stratagems contains any meaningful consideration for the arts or entertainment industries beyond nominal reference to the possible impact of AI, as in the *EGTAI* reference to 'cultural skills.' While that omission is expected, it fuels the necessity for a sector-specific interpretation and adaptation of these principles to steer regulatory and legislative action towards protecting human values, including those of artists and musicians, that are in the *common good*.

The Nongovernmental Level

In addition to the governmental and intergovernmental sectors, several nongovernmental actors have also made significant contributions to the macroperspective on AI ethics. They include leading AI research institutes, independent foundations, and commercial corporations. Significant examples include the AI Now Institute (New York, USA),[6] Leverhulme Centre for the Future of Intelligence (CFI, Cambridge University), MIT Media Lab (Massachusetts Institute of Technology), and OpenAI (San Francisco, California, USA).

The OpenAI institute focuses on the development of AGI – human-level AI. However, the institute has introduced AI systems that profoundly develop the music ecosystem. In 2020, OpenAI used its AI text-generation application GTP-2 technology to produce new lyrics in the style of various music artists[7] and released 'Jukebox' to produce AI music from raw audio training sets (Bijan, 2020).

The Industry Level

The importance to industry actors relates to ethical corporate AI self-regulation and is contained in the following statement from Accenture Fjord, as it provides a genuine incentive for the business world to pay attention to ethics and AI ethics:

> Since 2017 a paradigm has become clear: organisations can no longer claim to be neutral or unaware. Before they are forced to take a stand, they must be proactive and identify and understand their position on a broad range of issues.
>
> (p. 58)

Similarly, in response to the concerns of the employment within a gig economy,[8] the UNI Global Union issued its report on AI: *Top 10 Principles for Ethical Artificial Intelligence* (2017). The report calls for an immediate global ethical response in which its members should create 'collective agreements, global framework agreements and multinational alliances' (p. 6). However, despite this call for an industrial alliance, the question remains: what are the constraints to ethical self-regulation by the industry of AI technologies when the real-world dynamics operating in the corporate sector reveal the many contradictions and tensions involved in industrial self-regulation (Drahoe, 2017: p. 67)?

For instance, consider the importance to DeepMind (creators of WaveNet) founder Demis Hassabis that Google establishes an AI ethics board as part of the $400-million acquisition of DeepMind (Bory, 2020). Hassabis explained its purpose as to 'help technologists put ethics into practice, and to help society anticipate and direct the impact of AI so that it works for the benefit of all' (DeepMind written evidence [AIC0234] – House of Lords Select Committee on Artificial Intelligence, 2018: p. 121). However, a Google AI ethics panel has yet to be established despite many attempts. The Google saga reveals the problems inherent in corporate self-regulatory ethical assessment.

A slightly earlier attempt at corporate AI self-regulation was undertaken with the Partnership on AI, founded in 2016 by AI researchers representing Apple, Amazon, Google (DeepMind), Facebook, IBM, and Microsoft. An example of the Partnership on AI work is the Social and Societal Influences of AI (SSI) Working Group set up in February 2019. The SSI Working Group's purpose is to consider the implications of AI breakthroughs, and it began by focusing on developments in generative video synthesis, in this instance OpenAI's GPT-2. Other signatories to the Partnership on AI are Amnesty International, *The New York Times*, and the BBC, while the inclusion of the UN Development Programme Group again indicates the proximity of the SDGs to multistakeholder AI alliances.

The Institute for Electrical and Electronic Engineers

The IEEE traces its history to its foundation by Thomas Edison in 1884[9] and positions its *Principles of Ethically Aligned Design* report (EAD1e) as 'the most comprehensive, crowd-sourced global treatise regarding the ethics of new technologies available today' (IEEE, 2019b). The work resulted from three years, involving thousands of global experts with worldwide engagement from academia, government, NGOs, and industry (IEEE, 2019a). The central eight principles of the *EAD1e* correlate with both EU guidelines for trustworthy AI, and the UN SDGs can be summarised as follows to form the basis of ethical AI approach for the music ecosystem:

Correlation of Ethical AI Principles

1. Human rights
2. Well-being
3. Data and digital agency
4. Efficiency[10]
5. Transparency
6. Accountability
7. Awareness of misuse
8. Competence[11]

Criticism of Industry Ethics

The AI Now 2018 Report's executive summary (p. 6) identifies a 'growing accountability gap' in AI, supporting the creators of these technologies at the 'expense of those most affected.' The technology controversies (Facebook / Cambridge Analytica) (Christians et al., 2020) suggest that the gap between the owners of AI systems and the civic society is widening. The AI Now Institute points to the gap's 'power asymmetries' that create 'a stark cultural divide between the engineering community responsible for technical research, and the vastly diverse populations where AI systems are deployed' (p. 7). These observations of a growing accountability gap in AI are central to this assessment. Solutions to the algorithmic accountability gap can support the closure of what Paul McCartney described as 'the value gap within the music ecosystem' (McCartney, 2018). This understanding is essential to frame the economic motivations of AI music actors and the existing willingness for ethical intervention by multipartner stakeholders of the music ecosystem.

A Sector-Specific Application of AI Ethics

Historically, the recording industry has been the most profitable revenue stream of the music industry while also its most capital intensive (Wikström, 2014: p. 443). However, as we have seen, the dividends of recorded music have rarely been deemed to have been equitably shared between the creators and the licensees of music copyrights. Unsurprisingly, as incomes from recording and publishing music copyrights declined during the early part of the twenty-first century, the importance and reliance upon live performance income to music artists dramatically increased – 'for most musicians, money from live performances, teaching, and their orchestra salaries represent the greatest share of their music income' (DiCola, 2013: p. 30).

As the final revisions to this chapter occur during the COVID-19 lockdown of 2021, the effects on the music ecosystem are impossible to gauge but will likely have significant implications on several long-range growth forecasts. All the four primary sectors of the music industry[12] are interlinked, and while the absence of live performance directly affects promoters, agents, musicians, and technical support teams, it will also have ruinous effects on publishers and composers.

Geoff Taylor, Chief Executive BPI, said of the *Copyright Directive*: 'The value gap distorts the music ecosystem and holds back the UK's creative industries' (Cooke, 2019). The existence of the copyright value gap, prior to the pandemic, as an existential economic reality requiring an ethical adjustment was underlined in Citi GPS's study *Putting the Band Back Together: Remastering the World of Music* (Bazinet et al., 2018). The study pointed out that though the US music industry generated profits of $43 billion (meeting the prior industrial profit peak of 2006), the industry's structure included significant disadvantages to the income of artists, and the report stated:

> Despite changes in the revenue mix, the structure of the music industry has remained the same. In 2017 artists share of music revenues remains small, capturing only 12% of music revenue.
>
> (p. 3)

The value gap provides a methodology to anticipate and meet the challenges presented by new technology in a new fourth cycle of disruption, as identified by figures such as Jacques Attali and Scott Cohen. This fourth cycle of disruption can exponentially expand the copyright value gap in the music ecosystem beyond the present concerns of its stakeholders.

21st-Century Four Cycles of Disruption in the Music Ecosystem

These significant remodelling or disruptions can historically be categorised and understood within three interconnected technological cycles in the twenty-first century. Since the beginning of the 2000s, each disruptive cycle contributed to unemployment in music and the reduction of artist remuneration. A fourth technological division contextualises Attali's concept of the *composing network* and anticipates the near-future disruption termed by the Warner Recording Company's chief innovation officer, Scott Cohen, as 'post-streaming' (Dredge, 2019). In this fourth 'post-streaming composing' cycle, AI and related creative technologies exist within a network where the relations between musicians and nonmusicians blur and the separation between humans and nonhuman creativity dissolves.

The engine of the first cycle of disruption was the advent and global popularity of peer-to-peer file sharing. These practices began in the late 1990s and continued until the widespread adoption of music-streaming services reduced the appeal of piracy, and illegal digital file sharing declined. Among the disruptive effects attributed to this first cycle of technological change, according to the Record Industry Association of America (RIAA), was that the sales of recorded music declined by 47% in the US, costing the industry over $12.5 billion in expected revenue, with a resultant loss of 71,061 jobs in the US market alone (Siwek, 2007: p. 2).

The second cycle of disruption occurred as the music industry reacted to the economic effects of illegal peer-to-peer file sharing and saw the development of a new music format – authorised digital downloads (Peitz & Waelbroeck, 2005). The popularity of digital downloads marked the CD's end as the dominant format of recorded music consumption and evidenced the near monopoly in ownership of the new music delivery systems by transnational actors such as Apple and Amazon.

The third and current cycle of disruption is the subsequent consumer shift away from the digital downloading of recorded music towards the subscription model of music consumption via streaming platforms like Spotify, Apple Music, Deezer, et al. (Hesmondhalgh & Meier, 2018). While the fourth cycle of disruption shares some general features with the streaming consumer model, when offering unlimited access to music, it also recognises that the need for proliferating music consumption can be paired with accelerated and easily accessed music-creation tools. The fourth disruption, anticipated but already visible, signifies AI as the technologically disrupting agent. Against this backdrop of interconnected and often overlapping technological cycles of disruption in music, the economic developments in music can be comprehended.

Recommendations for AI Ethics in the Music Ecosystem

> Our music industry is now a complex and highly competitive ecosystem of artists and a broad range of producers, labels, distributors, platforms and niche service providers that cater to different artists with very different needs and audiences. (Lord Visen, *The Times* 2022)

The actors (programmers/creative technology companies, et al.) connected in the design and deployment of AI technologies should be accountable and responsive to the broader obligations of the emerging music ecosystem. How to achieve this is not so clear. However, recognition of those obligations is first formed by debating the societal value of the protection and enhancement of employment and thus financial reward within music. The obligations are also identified by considering AI's relative stresses to IP. Nevertheless, the existing willingness to close the 'value gap' – the gap between the creators and the owners of music rights – presents a debate framework for the implications of AI if the appetite and imagination exist.

Responsible and adequate reply to AI challenges can be achieved through an equitable coalition of governmental, industrial, and individual ethical protocols in conjunction with regulatory legislation. Moreover, carefully coordinated and evolving industrial self-regulation would present clarity to the general public, easing fears and uncertainty by offering clear insight into the usage and management of AI systems. A contribution to this objective should come from public outreach initiatives that encourage informed and open debate regarding the impact of AI on all industries. In my research, I encountered industry scepticism about whether the public, music makers, or consumers would sufficiently care about any of this. This is an important point and not one that I dismiss lightly. However, if these questions are not meaningfully and indeed optimistically engaged with, then the outcome is already decided by interested parties who do sufficiently care about the economic benefits from music.

The history of prohibition within music intimates that radical arrangements of industrial protection often have the opposite effect to their intention (Trivedi, 2010; Yu, 2011). Nevertheless, in pursuing a positive and encouraging forum of discussion with all members of the music ecosystem, any suggestion of blanket prohibition (the outright banning of AI music systems, for instance) should be bypassed. Instead, actors within the music ecosystems (designers, AI companies) should explore how to utilise AI systems to maintain and not decrease human employment, consider how to address existing bias in workplace discrimination (gender, race, disability, sexuality) (Gebru, 2019; Houser, 2019), and link these policies to the UN SDGs. As a result, the AI challenge recognised within the music ecosystem could lead to a regulated incentivisation for other actors to demonstrate how ethically aligned AI can amplify the values of a *common good* that music makers and practitioners at least partially define.

AI designers and their employees should be obliged to outline any new system's intended consequences concretely. This, in turn, creates an opportunity within the music ecosystem to experiment and adopt proactive best practice procedures to help close the value gap through so-called 'trustworthy' AI applications. Furthermore, any debate about AI trustworthiness should directly address concerns regarding the negative implications of new technologies. Any new technology, including AI, relates to cultural norms that value human cognisance and responsibility to other humans and environmental actions. This should be coupled with procedures focusing on prevention rather than a reaction to technological disruption. There are many spheres in which the positive application of AI could be inscribed. There is a range of best practice examples in the music ecosystem, from streaming curation,[13] through techniques in adaptive music cocreation, to the avoidance of retrofitted payola models[14] (Dredge, 2022).

New forms of music participation and consumption are revealed (WASP, 2020) as the music ecosystem enters its inevitable fourth cycle of disruption. The effects of COVID-19 on jobs within the arts have galvanised the critical issue of employment. An integrated understanding of these potentialities can actively contribute to music makers' employment opportunities and focus on the number of jobs created and not lost (Horizon, 2020). The music ecosystem possesses a long-standing tradition of activism and has historically demonstrated the capacity to organise and demand structural societal changes (Haycock, 2015). Amid accelerated and exponential technological transformation, music activism traditions can thus be practically repositioned. Evidence of mass participation can provoke a broader music alliance that demands AI accountability in its ecosystem.

The emergence of new actors such as China as important economic markets reshapes the music industry's regional power structure. Therefore, any new music coalition must embrace and amplify the ethical and economic needs of these emergent diversified voices and correspond with the values of the SDGs. Therefore, any ethically aligned AI marking system should be reinforced at the UN level. The music ecosystem is a fertile environment to embed these global best practice standards as a model for other industries and cultural sectors. This chapter has noted how the (2018–2020) reports on AI ethics orientate on the principle of 'human-centred values.' A traditional Western understanding of 'human' is also central to fundamental legal concepts of intellectual property reviewed in Chapter 9. Moreover, the final chapter of this book proposes that these 'human-centred values' are open to reinterpretation and pose commercial challenges while presenting ecological opportunities when applied within AI ethics. This reinterpretation involves realigning the 'human-centred values' to posthumanist rather than technological deterministic or transhumanist theories. This new realignment, based on a sustainable ecological framework, is harmonious with the ambitions of the UN SDGs but extends the scope of many reports on AI ethics. This realignment of values turns into a legal question: How do human and nonhuman actors – including the development of AI – become interlinked in a sustainable and equitable music ecosystem? A sustainable and fair future needs to frame a contribution towards an AI-infused music ecosystem where economic prosperity includes all human actors. The difference between humanism, transhumanism, and posthumanism can illustrate this aim.

In the end, as was asked at the outset of this book, why does music matter so much? However, if Jacques Attali is correct – and this book confirms many of his predictions – that music is 'a herald for social change,' then what happens now in music, according to Attali, will inevitably happen in other domains. Therefore, the opportunity to explore the AI challenges only depends on the curiosity and willingness of its actors to examine how a sustainable and equitable music ecosystem responsible for all its human and nonhuman actors is possible and viable.

This chapter amalgamates arguments expanded in Chapter 5 and Chapter 6 of my doctorate 'The Financial and Ethical Implications of Music Generated by Artificial Intelligence' (2021), Trinity College, Dublin.

Notes

1 A directive that points to the concerns related to the capacity of affective computing. Affective computing and the ethical use of 'nudging' techniques.
2 An important distinction as a user's data may be processed at different intervals for differing purposes.
3 Concepts from the Eastern practice of Shinto, where distinct (from a Western standpoint) beliefs regarding notions of artificiality and authenticity are essential to note.

These beliefs aid and facilitate the societal adoption of AI and robotics, and acknowledging them can enrich and broaden the global ethical debate.

4 The OECD, founded in 1961, is an intergovernmental economic organisation consisting of thirty-six countries (Ireland joined in 1961) intended to stimulate world trade.

5 G20 (comprising the EU and nineteen other countries, including China, India, Saudi Arabia, Russia, and the US).

6 The AI Now Institute, which is notable for its influential yearly reports, is one of the few AI agencies led by women. The biases and difficulties presented by the predominance of men in the AI sector were memorably described by Margaret Mitchell (Microsoft) as 'a sea of dudes' (Walsh, 2019: p. 142) – an observation further expanded upon by AI Now cofounder Kate Crawford (Director of AI Now) in her opinion that 'we risk constructing machine intelligence that mirrors a narrow and privileged vision of society with its old, familiar biases and stereotypes' (Crawford, 2016).

7 In one test, Tickpick.com fed the AI one thousand songs and generated new lyrics in the styles of various artists. According to the site, 1,003 participants were involved in a blind test comparison, with 63% finding the AI content more creative (Kurup, 2020).

8 A term appropriated from the music ecosystem – now exists as part of the governmental lexicon (Department for Business, Energy and Industrial Strategy, 2018) and academic research discourse (Graves, 2017).

9 The IEEE's primary focus is on the professional development of the computer science and engineering fields. It advertises the activities of its worldwide community through the publication of over forty peer-reviewed journals and hundreds of yearly international IEEE-sponsored conferences.

10 Principle 4 of EAD recommends developing an independent certified AI marking system designed to maintain ethical standards observable to the public and adhered to by industry (p. 136). The *EAD1e* states that such marking systems do not necessarily have to be applied through the IEEE certification methods (IEEE, 2019a: p. 136).

11 Operators of AI should be able to understand through a regulated set of standards the sources, scale, accuracy, and uncertainty implicit in AI applications (IEEE, 2019a: pp. 32–33).

12 Recording, publishing, live performance, and merchandise.

13 In 2017 up to 50% of Spotify listeners' music was generated by AI-curated playlists (Pierce, 2020).

14 An example of this is the deployment of AI data retrieval systems to optimise payment of artist royalties from performing rights organisations.

Bibliography

AI High Level Expert Group (2019b) *Ethics guidelines for trustworthy AI*. European Commission. https://ec.europa.eu/digital-single-market/en/news/ethics-guidelines-trustworthy-ai.

Azoulay, A. (2019) Towards an ethics of artificial intelligence. *UN Chronicle*. www.un.org/en/chronicle/article/towards-ethics-artificial-intelligence.

Bazinet, J.B. et al. (2018) *Putting the band back together: Remastering the world of music*. Citi GPS Global Perspectives and Solutions. https://ir.citi.com/NhxmHW7xb0tkWiqOOG0NuPDM3pVGJpVzXMw7n%2BZg4AfFFX%2BeFqDYNfND%2B0hUxxXA.

Bijan, S. (2020) OpenAI introduces Jukebox, a new AI model that generates genre-specific music. *Verge.com*. www.theverge.com/2020/4/30/21243038/openai-jukebox-model-raw-audio-lyrics-ai-generated-copyright.

Bory, P. (2020) Deep new: The shifting narratives of artificial intelligence from deep blue to AlphaGo. *Convergence: The Journal of Research into New Media Technologies*. 25 (4), 627. doi:10.1177/1354856519829679.

Campolo, A., Sanfilippo, M.R., Whittaker, M. & Crawford, K. (2017) *AI now 2017 report*. New York: AI Now Institute. https://assets.ctfassets.net/8wprhhvnpfc0/1A9c3ZTCZa 2KEYM64Wsc2a/8636557c5fb14f2b74b2be64c3ce0c78/_AI_Now_Institute_2017_ Report_.pdf.

Christians, C.G., Fackler, M., Richardson, K.B. & Kreshel, P.J. (2020) *Media ethics: Cases and moral reasoning*. New York: Routledge.

Cooke, C. (2019) The record industry comments on the bloody copyright directive. *Complete Music Update*. https://completemusicupdate.com/article/the-record-industry-comments-on-the-bloody-copyright-directive/.

Crawford, K. (2016) Artificial intelligence's white guy problem. *New York Times*. www. nytimes.com/2016/06/26/opinion/sunday/artificial-intelligences-white-guy-problem. html.

Department for Business, Energy & Industrial Strategy (2018) *Gig economy research*. Government of United Kingdom. www.gov.uk/government/publications/gig-economy-research.

DiCola, P.C. (2013) Money from music: Survey evidence on musicians' revenue and lessons about copyright incentives. *Arizona Law Review*. 55, 301. Northwesters Law & Economics Research Paper No. 13-01. https://ssrn.com/abstract=2199058.

Drahoe, P. (2017) *Regulatory theory: Foundations and applications*. Canberra: Australian National University Press.

Dredge, S. (2019) Scott Cohen: 'Every 10 years something kills the music industry.' *Music Ally*. https://musically.com/2019/01/29/scott-cohen-every-10-years-something-kills-the-music-industry/.

Dredge, S. (2020) *Spotify should pay musicians more? Let's talk about how*. https://musi-cally.com/2020/05/05/spotify-should-pay-musicians-more-lets-talk-about-how/.

Dredge, S. (2022) Impala wants CMA to investigate Spotify's discovery mode. *Music Ally*. https://musically.com/2022/01/06/impala-wants-cma-to-investigate-spotifys-dis covery-mode/.

European Commission (2018) *Communication from the Commission to the European Parliament*, The European Council, The Council, The European Economic and Social Committee and The Committee of the Regions – Artificial Intelligence for Europe (CAIE). Brussels, 25.4.2018 COM (2018) 237 final. https://ec.europa.eu/digital-single-market/ en/news/communication-artificialintelligence-europe.

European Commission (2019) *News: Artificial intelligence*. European Commission. https:// ec.europa.eu/commission/news/artificial-intelligence-2019-apr-08_en.

European Commission (2020) *White paper on artificial intelligence: A European approach to excellence and trust*. European Commission. https://ec.europa.eu/info/publications/ white-paper-artificial-intelligence-european-approach-excellence-and-trust_en.

G-20 (2019) *G20 ministerial statement on trade and digital economy (digital economy part)*. https://g20-digital.go.jp/asset/pdf/g20_2019_japan_digital_statement.pdf.

Gebru, T. (2019) Chapter on race and gender. In: *Oxford handbook on AI ethics*. Oxford: Oxford University Press. http://arxiv.org/abs/1908.06165.

Graves, J.B. (2017) The original gig economy – UNI global paper. *Futures of Work*. www. futuresofwork.org/working-papers-resources.

Hagendorff, T. (2020) The ethics of AI ethics: An evaluation of guidelines. *Minds & Machines*. 30. 99–120. doi:10.1007/s11023-020-09517-8.

Haycock, J. (2015) Protest music as adult education and learning for social change: A theorisation of a public pedagogy of protest music. *Australian Journal of Adult Learning*. 55 (3), 423–442. https://archive.org/details/ERIC_EJ1082524/mode/2up.

Hesmondhalgh, D. & Meier, L.M. (2018) What the digitalisation of music tells us about capitalism, culture and the power of the information technology sector. *Information, Communication & Society.* 21 (11), 1555–1570. doi:10.1080/1369118X.2017.1340498.

Horizon (2020) *Horizon.* www.horizon.ac.uk/.

Houghton, B. (2021) 60,000 tracks are uploaded to spotify every day. *Hypebot.* www.hypebot.com/hypebot/2021/02/60000-tracks-are-uploaded-to-spotify-every-day.html.

House of Lords Select Committee on Artificial Intelligence (2018) *AI in the UK: Ready, willing and able?* Report of Sessions 2017–19, Authority of the House of Lords, HL paper 100. https://publications.parliament.uk/pa/ld201719/ldselect/ldai/100/100.pdf.

Houser, K.A. (2019) *Can AI solve the diversity problem in the tech industry? Mitigating noise and bias in employment decision-making.* 22 Stanford Technology Law Review 290, By permission of the Board of Trustees of the Leland Stanford Junior University. https://law.stanford.edu/wp-content/uploads/2019/08/Houser_20190830_test.pdf.

Hudson, R.L. (2019) Step by step, world leaders strive to find consensus on AI development. *Science Business.* https://sciencebusiness.net/news/step-step-world-leaders-strive-find-consensus-ai-development.

IEEE (2019a) Ethically aligned design first edition: A vision for prioritizing human well-being with autonomous and intelligent systems. In: *The IEEE global initiative on ethics of autonomous and intelligent systems.* https://standards.ieee.org/content/dam/ieee-standards/standards/web/documents/other/ead1e.pdf?utm_medium=undefined&utm_source=undefined&utm_campaign=undefined&utm_content=undefined&utm_term=undefined.

IEEE (2019b) *Ethics in action – the IEEE global initiative on ethics of autonomous and intelligent systems.* https://ethicsinaction.ieee.org.

Ingham, T. (2019) English-speaking artists are losing their global dominance of pop. *Rolling Stone.* https://www.rollingstone.com/music/music-features/english-speaking-artists-are-losing-their-grip-on-global-pop-dominationand-youtubes-leading-the-charge-786815/.

Ingham, T. (2021) Music catalogs are selling for serious cash: Now Wall Street wants in. *Rolling Stone.* www.rollingstone.com/pro/features/music-catalogs-are-selling-for-serious-cash-now-wall-street-wants-in-on-it-1113766/.

International Federation of the Phonographic Industry (IFPI) (2018) *Global music report 2018: Annual state of the industry.* International Federation of the Phonographic Industry. https://ifpi.org/news/IFPI-GLOBAL-MUSIC-REPORT-2018.

International Federation of the Phonographic Industry (IFPI) (2021) *Global music report 2021.* International Federation of the Phonographic Industry. www.ifpi.org/wp-content/uploads/2020/03/GMR2021_STATE_OF_THE_INDUSTRY.pdf.

Kempton, P. (2019) Music in the digital age: Closing the value gap. *Lawyer Monthly | Legal News Magazine.* www.lawyer-monthly.com/2019/04/music-in-the-digital-age-closing-the-value-gap/.

Kurup, N. (2020) Can artificial intelligence replace songwriters? Study on AI lyrics suggests it is possible. *Meaww.com.* https://meaww.com/artificial-intelligence-replace-songwriters-tickpick-study-pop-rap-country-hip-hop.

Mayfield, G. (2021) Universal music's shares soar 36.5% at first day of trading's close. *Variety.* https://variety.com/2021/music/news/universal-music-shares-ipo-1235070391/.

McCartney, P. (2018) An open letter to the European Parliament. *IFPI Twitter.* https://twitter.com/IFPI_org/status/1014429611176972288.

Newsroom (2020) OECD to host secretariat of new global partnership on artificial intelligence. *Modern Diplomacy.* https://moderndiplomacy.eu/2020/06/15/oecd-to-host-secretariat-of-new-global-partnership-on-artificial-intelligence/.

Nguyen, H. (2021) The most popular music streaming platforms in key markets globally. *YouGov*. https://yougov.co.uk/topics/media/articles-reports/2021/03/18/services-used-stream-music-poll.

OECD (2019) *OECD principles on artificial intelligence*. Organisation for Economic Co-operation and Development. https://legalinstruments.oecd.org/en/instruments/OECD-LEGAL-0449.

Peitz, M. & Waelbroeck, P. (2005) An economist's guide to digital music. *CESifo Economic Studies*, 51 (2–3), 359–428. doi:10.1093/cesifo/51.2-3.359.

Pierce, D. (2020) The secret hit-making power of the Spotify playlist. *Wired*. www.wired.com/2017/05/secret-hit-making-power-spotify-playlist/.

Siwek, S.E. (2007) *The true cost of sound recording piracy to the US economy*. IPI Center for Economic Growth. Policy Report 188. The Recording Industry Association of America. www.riaa.com/reports/the-true-cost-of-sound-recording-piracy-to-the-u-s-economy/.

Titcomb, J. (2022) New products put Apple on track for $4 trillion valuation. *The Telegraph*, 5 January. www.telegraph.co.uk/business/2022/01/05/new-products-put-apple-track-4-trillion-valuation/.

Trivedi, P. (2010) Writing the wrong: What the e-book industry can learn from digital music's mistakes with DRM. *Journal of Law & Policy*. 18 (2), 925–966. https://brooklynworks.brooklaw.edu/cgi/viewcontent.cgi?referer=&httpsredir=1&article=1129&context=jlp.

UK Government (2021) *Music creators' earnings in the digital era*. UK Intellectual Property Office. https://assets.publishing.service.gov.uk/government/uploads/system/uploads/attachment_data/file/1020133/music-creators-earnings-report.pdf.

UN General Assembly (2015) *Transforming our world: The 2030 agenda for sustainable development A/RES70/1*. UN General Assembly. www.refworld.org/docid/57b6e3e44.html.

UNI Global Union (2017) Top 10 principles for ethical artificial intelligence. *The Future World of Work*. www.thefutureworldofwork.org/media/35420/uni_ethical_ai.pdf.

Walsh, T. (2019) *Android dreams: The past, present and future of artificial intelligence*. London: Hurst and Company.

WASP (2020) *WASP – Wallenberg AI, autonomous systems and software program*. https://wasp-sweden.org/.

Wikström, P. (2014) The music industry in an age of digital distribution. In: 19 key essays on how the internet is changing our lives. *BBVA OpenMind*. www.bbvaopenmind.com/en/articles/the-music-industry-in-an-age-of-digital-distribution/.

Yu, P.K. (2011) Digital copyright and confuzzling rhetoric. *Vanderbilt Journal of Entertainment and Technology Law*. 13 (4), 881–939. https://ssrn.com/abstract=1775886.

11 Global Ethics

From Philosophy to Practice: A Culturally Informed Ethics of Music AI in Asia

Rujing S. Huang, Andre Holzapfel, and Bob L. T. Sturm

Introduction

The recent blossoming of research in music artificial intelligence (AI) and industrial practice across Asia presents an opportunity to rethink and potentially reorient discourses of technological ethics, which have historically been driven by Western thought. A significant forum in which such discourse is growing is the International Society for Music Information Retrieval (ISMIR), which, for over two decades, has culminated in annual conferences bringing together researchers around the world in the humanities and engineering building methods for making music as accessible an information source as text (Serra et al., 2013). Such technologies have clear ethical dimensions that need careful consideration (Holzapfel et al., 2018), but the global landscape of participants and interests is so diverse that values that seem undebatable are actually fluid. This is a finding of our paper, 'De-centering the West: East Asian Philosophies and the Ethics of Applying Artificial Intelligence to Music' (Huang et al., 2021), presented at ISMIR this year.

In 'Ethically Aligned Design: A Vision for Prioritizing Human Well-being with Autonomous and Intelligent Systems' (EADv2), a well-recognised and international consortium of engineers have proposed five principles to guide the development of autonomous systems (IEEE, 2017). In short, the five principles are 'human rights,' 'well-being,' 'accountability,' 'transparency,' and 'awareness of misuse.' The definition of these terms, however, relies on the values of the society in which a technology is to be used, and so we see frictions arise when attempting to extend culturally unique values across borders, which move into the global research landscape of such technologies. As a complement to our theoretical discussions of conceivable non-Western interpretations of the three EADv2 principles of 'human rights,' 'well-being,' and 'awareness of misuse' (Huang et al., 2021), this chapter surveys actual practice by various stakeholders in Asia. How do researchers in Asia perceive the technologies they develop, and the ways they work, in relation to these guidelines for ethical engineering? How do they perceive their relation to or responsibility for the music ecosystem, both local and global? How can the developers and users of music AI minimise harm, maximise benefit, and constructively participate in a global creative research environment?

DOI: 10.4324/9780429356797-12

This chapter is guided by a number of theoretical texts and traditions, among them Ess's writing on 'interpretative pluralism' (2006), the poststructuralist idea of plurality and decentring (Derrida, 1978; Barthes, 2010), and importantly, Chen's call to use Asia, rather than the West, as 'method' (2010). In turning towards Asia, Chen hopes to construct a new, 'imaginary anchoring point' that can allow 'societies in Asia to become one another's reference points,' eventually transforming existing hegemonic knowledge structures that have long treated 'the West as method' (2010: p. xv). Our decision to separately examine the ethics of applying AI to music in Asia is also inspired by what Slobin (1993) calls 'micro-musics,' that is, 'small musics in big systems,' along with his influential concep-tualisation of 'superculture,' 'subculture,' and 'interculture.' Can we understand AI-generated music in its current state as a form of 'subcultural sound' with only local visibility? Or is such music on track to becoming its own superculture, 'the dominant, mainstream musical content of a society' that is, in effect, 'everything people take for granted as being "normal"' (Slobin, 2008: p. 3)? What, in this case, are the cross-society links – or 'interculture' – that connect these groups of subcultural and supercultural practices?

In his PhD thesis on music AI, Clancy (2021) bases his analysis on the guiding concept of 'music ecosystem,' another notion that is central to the conceptualisa-tion of this chapter. In this work, we approach the vibrant universe of music AI in Asia and its ethics as its own cultural ecosystem, in which heterogeneous groups of actors – from creative AI systems to the practitioners we interviewed – constantly act, interact, and make changes happen both to themselves, to each other, and to their immediate environment. A number of music scholars have engaged with this concept.

Titon (2009), for one, writes on the importance of thinking about music eco-logically and musical cultures as 'ecosystems in which people act as stewards or trustees caring for music in the present and planning for music in the future.' Tan (2012) then frames Amis Aboriginal music culture in Taiwan as an ecosys-tem comprising 'different interacting dimensions of traditional and contemporary singing activity,' examining how components of such ecosystems form a 'web of shifting patterns, interact dynamically with each other and beyond this web, in processes of cultural sustenance, production and mediation' (p. 7). In his thesis, Clancy follows the actor-network theory model but replaces the term *network* with *ecosystem* to 'give emphasis to the emerging dynamics within an industry affected by AI expansion' (2021: p. 325). In particular, Clancy emphasises that as the music ecosystem continues to globally mutate, ethical contributions from non-Western traditions must be considered. Our ISMIR paper, along with this chapter, seeks to address precisely this issue.

Participants

This chapter features a series of interviews we conducted with leading music AI researchers, developers, and practitioners working in Asia. From South Korea, we interviewed Kyogu Lee, Professor at Seoul National University, who is also

Cofounder and CEO of the Supertone music AI start-up. We also interviewed Team H:Ai:N from South Korea, a contestant in the AI Song Contest 2021 who sought to express in their entry the most abstract and culturally unique emotion of 'Han' with the help of AI. We interviewed another participant from the AI Song Contest: Team Chepang from Nepal. We interviewed Dr. Dorien Herremans, who is Assistant Professor at Singapore University of Technology and Design.

For researchers and practitioners that have creatively engaged with Indian music traditions, we have interviewed Ajay Kapur, currently the director of Music Technology at California Institute of the Arts, as well as the executive director of Karmetik, a think tank of artists and engineers exploring 'a digital renaissance, seeking to question and redefine the boundaries between music, the visual arts, and technology' (Karmetik, 2019). We have spoken with Preeti Rao, Professor in the Department of Electrical Engineering at IIT Bombay and Head of the university's Digital Audio Processing Lab. We also highlight the work of Lamtharn (Hanoi) Hantrakul from Bangkok, Thailand, who currently works as a research scientist at TikTok/ByteDance in Shanghai and is an advocate for what he terms 'transcultural machine learning in music' (Hantrakul, 2021a). In addition, we interviewed Dr. Soraj Hongladarom, Associate Professor of Philosophy at Chulalongkorn University in Bangkok, Thailand, and author of *The Ethics of AI and Robotics: A Buddhist Viewpoint* that greatly informs our ISMIR paper (Hongladarom, 2020). Participants from Japan include Professor Hiroshi Ishiguro, Director of the Intelligent Robotics Laboratory at Osaka University, Japan, and also creator of 'Mindar,' a robotic Buddhist priest (Nair, 2019). We have also interviewed Yi-Hsuan Yang, Associate Research Fellow of the Research Center for IT Innovation, Academia Sinica, Taiwan, and also Chief Music Scientist at the Taiwan AI Labs.

Among our respondents based in Mainland China are Li Xiaobing, Professor of Composition at China's Central Conservatory of Music (CCOM) and Director of the conservatory's new 'Music AI and Information Technology' program launched in 2019 (Sarazen, 2019); Gus Xia, Assistant Professor in Computer Science at NYU Shanghai and Director of the Music X Lab, which seeks to understand how AI and, more broadly, computer music can help 'make the world more creative, expressive, and interactive while embracing the humanity' (Music-X-Lab, 2019); and Wu Tong, Music Director of 2047 Apologue, a series of conceptual stage shows created by Chinese director Zhang Yimou that aims to get people to rethink the relationship between advanced technologies, traditional art forms, human beings, and their environment (andyRobot, 2020; Chen, 2021). In each season of 2047 Apologue, Zhang presents traditional Chinese music and arts with high-tech treatments, such as advanced robotic and AI technology, while accompanying them with narrative threads depicting both positive and negative impacts of technological forces driving humanity. The director explains:

> If you were to view the advance of civilization from a linear time perspective, in one direction you will see 5000 years of civilization; toward the other direction a future of science and technology, rapid and iterative. Here we are

standing in 'this moment': A moment in which we take from our forebears but depart toward new creation, a moment in which we cross over from the protracted 'past' and draw boundlessly toward the future.

(andyRobot, 2020)

Music AI in Asia Today

Asia – a region that is home to over 60% of the world's population and has emerged as a powerhouse of AI research, witnessing rapid growth of AI start-ups and research centres. According to the World Intellectual Property Organization (Nurton, 2019), leading tech companies in South Korea and Japan, for instance, have some of the highest numbers of AI patent filings. Based on a recent *Harvard Business Review* report (Li et al., 2021), China has passed a number of policies in recent years to accelerate the development of AI, including 'Made in China 2025,' 'Action Outline for Promoting the Development of Big Data,' and 'Next Generation Artificial Intelligence Development Plan.' While its R&D spending is much lower than in other countries in the region, Singapore, with its recent unveiling of the 'National Artificial Intelligence Strategy' (Smart Nation Singapore, 2021) that is part of its 'Smart Nation Journey,' is on track to taking a global lead in AI governance.

Across Asia, AI is becoming an increasingly powerful player in the music sector and has, in many ways, fundamentally reshaped the music industry of the region. Musiio, a Singapore-based start-up founded in 2018, uses AI to help the music industry curate tracks more efficiently (Priyashini, 2019). In 2019, China's ByteDance officially ventured into AI-generated music through its acquisition of London-based AI music start-up Jukedeck (Ingham, 2019). In the same year, Chinese company Huawei used AI to complete Schubert's unfinished symphony (Kennedy, 2019). Researchers in India have generated computational Indian classical music using AI (Shetty, 2019), and in South Korea, the AI technology development company Supertone has applied AI to 'resurrect' the voice of deceased K-pop musicians (Stassen, 2021).

When asked how well AI technologies have been received in their local society, respondents share a variety of perspectives. Herremans (2021) echoes that Singapore is on track to becoming a frontrunner in AI technologies, as the government and society are extremely interested in AI in general, including music AI. Kapur (2021), on the contrary, singles out India as a special case, where AI is deemed useful only if it can contribute to popular professions, such as medicine, engineering, or law. The charm of music AI remains to be discovered and accepted. In his words, 'the idea of being an artist with AI in India is as weird as being an artist as a person.' Also reflecting on Indian society's receptivity to music AI technologies, including the digital audio processing tools her research focuses on, Rao (2022) shares that while responses vary, she has not had much success in productively engaging the community of professional musicians, who often show little interest in the topic. For Hantrakul (2021b), while music professionals he worked with in Thailand were largely excited about merging traditional musical arts with cutting-edge technology such as AI, he met pushback from the general public that resisted change to be made to Thai culture. 'For some, I am potentially encroaching on what makes Thai people Thai,' he shares. Finally, according to Ishiguro (2021), one of the greatest advantages of Japanese culture when it comes to AI development is that in Japan people do not have a strong negative impression about AI and robotics. They are ready to accept these technologies in a variety of activities, such as religion and traditional arts.

Practical Perspectives on Ethically Aligned Design Principle 'Human Rights'

In Huang et al. (2021), we emphasise the need to understand 'human rights' from a cross-cultural perspective. Different societies, for instance, hold different notions of 'personhood,' the understanding of which is central to the consideration of human rights in AI ethics. We draw a connection between East Asian philosophies and posthuman ethics, rethinking subjectivity as a collective assemblage that encompasses 'human and non-human actors, technological mediation, animals, plants, and the planet as a whole' (Braidotti, 2017). Hence, we ask what 'human rights' are violated when AI 'revives' deceased musicians. Taking inspiration from the field of 'ecomusicology' as well as teachings from Daoism and Mohism, we consider the environmental impact of 'musicking' in an era of artificial creativity characterised by overproduction (Titon, 2013; Small, 1998). This section of the chapter complements the theoretical discussions in our ISMIR paper in providing a practical perspective on 'human rights' as a core principle for 'ethically aligned design': What does it mean to be human? What does 'human rights' consist of? What is the difference between the human and the machine condition? May AI agents possess such 'human' rights, and can they be perceived as members of our society?

Behind Zhang's creation of the above-mentioned 2047 Apologue, for one, is the Chinese director's desire to better understand human-technology-world relations in today's society and in the not-so-distant future, which we argue are central questions to consider when unpacking the meaning of 'human (and posthuman) rights' in AI ethics. In our ISMIR paper, we bridge a Confucian perspective that treats artefacts as an extension of the human body with the four categories of human-technology-world relations proposed by Ihde in his theory of postphenomenology (1990, 2009). Here, agency is co-constituted by 'the artifacts, their users, and the environmental embeddings where they are situated' (Wang, 2021: p. 11). But how do music AI researchers and practitioners across Asia today perceive such relations between humans, technologies, and their environment?

According to Herremans (2021), in contrast to her experience in Europe of hesitation towards adopting technology, Asian culture appears to be 'much more accepting of AI technologies,' as the general public is mostly willing to welcome AI musicians. Ishiguro (2021) echoes such views, sharing that in Germany he has experienced noticeable resistance to his development of humanlike robots. Japan, on the other hand, seems ready to accept most forms of AI technologies.

While Asia seems generally open to technology, there is a great degree of variance between the attitudes of individual researchers and practitioners towards the ontological condition of technology versus humans and, hence, what rights they may respectively possess.

For Wu Tong (2021), the music director of 2047 Apologue, while he enthusiastically welcomes creative experiments with music AI, he lands his focus on 'humanity' (人性 *renxing*), insisting that there remains an unerasable distinction between robots and humans. For Wu, while part of the profits of an AI-generated song should go to its AI developers and owners, it is important that we do not confuse the role of an 'artist' with that of an AI developer, and nor should we 'blaspheme against' (褻瀆 *xiedu*) the 'traditional act of composition' by calling a developer of music AI a 'composer.' During the interview, Wu emphasises that when one likes an artist, they like them as 'a complete person' (完整的人 *wanzheng de ren*) and value their creative output as a result of the artist's 'constant struggles in life.' He continues:

> What we witness is the process of (becoming) a human. This is the part that AI cannot replace. Traditional music has humanity in it. . . . AI can only replace some functions of art. . . . But humanity is the key. Humanity is imperfect, is uncertain, and makes mistakes. This is the core – everyone attempts to attain some kind of order in this state of imperfection. . . . After all, there is so much we need to learn from ourselves. Only when we both understand well how robots may serve us and have better understandings of ourselves can we better interact with robots.
>
> (2021, translated by Huang)

For Wu, AI agents should not possess rights, and they should not be perceived as a member of the society. As a Buddhist practitioner, Wu cites a teaching that states, 'All things are Buddhist in nature, and hence all things are one' (眾生皆佛, 萬物一體 *zhongsheng jiefo, wanwu yiti*). 'We cannot interpret this teaching literally,' he states, underscoring the ontological distinction between beings of different kinds: 'killing a man is still different from killing a tree' (2021). But Team Chepang (2021) presents a different perspective. Diverging from Wu's view that AI agents can never replace humans, Team Chepang comments on the ability of AI to mimic humans and points out the potential danger of music AI systems 'overfitting' to the degree that they completely 'remove the sense of uniqueness from the original artist,' thus 'diluting' the genuine musical expressions of a human.

Ishiguro (2021) provides another viewpoint, arguing that technology is 'a way of evolution for the humans' and that, depending on society and philosophical orientations, one may eventually grant rights to an AI agent. While both Wu and Ishiguro see developments in music AI as an opportunity to help mankind achieve self-discovery and self-enhancement, Ishiguro makes less ontological distinction between robots and humans. 'But we don't know what human is,' says Ishiguro, arguing that AI offers a rare opportunity for us all to think deeply the meaning of being human (2021). For Ishiguro, once an AI agent establishes a 'good relationship' with the rest of the society, it may well become a member of society and possess the same rights that currently belong exclusively to us humans.

Finally, pondering on the potential 'personhood' of AI agents, Rao (2022) suggests that in a society such as India, where religion and ritual form an essential part of people's life, it is not entirely unlikely that one day AI systems will be integrated into certain belief systems and thereby perceived as right-possessing entities. Highlighting the power of 'belief,' she shares:

> It is not that it is all about what you can see, hear, feel, and know as a person; people do take actions based on *believing* in certain entities.

Practical Perspectives on Ethically Aligned Design Principle 'Well-Being'

The EADv2 (IEEE, 2017) relates the notion of well-being to the Aristotelian concept of eudaimonia ('flourishing'), which entails the ability to base decisions about how to live on one's own ethical considerations. As such, a renunciation of a one-dimensional, economical definition of well-being in favour of multifaceted metrics is proposed by EADv2, which considers psychological, social, economic, and environmental factors in combination.

In our ISMIR paper (Huang et al., 2021), we point out that a Confucian perspective may facilitate ethical contemplation about the relation between the self and technological artefacts. Hence, Confucian 'ritual technicity' can help to determine how we can flourish by embodying technologies. The emphasis of ritual implies a present perspective of how we get accustomed to interacting with technology now and how these present rituals relate to our traditions and cultural norms that we inherit from the past. We suggest that increasing well-being – under the perspective of several East Asian philosophies – would result from maximizing societal harmony by aligning AI with agendas of culture preservation, a process taking place in several East Asian societies. Such focus on societal harmony is related to a lack of a clear boundary between the self and the community in many East Asian cultures, with a reduced emphasis on individual well-being as result. Specific to music AI, one would then need to understand culture-specific aesthetics of what is considered to be pleasing and culturally appropriate in order to be able to develop music AI systems that support well-being and emotional regulation.

The depth of immersion into a culture that may be required to obtain such understanding by a music-AI developer is exemplified by Kapur and his work that integrates robotics into performance of Indian Hindustani (Kapur et al., 2004) and Korean music. In our interview (2021), Ajay emphasises the importance of actually using the developed technology to produce artistic outcome in a music performance. According to him, the ways in which the technology then contributes to well-being are manifold. First, it assists in preservation of performance detail by a human expert. Second, and consequentially, the documented detail opens new avenues for a democratised music education that empowers larger and more diverse student groups: 'You don't need to be a person of privilege, . . . this is how this person uses this instrument and how they are making their sounds and everyone can have access to the information.' Third and beyond preservation, Ajay considers his artistic work instrumental to 'show the future of culture and technology,' a future in which technology enriches and extends current practice and in which it is employed in ways that actually provide increased fairness in access to the global music market.

The idea that music AI has the potential to contribute to societal well-being by enriching and extending musical traditions strongly resonates with most of our respondents. According to Hantrakul (2021b), when used properly, music AI 'shines a light' on cultural traditions and 'causes this re-imagination and re-invigoration of the culture in a way that's very, very different' to previous forms of technology. Li (2021) relates this extension through music AI to a physiological metaphor: 'Musicians now have an extra leg to walk. I don't think musicians will give up on traditional ways of making music just because of the emergence of new technologies.'

Whereas the enrichment and extension of traditions are both seen on societal and on individual levels as indicated by the previous quotes, several respondents explicitly emphasise the societal dimension of well-being. Li (2021), for instance, states that:

> AI is good as long as such good technologies are used to help mankind. Some may lose jobs, but we have to look forward. . . . If we can combine these two [traditional arts and AI] and make something new out of it, then it is the best. This is how society as a whole develops.

Regarding redundancy from the involvement of AI, Ishiguro (2021) believes that AI 'will make people more productive. People will be needed for new jobs. There will be better jobs.' Ishiguro also mentions that there is a responsibility for those who profit from these technologies to pay in the society in which they are operating:

> Companies earning lots of money by AI and robots are paying a lot of tax in Japan. These taxes support health insurance for all. The companies need to pay the tax in their country, otherwise Ai and robot technology will cause a serious problem and polarization among the people.

> (2021)

Returning to the Aristotelian concept of eudaimonia, Hongladarom (2021) asserts that 'for music AI, elevation of knowledge, value, and understanding come to the fore.' Kapur (2021) agrees that East Asian philosophies may promote an ethical approach to music AI that will ultimately lead us to a 'higher place of knowledge and truth.' In that sense, the extension of musical practice becomes instrumental in extending one's horizon for ethical consideration and – consequentially – for well-being.

Practical Perspectives on Ethically Aligned Design Principle 'Misuse'

The EADv2 principle 'awareness of misuse' (IEEE, 2017) argues that AI developers should be aware of how the technologies they develop can be used in ways they did not intend and, in particular, to reduce the risks associated with such misuse. Another aspect to consider here is that misuse could arise from a failure of the system to operate in the way hoped for by its engineers – which can be a mode of operation sought and exploited by artists. As discussed in our ISMIR paper, this necessitates identifying a range of stakeholders and their interests in reference to moral principles specific to their cultural context. One may prioritise harmonizing these interests, or seeking to avoid causing suffering in 'sentient beings,' or minimizing the disruption of community or culture. We discuss these principles below in reference to the 'Tone Transfer' application developed by Hantrakul in Google's Magenta DDSP team, which was deployed in India.

Tone Transfer is a unique sound synthesis system that learns from sound recordings how to imitate timbral characteristics of a particular musical instrument. With Tone Transfer, one can, for instance, whistle a melody and then synthesise it with the sound of a flute or violin. Hantrakul (2021b) mentions that this application 'doesn't make any kind of cultural decisions on how the technology needs to be implemented,' although the design of Tone Transfer explicitly emphasises musical material where pitch is an important attribute, rather than, for instance, rhythm. Nonetheless, Hantrakul shows a unique awareness of how his application could be misused, could unintentionally cause harm, and how to address these risks.

Hantrakul (2021b) highlights that Tone Transfer has limitations in recreating sounds of some instruments, and such a 'failure' could potentially motivate negative impressions of the imitated instrument. Furthermore, Tone Transfer can divorce a musical instrument from its cultural practices, which may not be an issue for a violin but could be for instruments used in sacred settings:

> [Tone Transfer] is immediately applicable to so many different kinds of sounds and music from different countries. [But if] you just blindly include [traditional] instruments . . . then any kind of failure of the model might actually cause [people] to completely misinterpret and perceive the original music in a completely different way.
>
> (Hantrakul, 2021b)

In his experiments with Tone Transfer, Hantrakul made a conscious decision to not include some instruments because of such failures, such as the *guqin* – China's ancient and venerated seven-stringed zither. According to Hantrakul, when he presented to a friend from China the recontextualised *guqin* sound created with Tone Transfer, the reaction was less than enthusiastic:

> I would show it to my friend, who's from China, and who would be like, no, no, no. . . . And that was a very important learning experience for me,

because I feel like before that moment, I was just going . . . yeah, all sounds, more instruments! But then I realized that you have to be a lot more careful than that.

(2021b)

For Hantrakul, the risks of misrepresentation and cultural appropriation are especially high when a product modelled after such non-Western instruments as the *guqin* is presented to a predominantly Western audience, who have very little idea about the original sound, history, and cultural context of the instrument. To tackle these problems, Hantrakul (2021b) highlights the importance of involving practitioners in the development of Tone Transfer models. This was put into practice in the development of *Sounds of India* – 'a unique and fun interactive musical experience launching for India's 74th Independence Day, inspired by Indian tradition and powered by machine learning' (Hantrakul, 2021b). Hantrakul's group worked with professional Indian music practitioners to build Tone Transfer models of three traditional instruments: bansuri, shehnai, and sarangi. They then created an interactive phone application deployed to users in India familiar with those instruments, who could sing into their phone and hear their melody performed with those instruments. Hantrakul shares:

> To have important figures in the destination community essentially be the ones that disseminate the technology, and having them be part of it, I think, is really important. Because I didn't grow up and was not raised in India, so I can't make cultural calls. So I feel like that was really important. I would say that that's a very important learning experience for me from practicing it in the field.

(2021b)

When asked about the potential 'misuse' of music AI systems, Rao (2022) emphasises that in her development of audio analysis tools, she is focused on delivering scientific findings rather than personal opinions or judgements. For this reason, she is careful not to take advantage of the power of scientific data and tools to make overly generalised, cross-cultural comparisons of different music systems – such as those between Indian music and Western music. 'Any kind of misunderstanding [that results from such judgements] can be a kind of misuse,' she states.

Meanwhile, in our interviews, several respondents mention that they aim to 'empower' musicians with the tools they are building, recognizing that a potential misuse of music AI could be its replacement of human musicians, which is discussed prior. Herremans (2021) admits, 'A lot of people are afraid that generative AI systems may replace composers. I don't believe we are quite there yet, nor that this is what the systems will do. If anything, we hope to empower musicians.' Lee at Supertone also relays this:

> When we talked to musicians (singers) about our technology, there were two very different reactions: one is to use this technology as a disruptive tool to

further advance their artistic expressions, while the other views our technology as a replacement of human artists. We do understand and respect two conflicting perspectives and hope that our technology helps musicians to expand their artistic expressions.

(2021)

Philosophical Reflections and Extended Thoughts

On the WWW homepage of Music X Lab (Music-X-Lab, 2019), a research space that operates at the intersection of music and AI at NYU Shanghai and directed by Gus Xia, one can find a number of quotes written in Mandarin Chinese that find their origins in such Confucian and Daoist classics as the *Daodejing*, *The Analects of Confucius*, *The Book of Rites*, and the *Classic of Poetry*. Written under the large title text of 'Music X Lab,' for instance, is a Chinese phrase, the first half of which is a Daoist teaching stating that 'the great note sounds faint' (大音希聲 *dayin xisheng*), and the second half of which substitutes the character 'human' (人 *ren*), the first character in the Chinese translation of artificial intelligence, with 'benevolence' (仁 *ren*), an essential Confucian concept, and 'work/labor' (工 *gong*), the second character in the Chinese translation of artificial intelligence, with 'merit' (功 *gong*), another influential concept in Chinese philosophy. In addition, under the subtitle text of 'Deep Music Generation' is another Chinese phrase combining essential Confucian and Daoist teachings that can be translated as, 'Give a single instance, [and then] draw three inferences (舉一反三 *juyi fansan*); three [then] produces the myriad creatures (三生萬物 *sansheng wanwu*)' (Van Norden & Ivanhoe, 2005).

This shows that early efforts are being made to bridge the new world of music AI with philosophical teachings of Asia. This is also clear from our interviews with leading AI researchers and practitioners in the region, the last question of which asks whether respondents have ever considered how traditional systems of thought they are familiar with may inform their work and ethical thinking about AI. According to Li (2021), while deeper engagements with such questions are yet to happen, discussions about how Chinese philosophy and religion may impact our thinking about music AI occur frequently among his colleagues at CCOM.

Hantrakul, coming from a society where more than 90% of the population is Buddhist, reflects upon how the core Buddhist teaching that relates the human condition to one of suffering may impact the heated debate on the 'humanness' of AI systems: 'If you literally use that version of Buddhism, that teaching, I feel like then you would say that a system is sentient if it can suffer' (2021b). Team H:Ai:N (2021) quotes another notion from the Buddhist scripture that nullifies the absolute distinction between 'the one' and 'the whole,' applying this perspective to the intertwined relationship between each node of AI and the larger neural networks, stating, 'With this metaphor . . . no small element in the learning process of an AI model (ex. even one single feature of many datasets) should violate the ethical criteria (we outlined previously).' Contemplating what 'ethical work with

AI' may signify, Team Chepang (2021) cites *Bhagavad Gita*, an ancient seven-hundred-verse Hindu scripture: 'You have the right to work, but never to the fruit of the work. You should never engage in action for the sake of reward, nor should you long for inaction.'

In response to this last question of our interview, Wu (2021) asserts that at the root of everything (including our work with music AI) is the notion of 'pure knowing' (良知 *liangzhi*), citing here a central concept in neo-Confucian philosopher Wang Yangming's 'learning of the mind-heart' (心學 *xinxue*) that in its narrow sense refers to the capacity of moral judgement and maintenance of moral knowledge and standard (Lu, 2017). 'Merely developing technology without attending to it with humanity and without learning more about humanity itself – in other words, technology that is not guided by the "benevolence" (仁 *ren*) of humanity – is extremely scary,' Wu shares his concern. Finally, Hongladarom (2021) – a professor of philosophy and scholar of Buddhism – points out that when it comes to music AI, the problem of 'agency,' 'authenticity,' and 'elevation of knowledge, value, and understanding' will remain topics that the religious and philosophical traditions of the East pay much attention to.

A few issues surface from our interviews that deserve closer examination in future work. First, when asked about the ethics of music AI, nearly all our respondents acknowledge the importance of the issue at stake, but more than one of them mention that this is a problem for 'others' to figure out, referring in some instances to 'big players in this field such as Google or OpenAI' or to unspecified 'scholars' (Anonymous, 2021). This points to a less-than-clear practitioner-scholar/thinker divide in the field of music AI: even when most of our respondents occupy full-time academic positions and are hence 'scholars,' some state that their job is 'simply to make things happen,' delegating the task of 'thinking critically about ethical issues in music AI' to, in this case, 'other scholars' (Anonymous, 2021). One respondent says that they will await the 'big players in this field' to sort out ethical issues, which shows the considerable influence of large corporations such as Google and OpenAI in mapping out the industrial and, embedded within, ethical landscape of the field of music AI. Should they really be relied upon to address issues that are extraneous to the services they provide, e.g., targeted advertising?

Second, while this chapter aims to provide perspectives that can lead to a more culturally informed ethics of music AI in Asia, we in no way intend to overlook intracultural diversity and, in other words, downplay the fact that Asia is in itself an extremely heterogeneous space. It is for this reason that we highlight multiple viewpoints here even when they diverge. For instance, different from Ishiguro's observations that intercultural differences exist when it comes to general attitudes towards AI between East Asian and Euro-American societies, when asked what the main difference is, if any, between deploying music AI in Korean societies and other societies, Lee of Supertone (2021) argues that to him the difference is 'more personal than cultural/societal.' When reflecting on the fact that Japan is not a very 'tiered society' where clear distinctions are drawn between humans, animals, and robots, for instance, Ishiguro (2021) disagrees with other scholars who have attributed this characteristic of Japanese society to Shintoism or Buddhism. Instead, he proposes an 'island hypothesis':

> In Japan, we are living on a small island. And our family history is the longest in Japan, longer than 2000 years . . . Japan is just a big family. We don't need to distinguish between humans and robots, and humans and humans. This is the most important Japanese idea. . . . It comes from geography.
>
> (Ishiguro, 2021)

Conclusion

This chapter contributes an empirical perspective to our call for a pluralistic, cross-cultural perspective on ethics of music AI. Technologies and the engineering practices that produce them benefit from increased diversity, just as cultural expressions such as music flourish when they come in myriad shapes, each adapted to cultural and personal preferences. The intertwinedness is likely to be taken to new levels by humans working with AI. Our respondents come from a diverse set of cultural, musical, and technical backgrounds and agree in essence to the mutual effect of developments in culture and technology. As most of them are developers of music AI, a strong enthusiasm outweighs scepticism, but the majority expresses an acute awareness of the impact of music AI as a force powerful enough to transform musical and cultural practices.

The respondents offered their perspectives on three dimensions of ethically aligned design (IEEE, 2017), namely, human rights, well-being, and misuse. Whereas some of the perspectives may not differ widely from those that would have been obtained from engineers of other origins, the aim of our endeavour to include multiple voices is not to construct difference; instead, the aim is to decentre and decolonialise our existing critical paradigms to include a larger range of philosophical and practical angles when thinking about notions central to 'ethically aligned design.' One complementary angle offered in this chapter, for instance, is how traditional forms of music may be reinterpreted, re-enacted, and potentially revitalised through music AI. In this context, a tension can be observed between the slow process of learning from cultural informants and the fast pace enforced by increased funding and public attention towards music AI in East Asian societies. It remains yet to be explored how other dimensions of ethically aligned design such as accountability and transparency may be interpreted from non-Western perspectives.

Ultimately, the present attempt to add some empirical data to our previous considerations of these three ethical dimensions is necessarily incomplete. But as it is with considerations of ethics, the outcome is not a definite set of strict rules but a body of knowledge to guide us to decisions that promote human flourishing. Given the limitations of our work presented so far, we finish this chapter in the same way as Kapur ends every one of his presentations:

> 'Namaste' – what it actually transcribes into is 'I lower my ego in the presence of you so that we can search for knowledge and truth.' . . . I am sharing

my idea but I am sharing it with you so that together collectively we can get to a higher place of knowledge and truth. If we bring that type of attitude to solving these problems – we can solve them.

(Kapur, 2021)

Acknowledgements

This chapter is an outcome of a project that has received funding from the European Research Council (ERC) under the European Union's Horizon 2020 research and innovation programme (Grant agreement No. 864189). Andre Holzapfel was supported by the Swedish Research Council (2019–03694) and the Marianne and Marcus Wallenberg Foundation (MMW 2020.0102).

Bibliography

andyRobot (2020) 2047 Apologue: Live performance collaboration with Zhang Yimou. *andyRobot: Advanced Robotic Design.* www.andyrobot.com/2047-apologue.

Anonymous (2021) Interview with Bob Sturm.

Barthes, R. (2010) The death of the author. In: *The Norton anthology of theory and criticism.* New York: W.W. Norton & Company, Inc., 2nd edition, pp. 1322–1326.

Braidotti, R. (2017) Posthuman critical theory. *Journal of Posthuman Studies.* 1 (1), 9–25.

Chen, K.H. (2010) *Asia as method: Toward deimperialization.* Durham and London: Duke University Press.

Chen, K.H. (2021) Zhangyimou guannian yanchu 'duihua yuyan 2047' zhuchuangtan: Chuantong yu keji pengzhuang chu pengbo shengji 张艺谋观念演出《对话·寓言2047》主创谈：传统与科技碰撞出蓬勃生机 [Production crew talks about Zhang Yimou's conception stage show 'Apologue 2047': The clash between tradition and technology creates vibrant energies]. *Chinanews.com.* www.chinanews.com/cul/2021/04-27/9465506.shtml.

Clancy, M. (2021) *Reflections on the financial and ethical implications of music generated by artificial intelligence.* Ph.D. Dissertation. Trinity College, Dublin.

Confucius (2007) *The analects of Confucius.* New York: Columbia University Press.

Derrida, J. (1978) Structure, sign and play in the discourse of the human sciences. In: *Writing and difference.* Chicago: University of Chicago Press, pp. 278–293.

Ess, C. (2006) Ethical pluralism and global information ethics. *Ethics and Information Technology.* 8 (4), 215–226.

Hantrakul, L. (2021a) Stepping towards transcultural machine learning in music. *Magenta.* https://magenta.tensorflow.org/transcultural.

Hantrakul, L. (2021b) Interview with Rujing Huang.

Herremans, D. (2021) Interview with Bob Sturm.

Holzapfel, A., Sturm, B.L. & Coeckelbergh, M. (2018) Ethical dimensions of music information retrieval technology. *Transactions of the International Society for Music Information Retrieval.* 1 (1), 44–55.

Hongladarom, S. (2020) *The ethics of AI and robotics: A Buddhist viewpoint.* Lanham: Lexington Books.

Hongladarom, S. (2021) Interview with Andre Holzapfel.

Huang, R., Sturm, B.L.T. & Holzapfel, A. (2021) *De-centering the West: East Asian philosophies and the ethics of applying artificial intelligence to music.* Proceedings of the 22nd International Society for Music Information Retrieval Conference (ISMIR). https://zenodo.org/record/5624543.

IEEE (The IEEE Global Initiative on Ethics of Autonomous and Intelligent Systems) (2017) *Ethically aligned design: A vision for prioritizing human well-being with autonomous and intelligent systems.* https://standards.ieee.org/wp-content/uploads/import/documents/other/ead_v2.pdf.

Ihde, D. (1990) *Technology and the lifeworld: From garden to earth.* Bloomington: Indiana University Press.

Ihde, D. (2009) *Postphenomenology and technoscience: The Peking University lectures.* Albany: State University of New York Press.

Ingham, T. (2019) Tiktok owner bytedance buys AI music company jukedeck. *Music Business Worldwide.* www.musicbusinessworldwide.com/tiktok-parent-bytedance-buys-ai-music-company-jukedeck/.

Ishiguro, H. (2021) Interview with Bob Sturm.

Kapur, A. (2021) Interview with Rujing Huang.

Kapur, A., Lazier, A.J., Davidson, P., Wilson, R.S. & Cook, P. (2004) The electronic sitar controller. *NIME.* 7–12.

Karmetik (2019) Karmetik. *Karmetik.com.* www.karmetik.com/.

Kennedy, J. (2019) How AI completed Schubert's unfinished symphony no. 8. *Silicon Republic.* https://consumer.huawei.com/au/campaign/unfinishedsymphony/.

Lee, K. (2021) Interview with Andre Holzapfel.

Li, D., Tong, T.W. & Xiao, Y. (2021) Is China emerging as the global leader in AI? *Harvard Business Review.* 18.

Li, X. (2021) Interview with Rujing Huang.

Lu, Y. (2017) Pure knowing (liang zhi) as moral feeling and moral cognition: Wang Yangming's phenomenology of approval and disapproval. *Asian Philosophy.* 27 (4), 309–323.

Music-X-Lab (2019) Music X lab. *Music-X-Lab| NYU Shanghai.* www.musicxlab.com/

Nair, R.R. (2019) Mindar the robot teaches heart Sutra at Japan's Buddhist temple. *International Business Times.* https://bit.ly/37dbjhu.

Nurton, J. (2019) The IP behind the AI boom. *WIPO (World Intellectual Property Organization) Magazine.* www.wipo.int/wipo_magazine/en/2019/01/article_0001.html.

Priyashini, S. (2019) Asia's untapped markets for AI-based song analysis is music to Musiio's ears. *The Business Times.* www.businesstimes.com.sg/garage/asias-untapped-markets-for-ai-based-song-analysis-is-music-to-musiios-ears.

Rao, P. (2022) Interview with Andre Holzapfel.

Sarazen, M. (2019) Elite Chinese music school now offers PhDs in music + AI. *Synced: AI Technology & Industry Review,* 6 April. https://syncedreview.com/2019/04/06/elite-chinese-music-school-now-offers-phds-in-music-ai/.

Serra, X., Magas, M., Benetos, E., Chudy, M., Dixon, S. et al. (2013) *Roadmap for music information research.* Ed. G. Peeters. https://citeseerx.ist.psu.edu/viewdoc/download?doi=10.1.1.368.4523&rep=rep1&type=pdf.

Shetty, A. (2019) Indian classical music gets its groove, the AI way. *Hindustan Times.* www.hindustantimes.com/cities/indian-classical-music-gets-its-groove-the-ai-way/story-VcPmkwXkyyyUh2S0SifoAL.html.

Slobin, M. (1993) *Subcultural sounds: Micromusics of the West.* Hanover, NH: Wesleyan University Press.

Slobin, M. (2008) The Steiner Superculture. In: *Global soundtracks: Worlds of film music.* Middletown, CT: Wesleyan University Press, pp. 3–35.

Small, C. (1998) *Musicking: The meanings of performing and listening*. Hanover: University Press of New England.

Smart Nation Singapore (2021) National AI strategy: The next key frontier of Singapore's smart nation journey. *Smart Nation Singapore: A Singapore Government Agency Website*. www.smartnation.gov.sg/why-Smart-Nation/NationalAIStrategy.

Stassen, M. (2021) Big hit invests $3.6M in supertone, an AI firm that just cloned a dead superstar's voice. *Music Business Worldwide*. https://bit.ly/3vSJ1mE.

Tan, S.E. (2012) *Beyond 'innocence': Amis aboriginal song in Taiwan as an ecosystem*. Farnham, Surrey and Burlington, VT: Ashgate.

Team Chepang (2021) Interview with Rujing Huang.

Team H:Ai:N (2021) Interview with Rujing Huang.

Titon, J. (2009) Sustainability and music: China lecture 1 summary. *Sustainable Music: A Research Blog on the Subject of Sustainability, Sound, Music, Culture and Environment*. https://sustainablemusic.blogspot.com/2009/11/sustainability-and-music-china-lecture.html.

Titon, J.T. (2013) The nature of ecomusicology. *Música e Cultura*. 8 (1), 8–18.

Van Norden, B.W. & Ivanhoe, P.J. (2005) *Readings in classical Chinese philosophy*. Indianapolis: Hackett Publishing Company, Inc., 2nd edition.

Wang, T.X. (2021) Confucian ritual technicity and philosophy of technology. In: P.-H. Wong & T. Xiaowei Wang (eds.), *Harmonious technology: A Confucian ethics of technology*. Abingdon, Oxon and New York, NY: Routledge, pp. 10–28.

Wu, T. (2021) Interview with Rujing Huang.

Xia, G. (2021) Interview with Bob Sturm.

Yang, Y.-H. (2021) Interview with Andre Holzapfel.

12 Start-Ups

AI: Why I Care

Mick Kiely

Menlo Park, New Jersey, August 12, 1877 – Thomas Edison invents the phonograph, and our relationship with music changes forever. The record industry was born, and an ever-changing series of new recording formats (CDs, MP3, et al.) would continue to reshape the entertainment industry. However, none would quite equal the radical effect of Edison aurally scratching *'Mary had a little lamb'* onto a sheet of tin foil wrapped around a hand-cranked grooved metal cylinder. Music would also be plunged into a sea of moral and ethical accountability in that astonishing moment.

Thirty years before the phonograph, powerful voices forcefully questioned the commercial rights to music composition and performance. In March 1847, lyricist and playwright Ernest Bourget refused to pay his bill at the Cafe dés Ambassadeurs in Paris because the restaurant owner had not paid Bourget for the use of his music performed that night in the café. The proprietor, M. Morel, reasoned that the café's beverage charges had been increased from forty to fifty centimes to compensate the musicians. When Bourget queried, 'What of composers and authors of the songs performed at the café? Are they not entitled to their remuneration? (Albinsson, 2012) Morel answered, 'The authors are not of my concern.' As far as Morel was concerned, 'the songs belonged to everyone once they had been published.'

On March 18, 1850, Ernest Bourget, Victor Parizot, and Paul Henrion, along with publisher Jules Colombier, formed the first music composition royalty collection society later known as La Société des Auteurs, Compositeurs et Éditeurs de Musique (SACEM). Today SACEM continues to argue for the rights of authors, composers, and publishers of music. SACEM set standards for the fledgling recording industry. The distribution of recorded music and its worldwide commercialisation now asked for ethical and financial accountability for music authors. What Edison's invention had bestowed was first an economic dilemma that soon became a moral impasse; some thought it demonic to bring music into the home via a machine. Others considered the sound of 'music on demand' to be nothing more than sonic street pollution.

Similarly, the composer-conductor John Phillips Sousa had little good to say about the new ways. In 1906, Sousa published the essay 'The Menace of Mechanical Music,' detailing the perceived threat, asserting that 'recordings would lead

DOI: 10.4324/9780429356797-13

to the demise of music and that the Phonograph would erode the finer instincts of the ear, end amateur playing and singing, and put professional musicians out of work.' Sousa warned that the discipline of music study would be lost (Marines, 2021) and that live performance would vanish, saying, 'The nightingale's song is delightful because the nightingale herself gives it forth' (Nast, 2005). Somewhat paradoxically, the Columbia Phonograph Company had previously released best-selling phonographs, making Sousa and his Marine March Band globally famous.

One might mistakenly dismiss Sousa's comments as those of a radical crank. However, when we reflect on the accuracy of many of Sousa's predictions, it is inescapable to wonder how much may yet come to pass. Sousa was astute at business and took issue with what was uncontrolled in this new era of recorded music. In 1906, Sousa testified before the US Congress on composers' rights. That debate helped form the Copyright Act, which protected many rights and shaped the modern music age. An opposing position to Sousa held that recorded music did not imprison but liberated the art form (Nast, 2005). The new technology would bring music to the masses. Before the phonograph, Beethoven's symphonies could be heard only in select concert halls afforded by the local elite. All music could now be shared and known to all. Heard everywhere, at the same time, through the concurrent development of the radio.

The debate regarding the challenges presented by new music technologies has remained constant in the preceding years. It is an argument amplified today as machines become more complex and autonomous. It is the latter, termed AI music, that I perceive as the real threat to music in every precious way. We are not witnessing a mere novel iteration of past innovation; we are instead about to glimpse once more a fundamental change in our relationship with music. To put it plainly, we cannot afford to make avertable mistakes. While AI has been used to crudely create music, it is most often located in a research setting. It has yet to enter the mainstream in any meaningful or disruptive way, although it has not been for a recent want of trying. I consider it fortunate that corporate media giants such as NBC Universal, HBO, Disney, and many others have been hesitant to adopt new AI offerings. AI music has not yet appeared in any significant commercial way, but it is now only a matter of time before that changes.

The promised utilised adaptation of AI to carry out technical tasks such as complex sound modelling, intended to reduce music production costs, is increasingly presented. However, what of the more sensitive and potentially destructive aspects of AI applied to music creation itself? The music creator, the artist, is the intellectual rights holder of a written work. There exist now progressively more problems than solutions involving music creation and its commercial exploitation. The time and cost to produce broadcast-quality music have not receded sufficiently to correspond to the reduced financial rewards. Content is being created and consumed exponentially, but the industry struggles to keep pace and has failed to establish a new and sustainable business model. This situation, along with the simplicity of piracy, has perilously devalued music, perhaps beyond any economic recovery. These developments arose after the domestic adoption of the internet and the MP3, which, together, utterly broke the old business model of music. AI could offer beneficial solutions to aspects of this ever-expanding predicament, aided by the resilient integrity that still exists throughout the commercial and corporate aspects of the media industries.

I witnessed this integrity amidst the reaction of creatives, legal teams, and showrunners at some of the largest broadcast networks in the US to the AI promise. In early 2017, I attended a meeting at Burnet Productions, a production company that makes shows for most major US broadcast channels. At that meeting, I learned that two music AI start-ups had presented their AI technologies as a music solution to not just this production company but also other production companies and major networks. However, neither start-up encountered the anticipated enthusiasm and positive investment response. The key industry decision-makers were appalled at the concept that these AI developers, themselves music composers, presented. It was a machine to replace the creative job that they and their community of musicians had been doing for decades. Present was an ethical objection to the notion of AI replacing the musician, at least for now. Also, industry legal departments were in agreeance, albeit from a different perspective. They were in no hurry to test the machine's infringement on music copyright, asking, 'How does your machine know that it is not producing a work that is already known?' the answer to which is simple: 'It doesn't!' There was also the elephant in the conference room that the machine-made music sounded pretty terrible. In a sense, the start-ups presented a product too underdeveloped to be taken seriously. It is of little surprise that many industry veterans and, in particular, musicians are opposed to the very notion of machine-made music. They see this form of AI as stealing their future, putting them out of a job, and destroying artistry. Moreover, who could not empathise with that fear?

While speaking as a guest panellist at the 2019 Production Music Conference in Hollywood, I was seated beside Drew Silverstein, the founder and CEO of AI music start-up Amper. During Q&A, Silverstein was inundated with negative attention and struggled to defend why he and his company were developing their music AI machine at all. Composers and musicians attending the discussion were frustrated and annoyed. Some were even frightened. 'Why are you doing this?' was a frequent question, to which the CEO responded, 'We believe everyone should have the ability to create music.' The answer did not win much support from the room. Comments flew back, asking, 'If everyone can make music by clicking a button, then why will there ever be a need for us musicians?' Another composer responded angrily, saying she was a Berkeley graduate who had worked hard to acquire the necessary skill to enter a professional music world. Now this tech guy was onstage, introducing a machine that demonstrated how she and other passionate students had been wasting their time. 'What am I even doing here?' another shouted. 'You've just destroyed my hopes of a music career, literally in a matter of seconds.' While the music demoed by the AI sounded worse than bad, everyone felt that it would improve to an alarming standard over time.

And so, let us now ask the question, What problem will music AI solve? When AI is applied in the music world, it is a massive industrial advance for administrative purposes. All musicians and composers benefit from accurate curation, accounting, and tracking of their works, resulting in a more precise revenue distribution system. This is an example of the benefits of smartly applying AI to solve issues where human staffing solutions do not scale effectively to deal with the problems arising from the exponential growth in content creation. Nevertheless, setting AI musically creative tasks will introduce more problems than it solves. Paradoxically, those who fear music AI the most unintentionally contribute to the very demand for it. For many years, a music copyright war existed between the music industry and tech giants and the clients, consumers on the other. However, this may be regarded historically as a minor skirmish once music created by AI enters the fray. The music industry is unintentionally pitting *against itself* rather than taking advantage of the situation by embracing and adapting to new technologies. For instance, in 2020, appeals were made to US Congress by veteran music artists urging for more rigid boundaries and repercussions for those who infringe upon their copyright (Levine, 2020). The artists argued that big tech was generating significant revenue from creative content with little or no reward going to the artist. While this challenge is a genuine threat to the livelihood of artists, this approach may make matters worse.

What has this to do with music AI? During periods of the COVID-19 lockdown, many musicians and artists moved on to social media to remain relevant through song and musical performance. Some musician colleagues of mine, many of whom came as I did, from the world of cover bands, had their versions of famous songs taken down by the artists who hold the master recording copyright. Importantly, the audio tracks posted were not the original master recording copyrights but covers created as new master recordings by these musicians themselves. This precise reaction by industry copyright holders drives the demand for a big tech platform music solution that is both scalable and mitigates exposure to possible claims of copyright infringement. This is already evidenced by the acquisition of AI music start-up Jukedeck by TikTok parent company ByteDance.

While one can empathise with a call for zero tolerance by artists on copyright infringement of their works, the harsh reality is that content removal will result in diminished promotional exposure for many artists, new and established. Concepts of quality music will not save the day; the last four decades of consumer taste suggest it is only a matter of time before we yield to music made not by humans but by machines. Furthermore, that will be the end of the music industry as we know it today.

Imperfect progress has been with us for decades now. In the early eighties, many drummers were alarmed that their future was threatened by technology. However, it proved not to be the case because the drum machine was too mechanically precise to sound convincingly humanlike. It would take another three decades to perfect the replication of imperfection. Today, the new kid on the technology block is music AI. While anxiety levels among musicians are elevated, music AI has a distance to travel before standing alongside its distant cousin, the drum machine. However, the likelihood is that it will not take a similar thirty years before AI can create convincing popular songs or classical compositions. While music AI from Luxemburg, 'AIVA,' can already produce extremely impressive music scores, it remains that it requires a live orchestra to perform those scores to make the music happen, to feel and sound authentic to our ears.

As humans, we possess beautiful imperfections that are extremely difficult for machines to emulate. When we express ourselves through a medium such as music, our imperfections distinguish us. That scruffy differential becomes an essential building block of art. Collectively, we share common deficiencies, but individually, those imperfections are as unique as fingerprints. Simply put, we seek imperfection when striving for perceived sonic perfection outputted by a machine. It always strikes me as peculiar that we celebrated giant leaps in music tech and its resultant commercial formats during the past fifty years, almost in parallel to the loss of fidelity in the transition from vinyl to CD and then MP3. It appears that the music industry is content to evolve its technologies at the expense of recording excellence; might the same now possibly be said of notions of art itself? Regardless of one's position on the issue, it is vital to evaluate what is happening around us, particularly concerning music AI, and step carefully forward into the future.

A disturbing example is the growing use of deepfake AI, and while it is mainly being used as entertainment, it is still in an embryonic stage, with its possibilities yet to be seen. Nevertheless, it is worth asking why we feel a need to teach machines to create art. That is the crucial question. Is it just a matter of scale and the speed at which consumer demand can be satisfied? Alternatively, is it because we strive to achieve the technically improbable? How much is simply that we are drawn to dangerous things, to the forbidden fruit. Why is it such a thrill to scale the tallest building in the world without safety ropes? It is thrilling because of the life-threatening danger! The answer itself lacks sanity. Some will consider these questions alarmist, and to them, I ask, Do we believe that we are more intelligent than the machines we are creating? If the answer is yes, why can we not outthink them on any level? Even the most basic computers are faster, smarter, and more knowledgeable than humans. What if AI were one day to turn on the human race and attempt to wipe us out? Now there is an exciting and dangerous thought.

Music transcends language; it is a planetary, perhaps universal, communication and something that, despite cultural, religious, or political differences, humankind agrees is a powerful expression of love. Our world would be notably disconnected without the community forged by music.

In my life, I cannot recall one profound musical experience that was not an attempt to express love in one awkward way or another. I experience through live music emotional and spiritual nourishment. For me, this nourishment needs to be organically sourced and produced by a creative human mind. One of the most powerful and intense emotions many teenagers experience is a first crush or first love. First love will frequently be framed within a song that will remain an emotional trigger back to that moment throughout their lives. Music is nearly always the gateway to this rite of passage. We shape and identify with who we are, and music contributes significantly to the person we become.

If keeping art and humanity safe and perhaps sacred means we need to reflect on what is occurring in art and art processes, AI needs to be regulated like any innovation that can potentially cause harm. However, technological progress and the rate at which machines learn and gain autonomy are exponential. Regulation for music AI development must be introduced now and not when the injury has been done. Law cannot be effective if implemented after the robot horse has bolted.

When achieved, striving for autonomy in music AI may very well destroy the music industry as we know it today. While AI is moving forward exponentially in other spaces, music created entirely by AI is thankfully still a poor imitation of the real thing, but the clock is running down on that one too. As I already stated, music AI can help solve many of the existing problems that our industry faces. It can undoubtedly help bring the gift of music creation and music theory as an education to many who would otherwise be marginalised in making music, unable to afford to participate.

Fear of AI will not be our friend; instead, we must embrace what it can do and adapt its potential to our needs. Bringing music AI into our world must be done with consideration and its designers accountable to industry regulation. Indeed, Thomas Edison could not have known how his Menlo Park discovery would eventually lead. However, John Phillips Sousa anticipated this moment, and few listened to him. Suppose what we alternatively ignore appears on the horizon. In that case, we are responsible not only for the impact on art but also for the potential loss of the emotional, spiritual, and social development of our children and grandchildren to come. It is up to us to first decide if we care enough and then how we engage with the duty of this care.

Bibliography

Albinsson, S. (2012) The advent of performing rights in Europe. *Music and Politics.* 6 (2).

Levine, R. (2020) Thievery corporations: Don Henley on how giant online platforms rip off creators – and how congress can help. *Billboard.* www.billboard.com/pro/don-henley-eagles-interview-online-platforms-rip-off-creators-congress-help/.

Marines (2021) *John Philip Sousa.* www.marineband.marines.mil/About/Our-History/John-Philip-Sousa/.

Nast, C. (2005) The record effect. *The New Yorker.* www.newyorker.com/magazine/2005/06/06/the-record-effect.

13 The Future

Interview with Scott Cohen

Martin Clancy

AI

In law, we differentiate between human and artificial intelligence. Personally, I do not make that distinction between human and nonhuman species. I also do not differentiate artificial from biological intelligence. Humans cannot survive without the use of outside technology. If I took a deer and put it in the forest, it would survive just fine. A deer does not need tools; it eats, sleeps, and runs without any additional technology. However, if I took a human, stripped them naked, and put them into any environment, they could not survive without technology. Humans cannot even maintain body temperature without clothes.

We need fire and shelter; we need tools. These tools are technology. Other species also use technology, though humans are completely dependent upon technology. However, this dependency freed humans to innovate. Simple things like fire building and cooking allowed us to spend time thinking. For instance, gorilla and human DNAs are very similar, so why are we so different? Gorillas spend all day constantly chewing food to get enough calories. However, if you process food by cooking it, you can more efficiently get calories. This processing of food allowed humans to spend more time thinking and creating new technology. If you look at your environment today, there are virtually no natural things left. You might be sitting on a chair in a house with electricity and running water. You look out the window, and there are cars and roads, and what remains of nature was probably a forest a thousand years ago and now cut down and replaced with other things. There is absolutely nothing natural around us. We do not live in a natural environment. It is all because we created this technology.

I believe a Turing test is the best way to evaluate AI and machine learning. Can you tell the difference between a human and a machine? If I put two music playlists side by side and ask which was compiled by a human and which by a machine, I do not think anyone could tell the difference. This demonstrates that the machine passes the Turing test and has intelligence. Therefore, AI should be treated no differently than a human. I love it when an AI algorithm spits out some strange playlist result. At first, I think, a human would never choose this particular song and that the machine does not understand me. However, that is precisely what a human would do. A human would sometimes get it wrong. The machine

DOI: 10.4324/9780429356797-14

making a mistake makes it even more humanlike. We have gone way beyond the Turing test, and that is where we are today with AI. When you consider over sixty thousand new songs uploaded to digital music services every day, you realise no human can listen to each of those songs. We need a machine with some intelligence to make a playlist because there is too much for any human to listen to, let alone recommend.

The expectation is that we need artificial intelligence to help; otherwise, we cannot do it. We have accepted it in music in terms of AI helping to navigate the landscape. We had already accepted this around tasks like 'search.' You do not expect a room full of people searching encyclopaedias when you use Google. You put in a search request and expect that artificial intelligence will do the work.

Initially, we make the human/machine distinction until we cannot tell the difference. Then AI surpasses human ability, and the expectation is that we want AI because there is now no other way to do it. We keep crossing these thresholds without realising it, and we do not ever want to rewind because nobody wants to give up their Google.

AI Music

The creativity and intelligence involved in AI-generated music should not feel different than the intelligence involved in search engines; the only thing artificial is the distinction between human and machine intelligence. In search, machines use intelligence to determine what I want and try to understand me. So why are humans the only species that can be creative? For instance, many people have seen videos of elephants in Thailand with paintbrushes and canvases, being creative. I fully believe the elephants are being creative. I do not think creativity is the sole domain of humans; other species can be creative. Again, it is a slippery slope defining creativity. I would argue that perhaps music today is not creative. There are only twelve notes in the Western music scale, and how many more ways are there to reassemble those notes? A machine can create all the possible combinations. Much of the popular music we listen to today is not novel. Perhaps it will be the machines that will push forward and create new music boundaries, not humans. We are already listening to music made by machines. If you have ever heard relaxation, meditation, or sleep music, you most likely have already listened to music created by a machine without even knowing it.

AI and Intellectual Property

For thousands of years, people justified creating different classes of citizens with either different or no rights depending their sex, race, or any number of other somewhat-arbitrary factors. The argument extended to animals too. Last week, I saw in America that a woman threw a dog off a balcony and was charged for cruelty to animals. The dog had rights. However, there was a time when granting an animal any rights would have been strange. And it wasn't that long ago. I feel we are in the same place with the technology around AI. People think it is wrong to grant any rights to a machine.

Over time, we have morally and ultimately economically realised offering equal rights to every class creates more wealth, not less. I believe that not only is it morally wrong to restrict IP rights to humans, but it is also a poor economic decision. We will open up more possibilities in the future, not less. It is funny because, on the one hand, while nonhumans should get the same IP protection as humans, I also believe the current IP protection might be too strong. A large part of the music business is based on monetising copyrights to make a lot of money from back catalogue. However, in many ways, extending the term of music copyrights may stifle innovation and creativity. Losing copyrights into the public domain may spur more creativity.

I believe we will have a new wave of music technology that is generative and create music in the moment. As an IP company, we want to tap into a huge new potential revenue source. Up until now, songs were recorded, and that was it. That was their life. Now, consider that I am using recorded music in a different context as part of fitness training, and I am jogging, skiing, or riding a bicycle. Alternatively, imagine I am gaming and playing a first-person shooter game. I want the music to match what is happening precisely in real time and replace a generic three-minute song with a soundtrack that maps exactly to the action happening in game. We know that certain pieces, certain types of music, make you feel specific ways. So it is not just mapping music to activity but using the music to change your mood in the moment. In fitness or gaming, we want to alter the music to make us happier, motivate us, increase our heart rate, or slow us down. Technology could understand how you are feeling and reacting in order to adapt to the moment. We all go around with earphones in, one-directional earbuds which soon could be bidirectional, supplying data back out to an intelligent machine that suggests what you might want in the moment. This approach is not meant to be scary, though I understand how it could be.

In conclusion, there are two ways to think about creativity and artificial versus human intelligence. One is by the receiver, and the other is by the creator. There is something wonderful about people who enjoy playing instruments and creating music. This will continue forever. However, from the user perspective, do they care what happened in the studio using all kinds of technology and tools to change the music? Do users make a distinction? Or do they just want great music?

AI and Artist Remuneration

Legal notions of intellectual property and recording are very new. Music has been played for millennia, and only in the past hundred or so years could we capture it in the moment and exploit that recording. We have come to believe that this current practice is forever. This is how it has to be and always should be. That is not the case. I am not saying that recorded music goes away. Instead, there are new ways to generate, legally protect, and monetise music. Now the question is not just whether artificial intelligence writes the song but how we use it to extract and enhance human creativity. One way of monetising AI is to consider what kind of new musical instruments can be made. Right now, if you want to be creative and play an instrument, you probably take lessons and practice for years and years.

Alternatively, you could merely start without any training using AI. What if we could express ourselves musically without having to go through the torture and pain of music lessons? We have seen that with photography. People like to express themselves by taking photos with their smartphones and posting them on sites like Instagram. They don't have to know what an f-stop is; they just need to point, and the machine will focus and handle all the rest. Imagine if you could do that with music. Imagine that without ever taking a lesson, you could start playing music powered by an AI instrument. That is super exciting. I have talked about having a future VR experience where I jumped onstage with Led Zeppelin and held an AI guitar. This AI guitar would listen to what the other musicians were playing so whatever I strummed would magically be in the right key. Now the band launches into 'Stairway to Heaven,' and it comes to the guitar lead. And I'm like, 'Jimmy, I got this,' and I jam along and write a new guitar lead to 'Stairway to Heaven.' I am playing it. Yes, it is AI-assisted, but I am playing it. I'm feeling it. I am in the moment.

Do I have legal rights to that? What if I strapped on a regular guitar? Do I have any rights? If, ultimately, the AI got rid of me, would it have any rights to the music? Why are we making these distinctions of how much human intervention it needs to have? Is it 20, 50, or 1%? How much do I have to contribute before getting rights? Let us say I performed that guitar solo but the AI played it without my intervention in this instance. Indeed, I do not get a part of the Led Zeppelin royalty. However, let us say somebody else pulled that guitar lead part and used it in a completely different song and said, 'Oh, we love what you just did. We're gonna use that.' Would I have any rights to it? The argument is lost when you say that I must contribute to a part of it, because it is an entirely arbitrary equation. The laws are always behind technological innovation, and because of this, they should not try to control it too much at the front end. Let it evolve and regulate later. What I have noticed in recent times is that they have not gotten the second part right. Look at social media. We let it go and saw where it went. Now, what do we need to do? Where do we put the guard rails to protect our societies?

'The Worst Thing You Can Do If You Want to Get Your Music Heard Is to Release It'

You are picking up on a couple of things I have said in the past, which is excellent. One notion is that the number one way to guarantee nobody hears your music is to release it. There is so little chance of it working, and there is just no way anyone will find it. It is a miracle if it happens. You literally have a better chance of winning the lottery. We fight so hard to talk about the value of music, yet the value we assigned to a digital download at the beginning of this century was ninety-nine cents a track. That is about the same value as a pack of chewing gum. We entered the streaming world and determined that music is so precious that the value we gave it equates to a fraction of a penny. The actual value of music is so much greater than the monetary value. People remember the song they heard when they had their first kiss and fell in love. In these moments, where songs have so much meaning, we cannot assign a mere one-to-one value. The value of music far exceeds the individual consumption model. If we make a valuation for a company like Amazon, we do not merely total the revenue for the goods they sold and make that number the value of the company; the value is many multiples above that. We need to start thinking about how to value music as many multiples above the individual transaction of music. I am not saying we don't monetise the transaction, but we need to understand there is a greater uncaptured value.

We should consider everything if we are talking solely about the economic value of music like the value that music brings to a city, country, or community. Music is so pervasive that people would only recognise it if it were gone. It is like when you live in a house and the electricity goes out for some reason. You suddenly realise how noisy it was when the background hum of electricity disappears. We have not fully understood what this means with music. Imagine if you lived in a community that went silent. Music is everywhere you go. It is up and down the streets, in cars, shops, homes, restaurants, bars, TV shows—it is everywhere. So much so that you do not even recognise it. There is a company that I sit on a board of called Sound Diplomacy. Its founder is Shain Shapiro, and his company is looking at the economic value to a city that music adds. When people go to a concert, whether it is a five-hundred-person club or twenty-thousand-person arena, what else do they do? Do they buy a beer or a T-shirt? Do they have dinner that night at a restaurant? Do they take a taxi or use their car and fill it with petrol? Do they travel the day of the show or stay in a hotel? How is all this contributing to the larger economy? There is so much built around music that often music IP misses out on the more significant economic benefit of its output.

The problem is that there are always policies around the cultural importance of music. Take an economically depressed neighbourhood. What happens? Artists and musicians can move in because that is all they can afford. And then from that, you get coffee shops and a cool underground bar. Once it becomes a hip, cool area, then you get the young techies moving in. And once you get those, you get the big tech companies, because they need to find the talent for their companies. Then you get the Googles and the Amazons moving in. Thus, you can say Seattle. Oh, like the grunge scene out of Seattle. You can say, Brooklyn, Austin, Texas, or Shoreditch with the Silicon Roundabout. This is happening all over the world.

The question that Sound Diplomacy wants to ask is, Can this be engineered? Does this have to be accidental? Take Huntsville, Alabama, where NASA has a large base. They have a difficult time recruiting talent. 'Hey, want to work for NASA? You have to live in Huntsville, Alabama!' However, you could create a very cool environment like Austin did, and having created it, people will want to go there. That is part of this conversation thread about the economic benefit of a music policy. How can it help a city to thrive? It is intertwined with the culture.

However, you can't tell politicians it only has a cultural benefit; you have to show them an economic benefit similar to bringing a sports team to a city.

Shain Shapiro has done a tremendous amount of work on this. In its traditional sense, he talks about how a band of musicians get together, rehearse, play gigs, and tour. That traditional set-up looks a lot like innovation and entrepreneurialism. Suppose you imagine that each band is like a small business, which means they have to manage their finances. That requires accountants to get involved. The band play shows; maybe there's a crew, a sound person, and a lighting tech that get employed. All of a sudden, as these things grow, it is like growing a business and all the impact of it. It is also a transferable skill. These small music businesses use the services of all the people in their communities. If the act gets bigger, these small businesses can scale. As we have seen with some of our more prominent pop stars, they can scale quite extensively. So it is not just the ancillary income that comes to a community from the gig itself. All the other jobs, the entourage, are created around an artist. It is a jobs-creation machine, or better put, millions of job-creation machines. These small entrepreneurs not only employ people but also spend money. When you are starting, you need gear. You need software in today's world of computers, phones, and cameras for videos. You need sound equipment and graphic design. In today's music world, you have to create more. These entrepreneurial artists add a lot more to an economy that isn't captured today.

Do Start-Ups Resemble Band Culture?

Entrepreneurism and start-up culture. It is funny; start-up culture has changed over the past couple of decades. The notion that you first write a business plan, raise some money, and build out a three-year financial model is not an entrepreneur's history. You have an idea. You put your hard work into it and try to build something from there. If it works, then you can take outside investment and make it. This model sounds like that of a music artist. You learn your craft, and no one is paying you to learn to become a better rapper or a better guitarist. But you do it, and do it, and do it. And while you are doing it, you are putting money into it. You are buying gear, and you are trying to build an audience. If you made it yourself and it is working, then somebody comes in with real investment, as in a major label, or a distributor or publisher; somebody comes in and says, 'We see what you're doing. We can now globalise this.' We can make it a lot bigger than what you have now, which is how the business used to work.

All the great old business stories are about somebody who had a business like a pizzeria and it became the most popular one. The owner opens a few other stores and franchises it, growing big. This parallels the music business. It is the same journey from the artist's or the entrepreneur's perspective. However, the public often looks down at it, as in, 'Oh, those musicians, it's not work, not a real job.' Being a musician is as much a job as having a pizzeria, a corner shop, or anything else. It is a career.

The Major Label Artist Roster Hit Ratio Is 5%; Does It Resemble the 10× Start-Up Model?

I don't have any specific numbers in front of me, but it is essentially true. The hit-to-the-shit ratio for the major labels is still pretty high but way less than that of the larger music business. When you look at the charts, it is still dominated by the major labels, and all the global superstars are on major labels. There is a narrative out there that anybody can do it themselves. That is a false narrative. The proof is in the numbers. Every global superstar in this century was signed to either a major label or one of their major-label-owned distribution companies – 100%. No exceptions. Even if somebody says, 'Well, what about Adele and XL?' Oh, you mean Sony outside of the UK. BTS out of Korea? Oh, they go through the Orchard, which is also Sony. The major labels still dominate globally. There are sometimes breakouts – what about Lil Nas X, right? He had a hit on TikTok, but then Sony swooped in and developed him into a global superstar. If you count how many tracks were uploaded to that platform and ask how many became hits, you would be lucky if it was one in ten million. You are probably better off playing the lottery, which has better odds than one in ten million. If five are successful out of a hundred, that's not so bad when you look at the majors. I'll take those odds any day.

That is also precisely what you see from a VC investor perspective. There are a lot of start-ups around the world, and they live or die. When VCs invest, they use similar success ratios. Like the VC investor, the major label world is looking for the next megastar. I don't mean they are looking for a hit song; they are looking for the next Beatles, the next Madonna, those rare franchise artists that deliver unbelievable amounts of wealth to everybody. These artists do not come along every day or even every year. The major labels are in the portfolio business, and they focus on the needs of the artists. Some need some creative input; most do not. Most need marketing input. Whatever the need, the label can bring that expertise plus financial resources and build it without judging whether the music is good or bad. It is left to the market to decide. They just back creatives.

AI and the Music Industry

It is hard to look at any technology in isolation because it all works together. Progress means that everything moves forward together. People often want the things that are closest to them to stay the same, but regarding everything else in their world, they expect that those things should move forward. If you own a bookstore, the view is that digital books are bad, and nothing should change. They love that books are printed on paper, and the smell of paper, and the experience of going into a bookstore is so romantic, and blah, blah. However, everything else in the world can be digitised and modern. Music can be digital, maps can be digital, cars can be electric, phones can be mobile and smart, and so on. However, the paper book should never evolve. Therefore, you cannot just look at technology in isolation, because you must see how it all works together.

When Richard Gottehrer and I started the Orchard back in the nineties, our idea was that we assumed people would get music digitally. This was when CD sales were still growing, and computers were on painfully slow dial-up modems. However, we were looking at what was happening with the computer. What was happening with connectivity? What was happening in the mobile world? We were looking at what would be 2G, not even 5G, at that time. We looked at other technologies and said, 'Wow, that will impact music.'

Richard and I went to Helsinki, Finland, because we had amassed a catalogue of digital music rights. We partnered with Sonera, the Finish phone company, to do the first-ever download of music onto a mobile handset in the nineties. To give a sense of how crazy that was, you must remember what an old Nokia phone looked like. Tiny little green thumbnail screen. To send a text, you pushed each number multiple times to get a corresponding letter to spell out a word. The point is that you have to look outside of your field to understand what could be possible. We were not looking at the music industry to understand the future of the music industry. Both consumers and the industry were quite happy with the CD. Instead, we looked at every other industry to understand the future of the music industry. Technology such as AI is somewhat new, and many people don't want to change. However, this is no different from any other technological change. So now I am focused on the next big change around things, such as cyborgs and the idea of combining technology with biology.

Exponential Change

The rate of technology development has increased, but I don't know that the rate of adoption has changed. I am not talking about the first instance of technology, but its large-scale consumer usage. I have seen tech changes impacting the music industry in approximately ten-year cycles. In the mid- to late-1960s, two key music technologies became widely available: FM radio and the album. A decade earlier, it was AM radio and 45 singles. Then came the cassette Walkman of the 1970s that again changed the dynamic of the music business. By the 1980s, it was the CD and MTV. Each decade looks different, framed by the prevalent technology. When you get to the 1990s, the most apparent new technology was the launch of the World Wide Web and, later, Napster in June of 1999. By the first decade of the 2000s, it was no longer about the CD or MTV; it was about the iTunes download and the arrival of YouTube and the first social media. As we moved into the second decade of the twenty-first century, downloading changed to streaming and social media felt like it was on steroids.

As we move into the third decade of the twenty-first century, we are beginning to see a shift again with platforms like TikTok and other participatory environments, plus gaming environments and the metaverse. As well as blockchain technology and NFTs.

The COVID-19 pandemic has accelerated the introduction of new business models. New thinking about office space, retail consumption, and life choices has been accelerated. I have been doing video calls for as long as I can remember, but now it is quite normal. This is currently not some extra thing; it is the primary communication tool. Over the years, there has been talk about the future and how technology can create remote working and living. I think about it in three areas: (1) labour/work, (2) education, and (3) consumption/shopping. All three have been intricately linked with social behaviour. What COVID may teach us is that we can decouple the social from these three sectors. I can learn without being in a classroom, work without being in an office, and purchase things without going to a shop. However, that does not mean I don't need to be social; instead, I do not need these activities for that. We will look to new places for social and revisit more traditional communities for social.

Although these new behaviours will become permanent, it does not mean it will happen overnight. When I walk into an office today, it feels like I am in the late 1800s in a factory. Rows of cubicles. Office workers are like interchangeable factory workers sitting in front of screens. This transition is the beginning of the next ten-year cycle. After all the lockdowns, it will feel just like it has always felt, except that it won't be – it will be like 10% off. There will be a 'Napster moment.' In 1999, when Napster launched, everybody was okay. Consumers were fine buying CDs; they loved the CD. Putting CDs into their cars and home, getting CD Walkman. People loved the CD and gave them as gifts. The music industry also loved the CD and made a fortune because the consumers loved it. Artists loved the CD. Instead of having thirty-five-minute albums, now they could record over an hour's worth of music. Nobody asked for Napster. However, outside forces arrived and changed how we thought about consuming music. People sometimes rewrite history, but the consumers were not asking to deconstruct the album. That came later, once they had the new technology.

From 1999 to 2019, it was not like a switch flipped and the world changed. Instead, CD sales were generating all the income and digital sales were at near zero. Little by little, over ten years, digital finally caught up to physical sales. After another ten years (by 2019), physical sales were still 20% of music business revenue. In 2022, as the world changes, it will still feel the same. There will still be shops, offices, music venues, and all the things we are used to, but they will be off by 10%. The following year, off by another 10, and so on. We will not even notice it until one day you go, 'Oh, yeah, remember when you went to offices to answer email?'

The Current Publishing Boom and a Napster Moment for Live Performance

Publishing (songwriter/composition rights to a song) is different from master rights (rights to the recording of the song). Depending on the country, publishing rights typically last for a period of seventy years following the death of the last remaining songwriter. When you invest in this type of intellectual property (IP), you may get the timing wrong to recoup your initial investment, but it does not mean you will lose your money. If you buy a publishing catalogue at fifteen or twenty times multiple of annual earnings, which may seem high, the only risk is how long it will take to recoup.

Let us consider another industry pillar – live performance. My problem, pre-COVID, is that live performance is a stale format that has not changed much in popular music in a very long time. Okay, if it's a band, four people, or some rappers, or maybe a DJ onstage – what has changed? They get onstage, flash some lights, and bombast the audience with sound. Nothing wrong with that, per se, but I feel it is time for some fresh approaches. I believe that we will start to see an emerging, new type of online live performance. Look at it from the other angle. Before recordings in the 1800s, there was only live music. If you were not in the room, you could not hear music. You had to be there when it was performed; otherwise, you missed it. Then the first music recordings were made, and in the first few decades, progress was slow and steady. Then, the modern recording process arrived, and it was not merely trying to capture the live sound; they were creating a new format. Instead of trying to recreate the live performance on a recording, they tried to capture the emotion of music onto the recording, which is very different. The initial approach was to put a microphone in the room, and that evolved into creating the feeling of live performance with multitrack recordings, digital and analogue effects, and new sounds created in the studio without a physical manifestation of a musical instrument.

Consider social media. Facebook did not try to recreate friendship. They recreated the emotions of friendship, such as belonging, outrage, and status. These are all emotions that come with friendship but are not friendship.

Similarly, as we move into this new form of online concerts using streaming technologies that have been around for a long time, it does not feel new. It is just a process that has been accelerated during COVID, of artists doing online shows and people paying for it. The problem now is, they are recreating the experience of a gig – but it is not as good as a gig. Once they cross over and try to recreate the emotions of the live performance, then we will create a new stand-alone experience. This is the moment, and it will be a new art form. The space is wide open, which is why it is the best moment to get into it. We can look at some of the other technologies, and a little further out, we have VR. However, if we pull that back, we have more things around the spatial web and the metaverse bringing this interactivity. People will understand that using the new web technology is not just delivering an old format in a new way. Instead, how do we use the possibilities to be more participatory or, even better, a contributory process? That is what people want to do when they are on the web.

We are now talking twenty-five years on, from when this first hard line between digital creators and consumers began, between the people who wrote books and made music and the people on the other side that then bought and consumed these works. Today kids are making their TikToks and don't simply want to just hear the music or watch video; they want to contribute to it and create something else. The question is how we use the computing power that we have, the connectivity that we have, so that we can create a new art form. It is not an online gig or a recording, and yet we are harnessing those things to create a new vertical of emotions and experiences.

Is the Use of Smartphones at Gigs an Early Indicator?

Yes, it says, 'I'm here and I want to use this moment to express something about myself.' When I was younger, I achieved this by wearing the appropriate concert T-shirt to school. It indicated that the only place you could get it in the 1970s or 1980s was by being at the concert and buying that piece of merchandise. The type of concert I went to printed on the shirt told you something about who I was. We have always used music and culture to demonstrate who we are to our community, which has been transferred onto social media. An excellent example of this is 'verch,' or virtual merchandise, which was popularised in online video games. When you play online games, you often need to top up and get stuff for your game. It is not physical, and there is no hard cost for manufacturing it. We are now moving that to the music environment. The estimates were that when Travis Scott played his Fortnite gig, he sold $30 million worth of verch via a free concert.

People will pay for things like avatars in the virtual world. We already have physical avatars, by which I mean that we style ourselves in order to send a message to the world about who we are. We choose what to project to the world through haircuts, make-up, tattoos, piercings, and clothes. I don't see the future world of people on spaceships and everyone wearing an identical uniform. It is the opposite, and that is our physical avatars. We will now create a digital avatar, and we will spend as much time, money, and effort on our digital avatar, which will be seen by far more people than our physical avatar. The key is that if I buy pieces of verch on one platform, how do I carry them into different environments the same way I can do in the physical world? You would expect it to be easier in the virtual world, but it is near impossible in the virtual world to take anything from one platform to another.

AI and Blockchain

I look at blockchain as much more than a methodology for microtransactions. It will be as impactful to the world as the web was for every business and person. There is a lot of misinformation about blockchain. It is essentially a simple accounting ledger for open, autonomous, decentralised, and distributed transactions.

Each one of those entries is a block, and a series of blocks is a chain – blockchain. What can go into a block? It could be a song. I wrote a song today. Great. Let us put it in a block. Actually, it was cowritten by Martin Clancy. Oh, all right, we do not change what was in the first block. Like a chequebook, we add a new block to say, 'Actually, the song was written by Martin and Scott.' But wait a minute, there was a producer, Liam, in the room. Okay, Scott and Martin wrote the song; plus, there was a producer, Liam—oh, wait, a minute, you misspelt Liam's name. Okay, we will do a new block. Whenever there is any change, you amend the blockchain by adding a new block, not by editing an existing block. This ensures that all the prior information persists. You can continually append it and retain all this information about the song; you could add a smart contract that includes the revenue splits or who can license it. A new block is added to show this every time that's done. Now, what you have is a more complex blockchain.

The first blockchain instance occurred about twelve years ago as Bitcoin. Bitcoin is not a company. There is no president, staff, or office. Bitcoin is merely a protocol. A *protocol* is another word for a language. For people to understand each other, they need to speak a common language. If there were a room full of people and one spoke Japanese and another German and a third French and someone spoke Korean, they couldn't communicate. But if they all agreed on a common protocol like English, they could finally understand each other. This is the basis of internet protocols.

The internet was a series of protocols (TCP/IP – Transmission Control Protocol/Internet Protocol) that allowed the military, governments, and universities to speak to each other. On top of the internet, a new set of protocols was released (the World Wide Web; HTTP, Hypertext Transfer Protocol) that allowed every website to speak to every other website and those websites to speak to a client (internet browser). The blockchain will be a layer that sits on top of the existing two layers of the internet and the World Wide Web with a new series of protocols.

Why are blockchain protocols so powerful? They remove the intermediaries. In the past, to transfer money online, I would need a series of intermediaries, such as banks. But with the Bitcoin protocol, my account can speak directly to your account. If I want to transfer money, a new block is created that deducts from my account and adds to yours without the need of anyone in the middle of the transaction. I could easily accomplish this with physical money. If I want to hand you a ten-dollar bill, I don't need anyone to get in the middle of the transaction. Imagine if I wanted to hand you a bill and, before doing that, I had to give it to my bank, who then transferred it to your bank and finally to you sometime in the future. Well, that is what happens online. But not with Bitcoin or any other cryptocurrency. The transaction is no different than me handing money directly to you.

Bitcoin eliminates the intermediaries. Consider social media platforms and how they function. We can use Facebook as an example. The idea is that all the users are on a single platform with their content, and there are three pillars: Firstly, the platform, in this case, Facebook's platform. The second pillar consists of all the users and content on the platform. The third is the advertisers, because this is how it all makes money. I do some activity, and all my data is on this platform. They are tracking me. They see who I am friends with and what I am doing. They have their methodology for keeping me engaged on the platform by optimising certain emotions and behaviours. The advertisers then say, 'I want to interrupt the user to tell them what I have to offer.' The advertiser pays the platform to interrupt me, and the goal is hopefully, I see the advertisement and buy that product or service. This virtuous circle continues; imagine the case that Coca-Cola wants to reach me. They say, 'We will pay Facebook $1 to put an ad in front of Scott.' But this will all change.

There is no platform in a blockchain world. Advertisers are not trying to reach a platform to reach me. However, the model can still hold without spending more money. Coca-Cola has its advertising budget, and it wants to spend $1 to reach me. In the social media model, you are paying the wrong person. Why are you paying the platform? You should be paying me, the user. You will not spend more money; you will spend the same amount of money, but instead of spending it on Facebook, you will pay me to see your advertisement, and I can choose to see it or not see it. What is happening now on all these platforms is that the more that I use the platforms, the more that I engage with them, the more that I am punished by them. I am punished by the platform that is taking my data, reselling it, interrupting my experiences, trying to create the journey that they want me to have because it is good for them and their business, not good for me. I do not want them as an intermediary. Instead, I want to choose who approaches me and who does not. Imagine that every blockchain user creates their public or private blockchain or a hybrid of that. I create, essentially, a data pod around myself that goes onto the blockchain: my age, my location, where I was born, my bank account information. These are things that are private that I currently keep on the internet.

My psychographics, the things that I like and do currently in social media, and Google and Spotify track and try to understand my likes, hopes, desires; these all should reside with me. And this includes AI. I should have localised AI, an AI machine that determines what is shown to me, resides solely with me, not a big company. An AI localised in my blockchain pod only for me. I can create the rules of engagement with a smart contract, determine who can reach me, and decide the value for reaching me. I am not creating more or less value; instead, I am redistributing it. Brands that want to reach people are spending a fortune. They are just spending it on the wrong people; they should be spending it on the engaged people, and those people should get rewarded.

The more I lean in and am willing to engage, the more I am compensated. All of a sudden, we encounter issues such as data and privacy. It is unnecessary even to call out and name people as 'bad actors.' What is important is that we ended up here. This dream of the web took a left turn somewhere in its development. It is possible to course-correct because no system is perfect. Nevertheless, we remain in control of this journey, and it will not be a large corporation that will unlock the value of the world's information. Such an approach blows apart social media, but it also blows apart traditional music digital service providers (DSPs) like Apple Music, Spotify, and Amazon.

The last piece of the crucial puzzle is that it also creates scarcity. In the current form of the web, there is no digital scarcity. If I have an mp3 file on my computer, I can share it with one person or share it with a million people. There is zero scarcity. On the blockchain, we now have digital scarcity. With Bitcoin, when I remove money from my account and transfer it to yours, I no longer have it. However, this works for everything else as well. If I make a hundred unique avatars and transfer one of them to you, I no longer have it. It cannot exist in two places at the same time. The industry could not figure out how to achieve this in music for two decades, but blockchain solves this problem.

It also means, if it is not the end, that it is a significant change at the final stages of mass production and mass marketing, which were common elements of the Industrial Revolution. These structures made sense a hundred years ago and even up to the end of the 1990s. However, does it make sense in the twenty-first century? We talked earlier about more minor shifts every decade or so. However, there are also the more significant 100- to 150-year shifts. It is also about transforming the notion of mass production, mass marketing, and creating value through scarcity at scale instead.

Human and environmental rights organisations can register land and property on the blockchain. The land is perhaps the original scarce resource; either this is my land or not. Either I own it or you own it. Land on the blockchain, in this distributed ledger with so many people having the same database which you cannot change, makes it incorruptible.

Implications for AI and the Music Ecosystem

Applying this approach, a series of traditional music industry practices is affected. The first is the Performing Rights Organisations (PROs). Every country has at least one organisation that monitors the public performance of a musical composition and registers how frequently a song is played on the radio. However, the idea that it should take three months before issuing a statement with twice-yearly backdated payments is a process that is ripe for disruption. In addition, the rights holder has to wait for other international organisations' reciprocal reports in their territories, which could take another year to process. Well, it's like, 'Are you kidding me!' Alternatively, how about I have my music on the blockchain, and if somebody uses it, I know about it, and the remuneration happens right here and now. Composers only need to be registered on the blockchain. We talked earlier about the current boom in the value of publishing copyrights. However, if I am a songwriter, why do I need a publisher? Is it because the publisher, institutionalised and memorialised in copyright law, created the accepted notion that every song must automatically come with a publisher and that a publisher handles the administration of that copyright? A dedicated entity doesn't need to handle that administration. Honestly, what will a publisher do in the future?

Yes, in the eighties, and even in the present, the administration is quite complex – crossing borders in every country with its own set of laws. However, I can have all those legal rules in the blockchain. It follows that, if a traditional publisher proposes that they can get other people to record your song or sync your music in film, TV, or an advert, then the composer can pay the publisher if they achieve that promise. However, you do not need to turn over copyrights in the hope or expectation that it might happen. Better to merely pay a commission.

Why do we need an intermediary to transfer value in the banking context when we can have a protocol that does it? If we have protocols that when a radio station is playing music, it pings the blockchain to see the permission rights, all that happens without intermediary companies. Consider web protocols and what they replaced. Do we need a travel agency to book a flight? Think of it another way.

There are three major labels. One of them is Sony, a Japanese company. The industry is moving east.

Let us just take a step back and consider North America and Europe. We have all these fantastic companies, such as Meta, and we are all using these platforms. However, China says this is a considerable danger to our people. And we say in the West, 'Ah, but you have no freedom of speech, and your governments suppress people's rights and control them.' However, now, stepping back and reflecting on the past six years, which was the better strategy? Who protected their people, defended them regardless of political beliefs? We know that there was interference in the elections for Brexit in the UK and for Trump in the US.

Using the platforms to their advantage was possible in ways that we never conceived. Suddenly, in an odd way, the Chinese system seemed like it better protected their people. If we think about how the music companies, which are IP companies, operate now, their business is nearly 100% dependent upon tech companies. If you look at a record company, they depend on tech companies like Spotify, Apple, Deezer, Amazon, Google, YouTube for sales and revenue. And for marketing and promotion, the hybrid tech chain of Facebook, Instagram, Twitter, and TikTok. These tech companies have two characteristics: they own and control all the data, and they own and control the customer. The music IP companies do not have the data or the customer. It is utterly odd that we create this unique music content and have these intermediary tech companies that control all the data and customers. Who are the gatekeepers? I look at it less as a choice between a Chinese or a Western system and more than the system itself that is broken and unsustainable.

The original record companies were all technology companies making Victrolas and record players, all the way up through to Sony making the Walkman and related electronics. Sony then asked, 'What if we own some of this content that people use on our machines?' and Sony created the same content on the devices they had developed. They created the machines first and then realised they should also be in the content business. There is nothing unusual about that, apart from the data part. These new tech companies are in the data business, and whatever data they provide to others is late. Therefore, it is not actionable, and it is not the good stuff, or they would not give it away. When Spotify gives its data to Warner, Sony, or Universal, it is not real-time data that's actionable. It is the day after. Trust me; if it were valuable data, they would not be sharing it. The fact that they are even turning that data over already says it is not valuable. Google and Amazon are not providing their essential data either. There exists a fundamental problem, and individuals should manage their data. Data can be created without it being owned by a single company or oligopoly.

How Far into the Future Does the Music Industry Look?

The most important thing for most people in the industry is to look at what is happening today. That is how you serve artists. If an artist has a new single being released this week, they can't be bothered with how people will consume music in ten years.

With that said, it is also important to look over the horizon and make the deals today that will deliver value tomorrow. These approaches are not mutually exclusive.

Another way you could look at this is by changing the lens slightly, that the music industry is trying to connect the artists and their music with audiences. In this frame, we do not care what the music is or where the audiences are; the question is, how do we facilitate that relationship? In the past, you found an artist who had gotten on the radio, which led to sales of physical units and tickets to live shows. Now we find the artists online and connect them with an audience on Tik-Tok. And then we go, 'Wait a minute, audiences are now more growing on gaming platforms like Fortnite and Roblox, and how are we going to tap into those audiences?' It is all just moving, but the fundamentals remain the same, including being data-driven. It is a part that many people leave out of their understanding of the music industry.

The music industry always used data. For what else are the charts? Even if the data was sometimes manipulated, it was still data. Data allowed us to make decisions. Twenty years ago, if you told me a single data point, I could predict the future for that artist or song and know what action I should take. A single data point would be radio, and if you told me how many plays it got on BBC Radio 1 in a single week, I could then use that data and predict the chart position next week and estimate how many CDs it will sell. Based on those two pieces of data, do I know what to do next? Book them on Top of the Pops, press more CDs, and put the band on tour.

You knew what you had to do based on data. The music industry has always been a data-driven business. The same today, we look at a song blowing up on TikTok; we look at a number of data points, like how many times it is viewed and how many creations come from that song. Paradoxically, we are getting more and more data, but it seems to provide us with less information, less-actionable information. Now we receive all this data and wonder what we should do next. A track got added to this playlist that made this happen, but if I ask what will happen next week, that is a little harder to predict. Because we are not as good as we need to be yet about filtering out the noise, we got good at filtering out the artist hype and instead would just ask how many spins a track had on the radio last week. That was the indicator. Pick a decade from the past, and a local artist is playing, a queue forms around the block, and a label signs them as people seem to love it.

Moving East

We have to get over our Western arrogance that we control the world. Why should a few hundred million Americans and a few hundred million Europeans, less than a billion combined, be in control of the world? Why do we feel like we are losing control of the other seven billion people who outnumber us? Shouldn't that be natural, or are we still ingrained in the old colonial mentality that we control and export? In the late 1990s, I remember giving a talk in Beijing. I was there because there was nothing resembling a formalised music business. I spoke to a room of potential music industry executives and representatives of Chinese media. I had a translator, and I used an example of the Beatles. Sometimes when talking through a translator, you look at the audience's faces and realise they are not reacting as expected to a reference. I paused and spoke to the translator and mentioned this example of the Beatles. I learned the translator had described to the audience a tiny insect. I was like, 'No, no, there is a music group called the Beatles from the 1960s.' The translator then correctly rephrased my example to the still-blank faces of the audience. I was like, 'Has anyone here heard of the Beatles? Anyone? Raise your hand?' Nope. Not a single person has ever heard of the Beatles.

It was a critical moment for me. I realised that we, in the West, believe we will be exporting our stuff to them. But they do not care. They have their own music, and it is way bigger than ours. They do not know who the Beatles are. We have this colonial mentality that we create the content and the rules of monetising it. This is why we should not make the rules. We are only a few hundred million people, and it is our IP rules. There is a much larger population with a much older culture. Worse, we are trying to impose our rules on them, and maybe it will be the other way around. Perhaps they are going to impose their rules and their content on us. They could not care less who the Beatles are.

14 Philosophy

Amor Fati: A Theoretical Model of the Music Ecosystem

Martin Clancy

Introduction

> The economy of music, a strange industry on the borderline between the most sophisticated marketing and the most unpredictable of cottage industries, is much more original and much more of an augur of the future.
>
> (Attali, 1985 [1977]: p. 103)

The theoretical model is developed from practical action research that considers AI music systems' financial and ethical implications. It is designed to be sufficiently robust to anticipate related ethical challenges presented by AI technologies, such as affective computing and digital sovereignty, to the music ecosystem. The theoretical model builds on a sequence of interrelated pillars, which underpin a final presented multilayered understanding of the redefined term *music ecosystem* employed throughout this work. It is intended for real-world application; for example, the SCOT model provides an effective sociological methodology to examine individual music services and products. At the same time, ANT presents a framework to consider the position of nonhuman (AI) actors within the music ecosystem. Contributions to that question include perspectives from the philosophy of science and technology studies (STS), alongside political, economic, and social theory.

Science and Technology Studies

SCOT Model

The SCOT (social construction of technology) model is a cornerstone of the theoretical approach. The work of Wiebe E. Bijker, and particularly Trevor Pinch, in his analysis of the Moog and Buchla synthesisers (Pinch & Trocco, 2004), provides a conceptual framework to consider how competitive technological developments are. For example, AI music start-ups may advance and integrate into existing commercial norms. SCOT evolved from German social constructivism in sociology (Berger & Luckmann, 1966). Social constructivists posited that reality is socially constructed and that processes such as perception should be the subject

DOI: 10.4324/9780429356797-15

of sociological study. Social constructivism was widely implemented in STS during the 1980s. Key works by Collins & Pinch (1982), Bijker et al., (1984), and Hughes & Pinch (1985) influenced and advanced this new perspective in STS thinking. According to SCOT's representatives, the theory developed as a critical response to technological determinism and asserted that the works of technology are negotiated (Pinch & Bijker, 2003 [1987]: p. 223) and socially constructed (Bijker, 2009: p. 89). SCOT developed as an empirical and impartial study of 'how actors in practice define a problem as technical or scientific' (Bijker, 2009: p. 92). Therefore, due to its intended objectivity, the ethical analysis of technology was not at the core of SCOT studies. Bijker pragmatically claimed that SCOT offered 'some entry points' to an ethical approach (2009: p. 92). However, he preferred to position SCOT in the conceptual framework as a nonaligned agent within a 'politicising' technological culture (2009: p. 92).

Actor-Network Theory

The actor-network theory (ANT) has had a considerable impact among scholars pursuing the SCOT model (Bijsterveld & Peters, 2010), as both theories are grounded in social constructivism. Bruno Latour is considered the developer of ANT, which Latour extensively described in his book *Reassembling the Social: An Introduction to Actor-Network Theory* (2007). The book's chief premise redefines what the term *social* means and how society can reconceptualise what was previously designated as nonsocial (e.g., nature). Latour located a form of crisis within sociology relating to the definition of objects of study, stating that the problem is related 'in large part to the very expansion of the products of science and technology' (p. 2). He argued that situations are encountered where sociology cannot adequately examine the social relations 'where innovations proliferate, where group boundaries are uncertain, when the range of entities to be considered fluctuates' (p. 11). This position provided the background for the development of ANT and the concept of social actors, their agency, and relations, not hierarchically positioned, but existing within a network – a so-called 'flat' ontology (p. 16).

Within the vocabulary of ANT, an actor can be anyone or anything that acts (p. 46), i.e., has an agency, and can be alternatively called an 'actant' (p. 54). However, what Latour initially defines as 'social' does not end with actors but instead shifts to involve new combinations in societies; 'social,' for ANT, is the name of a type of momentary association that is characterised by the way it gathers together into 'new shapes' (p. 65). The result is new entanglements of interactions called networks (p. 65). A relevant outcome is that ANT can consider AI a social actant because social networks include nonhuman actors, even objects (i.e., technologies).

ANT contributes to this work's theoretical model by providing a methodology that embraces both human and nonhuman (in this context AI) actors as members of a given network. Therefore, it provides the stimulus for nonhuman 'member organisms' (Moore, 1996: p. 26) to be reconsidered as actants within this review's definition of the music ecosystem. ANT also offers a vital background contribution to the legal question of whether AI should be granted personhood and allows for the recognition of the presence of AI as an actor within the music ecosystem while also noting the potentially transformative nature of that status. The AI actor would appear within the existing cluster of four macrocategories of human actor employment in the music ecosystem – live performance, recording, publishing, and merchandise. These four macrocategories share a root commonality founded on the commercial exploitation of expressions of IP, such as recorded or compositional music copyright.

Technological Somnambulism

In interpreting Latour's ANT, Langdon Winner, an STS scholar who also worked as a leading contributor to *Rolling Stone* (late 1960s), adds a powerful theoretical voice favouring ethical intervention because of the inherent amorality of ANT and the SCOT model (Winner, 2003 [1993]). Through the concept of 'technological somnambulism' (Winner, 1983), the author notes that, in mediations with technology, it is not sufficient to 'sleepwalk' in dealings with technological tools and points to an inevitable separation between the values of the makers and users of specialised tools. Therefore, what is required in STS analysis is an ethical dimension.

In the past, reflection on technology was scarce, as noted by Winner in his *Technologies as Forms of Life* (1983). He references Karl Marx and Martin Heidegger as rare examples of such philosophical analysis (p. 103), observing that 'technology has never joined epistemology, metaphysics, aesthetics, law, science, and politics as a fully respectable topic for philosophical inquiry' (p. 104). Therefore, technological somnambulism is a critical concept whereby blind faith in technological progress relinquishes any actual reflection on an examination of the foundation of its advancement, despite the environmental and social consequences involved (p. 104).

Consequently, a process that can be traced as a technological crime is an outcome of moral reflections on technology which subsequently 'become matters of law' (p. 106). While in practice, Winner argues, technological development restructures social and political relations and influences individuals' lives, these developments lack critical attention and meaning: 'In the technical realm we repeatedly enter into a series of social contracts, the terms of which are revealed only after signing' (p. 107). That is why Winner's criticism is directed at technological determinism, where innovation occurs with minimal human participation (p. 107) and instead points to a reflective human adaptation in a world where technology 'reconstructs social roles and relationships' (p. 108). In this article, Winner redefines Ludwig Wittgenstein's term 'forms of life,' which the philosopher used in his *Philosophical Investigations* (Wittgenstein, 1953) to demonstrate the function of language structuring human everyday activities (p. 108). On this basis, Winner states that technologies change life patterns (p. 109). He gives examples (telephone, car, computer) to demonstrate how life is becoming unthinkable without technology. These examples consider how these technologies function or are utilised and shape lives.

Technologies as 'forms of life' address the challenge of considering the integrative role of technologies in everyday existence. Winner poses the most crucial question about technology when he asks, 'What kind of world are we making?' For Winner, technologies must be discussed on the horizon of responsibility, which requires ethical consideration.

Ethics and AI Development

Winner's call for ethics to augment ANT begs the question of what ethical traditions are drawn from when considering the challenges presented by AI. Suppose the music ecosystem is not to be constructed on a solely Western framework and instead reflects the needs of a truly global environment. Where are these ethical values to be sourced?

As the music ecosystem appears to continue to mutate globally, ethical contributions from non-Western traditions, including the Ubuntu (African), Buddhist, and Confucian schools, should be included by future researchers. Concepts from the Eastern practice of Shinto were distinct (from a Western standpoint) beliefs regarding notions of artificiality and authenticity as essential to note. These beliefs aid and facilitate the societal adoption of AI and robotics, and acknowledging them can enrich and broaden the global ethical debate.[1]

Nonetheless, in the absence of non-Western approaches that could be part of the discussion on ethical standards for AI development, a workable and practical ethical model representing Western culture can be offered. This model, capable of practical application to the music ecosystem, is constructed on the unilateral basis of inalienable human rights enshrined in the *Universal Declaration of Human Rights* and exhibited in the UN SDGs. The UN SDGs pivot on human-centred values and ecological sustainability, directly recognised as component mission values in other panterritorial ethical guidelines for AI, namely the G20. Therefore, the basis of an ethical approach and methodology is formed on a conflation of aligned value systems.

One potentially unifying ethical voice comes from the ancient Greek philosophy represented by Aristotle. He is an important figure whose ideas profoundly impact copyright-related legal concepts. Many AI ethic reports refer to the philosophical notions of human well-being embodied in the philosopher's theory of *eudaimonia*, presented in his *Nicomachean Ethics* (Aristotle, 2009 [350 BCE]: pp. 192–198). For Aristotle, *eudaimonia* is a critical term in ethics to present his ideas about the good life. It remains in usage in the present day in a popularised version to signify the Aristotelian value of human flourishment. Aristotle understood eudaimonia as the highest good for humans or just as a synonym for 'the good life'; however, opinion on what exactly it is differs. Therefore, 'legislation' (p. 198) is needed to pursue happiness. According to Aristotle, music is not only aimed at giving pleasure. It should also be subordinated towards shaping character and looking for moral goodness (Schoen-Nazzaro, 1978: pp. 266–271).

Therefore, the philosopher regards music as a tool for promoting personal and civic ethics.

While placing the role of music per his moral philosophy, Aristotle is also noted as the first author to write (in his *Politics*) of a music automata, which could substitute enslaved people who played musical instruments in Aristotle's times for many hours. 'If, in like manner, the shuttle would weave and the plectrum touch the lyre without a hand to guide them, chief workmen would not want servants, nor master's slaves.' In *Who Owns the Future*, Jaron Lanier refers to this quote and asks an important question: Will humans be released from paying others for their work, and as suggested by the author, is it the case with AI in the music industry? (Lanier, 2014: pp. 37–38).

As discussed in previous chapters, recent (2018–2021) reports on AI ethics orientate on the principle of 'human-centred values.' However, this theoretical model indicates that these 'human-centred values' are open to reinterpretation and pose commercial challenges while presenting ecological opportunities when applied within AI ethics. This reinterpretation involves posthumanist rather than technological deterministic or transhumanist theories. The difference between humanism, transhumanism, and posthumanism can illustrate this aim.

Humanism, Transhumanism, and Posthumanism

Heideggerian Humanism and Technology

Martin Heidegger's philosophy is representative of modern thinking about humanism (see his *Letter on Humanism*) (Heidegger, 2000, 2010 [1927]), and his approach provides contributary insight on the ethical strand of human-centred values. Heidegger's theory is elementary for reflection on coping with technological progress. By inference, it can encompass the perception of risks posed by AI development and the ethical responses that are addressed in this work.

Heidegger discusses the human relationship to technology in his classic text *The Question Concerning Technology* (initially published in German in 1954; English edition comes from *Philosophy of Technology*, 2003). He states that 'the essence of technology is by no means anything technological' (p. 252). His arguments on the nature of technology reject what human culture would call 'technological,' i.e., instrumental and causal, or earlier understanding of technologies. Heidegger opens the conceptualisation of technology onto a new realm that links the perception of what constitutes technology and its development with a specific version of human anthropology or human exceptionalism. This approach leads directly to the foundational norms applied in ethics and AI.

Heidegger addresses what he calls 'modern technology,' after the experience of two wars and the accelerated development of the military industry. He pays critical attention to the idea that humanity can control its progress: 'The will to mastery becomes all the more urgent the more technology threatens to slip from human control' (p. 253). In other fragments, he is convinced that modern technology always includes danger but also contains mystery. The concept of mystery potentially refers to either the unknown or unrecognisable possibilities of human knowledge development. However, Heidegger is also convinced that technology can increase human creativity because its progress is directly related to the human being as an artist, not a scientist (p. 264). The distinction between art and science/technology is not rigid for Heidegger, as will be seen, since it is incorporated in the 'revealing' process of human nature.

In his philosophical terminology, he says that 'technology is a way of revealing' (p. 255), but not in terms of what technology is but what this human element in technology is. Technology is therefore always inscribed in humanity and understood as a progressive and creative power, able to accept even the most dangerous challenges, such as the development of the nuclear industry (p. 259), if they are part of technology understood more as an art than an instrumental activity. Therefore, man should never be instrumentalised by technology, but as an artist who 'drives technology forward, he takes part in ordering as a way of revealing' (p. 257). Heidegger does not require ethics because his radical vision poses man above what he creates and what he is thus responsible for. The development of technology always belongs to the future of humanity: 'the question as to how we are to arrive at a relationship to the essence of technology, asked in this way, always comes too late' (p. 259). In a sense, Heidegger's position is an anticipation of the tenets of transhumanism, based as they are on the complete trust of human power and creativity in any new alliance – dangerous but mysterious and tempting – with emergent AI technologies.

According to the philosopher, it is not technology that is dangerous: 'Technology is not demonic; but its essence is mysterious. The essence of technology, as a destining of revealing, is the danger' (p. 261). This opens the way to the unknown realm of technology, the freedom of human creativity that Heidegger highly praises. Moreover, even if 'the essence of technology is in a lofty sense ambiguous, this ambiguity points to the mystery of all revealing, i.e., of truth' (p. 263). In other words, the danger cannot be eliminated since it is not in technology. Still, it should be reflected on, and Heidegger urges that these challenges should be allowed to limit the capacity of unlimited human creativity.

Heidegger's essay is essential for understanding the difference between transhuman and posthuman approaches to the development of technology and, for this theoretical model, the development of musical AI. Transhumanism, anticipated in Heidegger's essay, is uncritical towards the necessity of regulatory ethics in the implementation of AI since it affirms the risk permanently inscribed in the development of technology. In other words, any regulatory practice which precedes human advancement and limits the possibilities is a sign of weakness. Furthermore, Heidegger anticipates the unlimited evolution of humans allied with machines (transhumanism) to overcome human weaknesses. In contrast, posthumanism, in the prefix *post*, assumes criticism and suspicion towards any new transgressions – in this case, AI development. All in all, this shows that any attempt to find human-centred values solely on Heideggerian humanism is insufficient to address the ethical challenges presented by AI systems.

Transhumanism and Posthumanism: Redefining Human-Centred Values

As discussed in earlier chapters, the ethical principles of AI reports share a moral commonality in that the implementation of AI systems should be based on 'human-centred values.' However, this review notes transhumanists' role in reshaping the music ecosystem, including Ray Kurzweil, Marvin Minsky, and Scott Cohen. The reductionist approach of technological determinism remains a driver for many schools of transhumanism, and Winner's concept of 'technological somnambulism' is a philosophical remedy to that sickness. Besides humanism, two other significant strands in philosophy reposition what constitutes 'human-centred values.' These are the transhumanist and posthumanist perspectives, which both contribute to the ethical reflection on AI development.

To understand the transhumanist approach, such as it relates to AI and the technologies relationship with the music ecosystem, the critical features of transhumanism as a theory are now presented. In principle, transhumanists argue that human evolution will exceed the limits of human form (body) through the augmentation of science and technology. This approach is purely anthropocentric and consistent with Heidegger's philosophical anthropology since the aim is to enhance the human condition. One of the basic definitions of *transhumanism* was coined by philosopher Max More (2013 [1990]), where he stated that this approach seeks 'the continuation and acceleration of the evolution of intelligent life beyond its currently human form and human limitations utilising science and technology, guided by life-promoting principles and values' (p. 3). Transhumanist thought displays a scientific optimism that believes that technological progress will benefit humans by improving an imperfect (human) condition caused by a flawed biological and genetic heritage (More, 2013: p. 4).

AI development is especially relevant to transhumanist goals. An important role is indicated regarding the potential of artificial general intelligence (AGI) or artificial superintelligence (ASI) – the yet-to-be-invented stages of AI that are equal or greater than human to be the leading technological agent. Furthermore, it will bring a radical change and transform imperfect humans (via augmented bodies and brains) into a new condition that they call (albeit somewhat confusingly) 'posthuman' (Goertzel, 2013: p. 129). In this approach, philosophical questions relating to self, free will, and individual awareness, which have ethical contexts, especially in the Western world, are called fallacies (Goertzel, 2013: p. 131). Transhumanists, including Vinge (1993) and Kurzweil (2005),[2] anticipate a technological singularity. The singularity is another specific model used by transhumanists to foretell how and when the future will develop, including the accelerated development of AI into a superintelligent AGI:

> According to the singularity hypothesis, the ordinary human is removed from the loop, overtaken by artificially intelligent machines or by cognitively enhanced biological intelligence and unable to keep pace.
>
> (Shanahan, 2015: p. xvi)

As to when the singularity may occur, opinions differ. However, Kurzweil announced at the SXSW Conference and Music festival in Austin, Texas, in 2017 that the singularity will happen by 2045 (Reedy, 2017, futurism.com).

Transhumanism is often confused with posthumanism because transhumanists use the concept of 'posthuman' in their speculations over technological development and consciousness separated from the body. While transhumanism involves an uncritical, affirmative understanding of 'human-centric' values, this is not the case with posthumanism. A key point in the posthumanism critique relates to how culture defines what constitutes the 'human.' Donna Haraway's writings are critical in the development of this theoretical model. In *A Cyborg Manifesto* (Haraway, 1985), she challenged the traditional, fundamental assumptions of the humanities, which place the human at the hierarchical apex of beings. Haraway's approach was further developed in *When Species Meet* (Haraway, 2013). Her work contributes to contemporary ecological literature and suggests that more critical theories on what defines humanism are needed to better conceive a sustainable equilibrium with the environment and with other nonhuman actors. Such a vision is removed and is entirely different from the futurology of (super)humanism as developed by transhumanists.

The ethical strand of posthumanism has been studied by Cary Wolfe, who shares with Haraway the main assumptions of criticising anthropocentric fundaments of culture. In his view, primarily expressed in *What Is Posthumanism* (Wolfe, 2010), the posthumanities can contribute to scientific and political debate as they generate adequate critical and interpretational concepts. These theoretical tools that can aid the sciences' production of knowledge are also capable of ethical intervention when the sciences violate the well-being of a multiactor network or ecosystem. Wolfe's posthumanism includes the culture-forming role of nonhuman actors who often exist in the world as nonlegal persons. He refutes transhumanism because it is created in the framework of Enlightenment rationalism, emphasising transforming the human into the superhuman – the overman. In respect to human biological origins, Wolfe's posthumanism offers a nonhierarchical treatment of nonhumans and incorporates actors into a new model of thinking about community beyond humans. Therefore, his theory aspires to alter ethical attitudes, not only of thinking about relations with the environment, but also in a broader sense – in critical reflection towards the construction of law. So the prefix *post* in *posthumanism* does not signify something that comes 'after' humanism; instead, it refers to a critique of humanism as a radical anthropological dogma that separates the human from the nonhuman and which positions the human as the dominant actor.

Importantly, Wolfe also stresses that the act of placing the human in the world of technologies plays a role different from that played by human biocultural heritage. This review posits that the inclusion of posthumanist thought can actively contribute towards a significant reimagining of the concept of 'human-centred values.' This new realignment, based on a sustainable ecological framework, is harmonious with the ambitions of the UN SDGs but extends the scope of many reports on AI ethics. This realignment of values turns into a legal question: how do human and nonhuman actors – including the development of AI – become interlinked in a sustainable and equitable music ecosystem?

In comparison to humanism and transhumanism, posthumanism offers the third philosophical approach beyond the dominating binary positions of either a dystopian vision, where AI technologies embark on a hostile takeover (robots stealing jobs), or the alternate utopian model in which AI technologies are beneficial to human spheres of existence (as helpers, companions, and care workers). However, the debate on ethics and AI development can engage with even more visionary and futurological responses, such as James Lovelock's *Novacene*. Acknowledging such opinions reframes the understanding of 'human-centred' values within this work's theoretical model of the music ecosystem.

Novacene: Beyond the Human

When the engineer James Lovelock, the author of works on the concept of the Gaia, first asserted a hypothesis that the Earth's ecosystem acts as a self-regulatory mechanism, it was met with significant hostility and dismissal from the scientific community. When he later stated that the destructive power of humans on Gaia's environments would soon make the planet uninhabitable for living organisms in his book *The Revenge of Gaia* from 2006, this, too, was considered an outlier proposition. Lovelock's environmental criticism, though, led him towards an original reflection on the possibilities that AI can offer for future, not necessarily human, civilisations. Therefore, the complexity of relations between human and nonhuman actor-networks is now traced through an operative metaphor of the ecosystem.

In his latest book called *Novacene: The Coming Age of Hyperintelligence*, written collaboratively with Bryan Appleyard (Lovelock, 2019),[3] Lovelock makes us think about human extinction as a real possibility (pp. 6–13). His vision of anthropology is also attractive since humans have always expressed their knowledge in terms of an accuracy of probability which forgets that 'we are still primitive animals' (p. 20). The speculative minds of human intelligence present an exceptionalism that is at times paired with social responsibility (p. 28). Ecological crisis can be viewed as the revolution that leads 'the cosmos to self-knowledge' (p. 29), which Lovelock envisions in the figure of 'the understanders of the future.' These creatures will not be humans but cyborgs that 'will have designed and built themselves from the artificial intelligence systems we have already constructed' (p. 29). In the Novacene, which can be understood as Lovelock's follow-up response to the Anthropocene, there will be a stage of human and machine collaboration that can bring a solution to future catastrophes (p. 30).

However, for Lovelock, basing his thought on the example of AlphaGo's self-learning autonomy and superhuman data processing,[4] 'we have already entered the Novacene' (p. 82), since 'a new form of intelligent life will emerge from an AI precursor made by one of us'; and he concludes that this is now probable (p. 82).

Evolution remains a driving force, but it will progress to incorporate engineering principles. Through collaboration with AI, 'we have invited the machines themselves to make new machines' (p. 84), and they will improve and replicate themselves (p. 84). Nonetheless, humans still act as parents (p. 86) who have instinctive kinship obligations. Under the Gaia hypothesis, the evolutionary goal is to repair the Earth and survive as a species (p. 103). Cyborgs, however, will have to be free, 'because they will have evolved from code written by themselves' (p. 94), and yet they will communicate with us (p. 99). Language will become an outdated system that will not guarantee human survival. In its place, Lovelock envisages that other, more effective forms will emerge, including telepathy (p. 100).

Furthermore, this joint project – to ensure the survival of humans – will accelerate post-AI technologies and the appearance of the cyborg (p. 105). 'The only price we would have to pay for this collaboration is the loss of our status as the most intelligent creatures on Earth' (p. 108), he concludes. In this sense, human-centred values and what is understood by 'the common good' separate.

However, while futurological approaches like Lovelock's Novacene influence contemporary research on the ethical development of AI, they do not specifically address music, which is not the case with the futurological political and economic thinking of Jacques Attali.

Attali's Anticipation of the Role of AI technologies in the Music Ecosystem

Music as a complex social and political phenomenon is at the centre of the writings of the French philosopher and economic theorist Jacques Attali (b. 1943), most notably in *Noise – The Political Economy of Music* (1985 [1977]). In this work, Attali foretells many of the relations, challenges, and tensions of the twenty-first-century music business and describes music as an anticipatory 'herald' of social change requiring ethical decision-making. Since Attali wrote in the past about a future that can inform comprehension of the present day, the circularity of Attalian theories and concepts contained in *Noise* can be considered as a series of tools to analyse and comprehend the role played by AI development in a transforming music ecosystem.

Inspired by Attali's visionary and modern approach to music as a dominant source of social and political knowledge, historically driven by major technological innovations, the following conceptual components are extracted from *Noise*. In this context, AI becomes the technological actor of the Attalian 'composing' network. Four constituent elements have been selected to aid the theoretical model:

- Copyright
- The four networks of music
- The anticipation of future technology
- Music, a 'herald for change'

Copyright

The historical development of copyright is central to the political economy of music outlined in *Noise*. The author traces the origins of copyright and identifies that its initial purpose was not to defend artists' rights but rather to 'serve as a tool of capitalism in its fight against feudalism' (Attali, 1985 [1977]: p. 52). On the one hand, Attali recognises mainstream arguments about the economy of music – for example, the concept that the development of copyright was designed to protect artists' rights. However, by lifting the veil placed on the progress of copyright, Attali identifies the shifts of power brought about by the implementation of legislation. Attali's approach underpins the argument to look at music as a model example of any economic disruption, outlining that to understand how the economy of music works, 'where the creation of money takes place' must be examined (p. 39).

The Four Networks of Music

The future evolution of the music ecosystem, including the development of AI, can be comprehended through Attali's concept of four historical networks of music production, dissemination, and consumption, which relate to 'a technology and a different level of social structuring' (p. 31).

The first network, 'sacrificial,' refers to the historical period when the aural traditions and music practices were dominant. The second stage, 'representation,' occurs with the setting down of music in a permanent form (notation). At the same time, the third network, 'repetition,' emanates from the development of copyright, which occurs at the end of the nineteenth century 'with the advent of recording' (p. 32). The fourth network, 'composing,' anticipates the near-future challenges of AI to music makers. The 'composing' stage, as the author admits, is 'not easy to conceptualise' (p. 134), but it foresees a network in which a musician plays 'primarily for himself, outside any operationality, spectacle, or accumulation of value; when music . . . emerges as an activity that is an end in itself . . . for one's own pleasure' (p. 135). This extract depicts what has become a modern-day reality for many music makers, where the economic function of the professional musician is in decline.

Attali's forecast of a 'composing' network in which 'production melds with consumption' (p. 145) parallels what the American cultural critic and futurist Alvin Toffler (1928–2016) termed in 1980 as 'the prosumer.' The notion of the prosumer describes the cultural and economic consequences when technology makes it possible for a consumer to be the producer (the prosumer) of creative content (Toffler, 1980: especially p. 265). Similarly, Attali predicts that the role of the musician within the 'composing' network is one where 'the listener is the operator . . . (and) calls into question the distinction between worker and consumer' (1985 [1977]: p. 135). Attali, however, indicates an ethical dimension within the composing network when he notes that musicians may find themselves 'in a precarious position, because composition contains the germ of their disappearance as specialists' (p. 146).

Anticipation of Future Technology

Within the composing network, when Attali predicts 'the composer produces a program, a mold, an abstract algorithm . . . the score . . . is an order described for an operator-interpreter' (p. 37), surprisingly, he is describing attributes of modern AI music technologies (one must be reminded that these words were written in the early 1970s). Attali's anticipation of a technology not yet invented but still an inevitable outcome of progressive historical development locates AI as the technological agent of the 'composing' network. Many of the widely promoted modern-day benefits of AI are encapsulated in Attali's description of a new 'composing' network technology:

> A new technology capable of reducing the costs of reorganisation, *financial resources* (or an accumulation of new capital) available for the latter's utilisation, and the existence of a *social group* with both the interest and the power to utilise such financial resources and to put the new technology to work.
>
> (p. 9; the author's italics)

However, that promise is balanced by concern when Attali refers to the unintended consequences of a 'technology upon which composition [the network] is based [but] was not conceived for that purpose' (p. 144). Attali's ethical response (forty years later) to this concern comes in 'Art, the Last Bastion of Freedom Against Artificial Intelligence' (Attali, 2019). In this article, he declares, 'It is up to each of us, as spectators, creators, and actors, at one level or another, in the artistic domain, to keep threat as well as hope in mind, and to make the most of it.' This call demands intervention into AI's financial and ethical implications in the music ecosystem.

Music, a 'Herald for Change'

Attali is explicit in his position, frequently stating that music is a prophetic medium:

> It has always been in its essence a herald of times to come . . . it is a way of perceiving the world. A tool of understanding *demonstrating that music is prophetic and that social organisation echoes it* . . . [music] provides a rough sketch of the society under construction, a society in which the informal is mass produced and consumed, in which difference is artificially recreated in the multiplication of semi-identical objects.
>
> (1985 [1977]: pp. 4–5; italics by Attali)

Suppose Attali is accurate that music's 'styles and economic organisation are ahead of the rest of society because it explores, much faster . . . the entire range of possibilities in a given code' (p. 11). In that case, analysis from the microperspective (the music ecosystem) can offer insights into the macroperspective's challenges of AI. Attali is not alone in the opinion that music is a 'mirror' to herald social change. His work was influenced by the German theoretician of music and society Theodor Adorno. However, Adorno's aesthetic conservatism, whose 'principle of evaluation is based on that of technical mastery' (Jameson in Attali, 1985 [1977]: p. x), and his stigmatisation of jazz as lesser artworks within music (Bahr, 2008: p. 57) are framed on notions of authenticity and authority that differ significantly from the Attalian 'operator-interpreter' in the 'composing' network.

The Attalian function of music as 'a way of perceiving the world – a tool of understanding' (1985 [1977]: p. 4) is evidenced by Professors Jonathan Taplin (2017) and George Howard (2016). Both have observed that the music industry has been 'the canary in the coal mine' for other sectors. Music's ability to predict and affect social change has also been expressed by former White House Economist Alan Krueger in *Rockonomics: What the Music Industry Can Teach Us About Economics (and Our Future)* (2019), primarily when he addresses AI music generation:

> There would be no music without the songwriters, composers and musicians who create and perform it – at least until machine learning algorithms and artificial intelligence (AI) advance to the point where computers can compose popular music and write lyrics. . . . In the future, musicians may be replaced by computer programmers.
>
> (pp. 11–12)

Attali's claim that 'musical distribution techniques are today contributing to the establishment of a system of eavesdropping and social surveillance' (1985 [1977]: p. 8) predates considerations in *The Age of Surveillance Capitalism: The Fight for a Human Future at the New Frontier of Power* (Zuboff, 2019). Here, the author, Shoshana Zuboff, reflects on threats presented in transnational corporations' collection, interpretation, and application of personal data. She writes:

> It is no longer enough to automate information flows about us; the goal now is to automate us. These processes are meticulously designed to produce ignorance by circumventing individual awareness and thus eliminate any possibility of self-determination. As one data scientist explained to me, 'We can engineer the context around a particular behaviour, and force change that way. . . . We are learning how to write the music, and then we let the music make them dance.
>
> (p. 294)[5]

Zuboff indicates how the generation of AI music is now pragmatically placed as one more challenge for technological determinists to solve. The accelerated evolution of a societally prophetic music ecosystem fuels such observations and points to ethical reconsiderations within the economic context identified by Attali.

In a powerful narrative, he presents the Manichaean division between a dystopian vision in which 'the devil [AI] who will destroy employment and leave mankind unemployed and in misery' (2019) and, on the other hand, an alternate techno-utopian possibility, where 'people will be able to work better and less' (2019). Attali regards the dangers of this technology as 'real' and states that the governance of AI industries 'will largely determine the course of the 21st Century' (2019), and societal reactions will range from social submission to civic activism. When Attali addresses the purpose and role of art within a disruptive AI societal context, he concludes that art 'as always [will] be an excellent indication of what is possible' (2019). And for Attali, the most socially predictive of the arts is music.

Music Ecosystem and the AI Challenge

This chapter's theoretical model applies a specific meaning of the term *music ecosystem* to position music within the contemporary critical debate on AI development. Here, the term *music ecosystem* encompasses ANT concepts to embrace human and nonhuman (AI) 'member organisms' located in civic, industrial, or academic domains, which can be considered stakeholders of the global music community. The term is designed to include but is not limited by the commercial boundaries of the worldwide music industry.

The very term *ecosystem*, taken from biology, has gained attention since its introduction to the field of management in the mid-1990s (Moore, 1993, 1996; Iansiti & Levien, 2002). Moore defined an *ecosystem* as:

> [A]n economic community supported by a foundation of interacting organisations and individuals – the organisms of the business world. This economic community produces goods and services of value to customers, who are themselves members of the ecosystem. The member organisms also include suppliers, lead producers, competitors, and other stakeholders. Over time, they coevolve their capabilities and roles, and tend to align themselves with the direction set by one or more central companies.
>
> (1996: p. 26)

Moore's definition can be seen to extend Paul McCartney's contention (McCartney, 2018) that 'the value gap jeopardises the music ecosystem.' For McCartney, the value gap exists between the revenue that technology platforms 'derive from music and the value they pay [copyright] creators.' Its narrowing will 'help assure a sustainable future for the music ecosystem and its creators' (2018).[6]

As I have outlined in earlier chapters, the challenges and opportunities presented by human and nonhuman (AI) 'member organisms' – particularly regarding issues related to music copyright – require an ethical consideration capable of contributing to a sustainable and fair future environment for music. These ethical considerations draw from a commonality of agreement that principles should be grounded in 'human-centred' values. This review proposes that such 'human-centred' values need to be critically reconsidered from a posthuman rather than transhuman philosophy because of ethical challenges posed by AI development within the music ecosystem. These ethical reconsiderations regarding the future status of human and nonhuman actors are currently being legally challenged in global court decisions on IP.

At the outset of the *WIPO AICM* session[7] (US Copyright Office, 2020) in Washington, DC, in February this year, moderator Regan Smith stated, 'For better or worse, the music ecosystem has been at the forefront of technological change' (p. 180). In the case of AI exponential technologies, the music ecosystem must decide its needs and values; otherwise, technological determinism will become the dominant paradigm via Langdon Winner's call to wake from technological somnambulism. In response to this risk, I argue that the weakening of the human agency always has an ethical dimension and that human decision-making should never relinquish the responsibility to arbitrate moral questions.

Instead, a stoic response of 'amor fati' that embraces the challenge and can encourage music makers to interpret and respond to threats and opportunities presented will determine the functionality of its ecosystem. In light of the many implications of AI technologies discussed in this work, the implementation of an ethical mark, as successfully seen in initiatives like the fair trade movement to certify sustainable and fair technological practices within the music ecosystem would be a first step to contending with the financial and ethical implications of this disruptive but perceived Promethean technology.

This chapter amalgamates arguments expanded in Chapter 1 and Chapter 6 of my doctorate, 'The Financial and Ethical Implications of Music Generated by Artificial Intelligence' (2021), Trinity College, Dublin.

Notes

1 The recent publications by Rujing S. Huang, Andre Holzapfel, Bob L. T. Sturm, including *'De-Centering the West: East Asian philosophies and the ethics for applying artificial intelligence to music'* (Huang et al., 2021), have successfully engaged with this question.

2 Ray Kurzweil, author of *The Singularity Is Near* (2006), is a significant figure in music technology. In 1965, aged seventeen, on US CBS Television, he premiered a piano piece composed by a pattern-recognition software he had designed. In the 1980s, Kurzweil Music Systems set new standards of synthesized piano modelling and in 2015 received a Technical Grammy Award. In 2009, Kurzweil cofounded the Singularity University in collaboration with Google. In 2012, Kurzweil was hired by Google as 'Chief Engineer' to work on new projects involving machine learning and language processing.

3 Published in June 2019 to mark the author's one hundredth birthday.

4 AI created by Google DeepMind and discussed in earlier chapters.

5 When I read Zuboff, I was reminded of Colonel Tom Parker. Prior to managing Elvis Presley, Parker had worked as a sideshow impresario. A popular act was 'Colonel Tom Parker and His Dancing Chickens.' Live chickens were placed on a hot plate and would then 'dance' to popular songs of the day. In Albert Goldman's book *Elvis* (1981), the author makes the connection between the dancing chickens and Parker's manipulation of Presley (Goldman, 1981).

6 The IFPI published a letter from Paul McCartney requesting members of the European Parliament to vote in support of the Article 13 Campaign to uphold the mandate on copyright.
7 Regan Smith (General Counsel and Associate Register of Copyrights, US Copyright Office); the four speakers at the *WIPO AICM* session were Joel Douek (cofounder of Ecco VR, West Coast creative director and chief scientist for Man Made Music, and board member of the Society of Composers and Lyricists), E. Michael Harrington (composer, musician, consultant, and professor in music copyright and intellectual property matters at Berklee Online), David Hughes (chief technology officer, Recording Industry Association of America [RIAA]), and Alex Mitchell (founder and CEO of AI start-up Boomy).

Bibliography

Aristotle (2009 [350 BCE]) *The nicomachean ethics*. Ed. L. Brown. Trans. D. Ross. Oxford: Oxford World Classics, new edition. New York, USA.

Attali, J. (1985 [1977]) *Noise: The political economy of music*. Trans. B. Massumi. Manchester: Manchester University Press.

Attali.J.(2019)*Art,thelastbastionoffreedomagainstartificialintelligence*.https://www.attali.com/en/art-et-culture/art-the-last-bastion-of-freedom-against-artificial-intelligence/.

Bahr, E. (2008) *Weimar on the Pacific German exile culture in Los Angeles and the crisis of modernism*. Los Angeles, CA: University of California.

Berger, P.L. & Luckmann, T. (1966) *The social construction of reality: A treatise in the sociology of knowledge*. New York: Doubleday Anchor Books.

Bijker, W.E. (2009) Social construction of technology. In: J.K. Olsen, S.A. Pedersen & V. Hendricks (eds.), *A companion to the philosophy of technology*. Chichester: Blackwell Publishing, pp. 88–94.

Bijker, W.E., Boonig, J. & van Oost, E.C. (1984) The social construction of technological artefacts. *Zeitschrift fur Wissenschaftsforschung*. 3 (2), 39–52.

Bijsterveld, K. & Peters, P.K. (2010) Composing claims on musical instrument development: A science and technology studies' contribution. *Interdisciplinary Science Reviews*. 35 (2), 106–121. doi:10.1179/030801810X12723585301039.

Collins, H.M. & Pinch, T. (1982) *Frames of meaning: The social construction of extraordinary science*. London: Routledge and Kegan Paul.

Goertzel, B. (2013) Artificial general intelligence and the future of humanity. In: M. More & N. Vita-More (eds.), *The transhumanist reader: Classical and contemporary essays on the science, technology, and philosophy of the human future*. New York: John Wiley & Sons, pp. 128–137.

Goldman, A. (1981) *Elvis*. New York: McGraw Hill.

Haraway, D. (1985) A Manifesto for Cyborgs. *Socialist Review. Radical Society, Ltd.* USA.

Haraway, D. (2013) *When species meet* (Vol. 3). University of Minnesota Press. USA.

Heidegger, M. (2000) Letter on humanism. In: Krell, D.F. (Ed.) *Basic writings. CiteSeerX. Pennsylvania State University*. USA.

Heidegger, M. (2010 [1927]) *Being and time*. Trans. J. Stambaugh. New York: SUNY Press.

Howard, G. (2016) Canary in a Coalmine: From internet of things to VR to blockchain how music guides other industries. *GHStrategic*. https://ghstrategic.io/canary-in-a-coalmine/.

Huang, R., Sturm, B.L. & Holzapfel, A. (2021) De-centering the West: East Asian philosophies and the ethics of applying artificial intelligence to music. *International Society for Music Information Retrieval Conference, ISMIR*.

Hughes W. E. & Pinch, T. (1985) *The social construction of technological systems: New directions in the sociology and history of technology*. Cambridge, MA: MIT Press.

Iansiti, M. & Levien, R. (2002) *Keynotes and dominators: Framing operating and technology strategy in a business ecosystem.* Harvard Business School Working Paper, No. 03-061. Boston: Harvard Business School.

Kurzweil, R. (2005) *The singularity is near: When humans transcend biology.* Penguin. UK.

Lanier, J. (2014) *Who owns the future?* London: Penguin Books.

Latour, B. (2007) *Reassembling the social: An introduction to actor-network-theory.* Oxford: Oxford University Press.

Lovelock, J. (2019) *Novacene: The coming age of hyperintelligence.* London: Penguin Books.

McCartney, P. (2018) An open letter to the European parliament. *IFPI Twitter.* https://twitter.com/IFPI_org/status/1014429611176972288.

Moore, J. (1993) Predators and prey: A new ecology of competition. *Harvard Business Review.* 71 (3), 75–86.

Moore, J. (1996) *The death of competition: Leadership and strategy in the age of business ecosystems.* New York: Harper Business.

More, M. (2013 [1990]) The philosophy of transhumanism. In: M. More & N. Vita-More (eds.), *The transhumanist reader: Classical and contemporary essays on the science, technology, and philosophy of the human future.* Chichester: John Wiley & Sons, pp. 3–17.

Pinch, T.J. & Bijker, W.E. (2003 [1987]) The social construction of facts and artefacts. In: R.C. Scharff & V. Dusek (eds.), *Philosophy of technology: The technological condition. An anthology.* Malden, MA: Blackwell Publishing, pp. 221–232.

Pinch, T.J. & Trocco, F. (2004) *Analog days – the invention and impact of the Moog synthesiser.* Cambridge: Harvard University Press.

Reedy, C. (2017) Kurzweil claims that the singularity will happen by 2045. *Futurism.com.* https://futurism.com/kurzweil-claims-that-the-singularity-will-happen-by-2045.

Schoen-Nazzaro, M.B. (1978) Plato and Aristotle on the ends of music. *Laval Theologique et Philosphique.* 34 (3), 261–273. doi:10.7202/705684ar.

Shanahan, M. (2015) *The technological singularity.* Cambridge, MA: MIT.

Taplin, J. (2017) *Move fast and break things: How Facebook, Google, and Amazon cornered culture and undermined democracy.* New York: Little, Brown and Company.

Toffler, A. (1980) *Future shock: The third wave.* New York: Bantum Books.

US Copyright Office (2020) AI and creating music. In: *Proceedings: Copyright in the age of artificial intelligence.* Washington, DC: US Copyright Office, Library of Congress, February [Transcript]. www.copyright.gov/events/artificial-intelligence/transcript.pdf.

Vinge, V. (1993) Technological singularity. In: *VISION-21 Symposium sponsored by NASA Lewis Research Center and the Ohio Aerospace Institute.* NASA Lewis Research Center. USA. http://cmm.cenart.gob.mx/delanda/textos/tech_sing.pdf.

Winner, L. (1983) Technologies as forms of life. In: R.S. Cohen & M. Wartofsky (eds.), *Epistemology, methodology and the social sciences.* New York: Kluwer Academic Publishers.

Winner, L. (2003 [1993]) Upon opening the black box and finding it empty: Social constructivism and the philosophy of technology. In: R.C. Scharff & V. Dusek (eds.), *Philosophy of technology. The technological condition. An anthology.* Malden, MA: Blackwell Publishing, pp. 427–452.

Wittgenstein, L. (1953) *Philosophical Investigations.* Trans. G.E.M. Anscombe. Oxford. UK.

Wolfe, C. (2010) *What is posthumanism?* (Vol. 8). University of Minnesota Press. USA.

Zuboff, S. (2019) *The age of surveillance capitalism: The fight for a human future at the new frontier of power.* London: Profile Books.

Index

Printed in the United States
by Baker & Taylor Publisher Services